James H Monroe

Standard Decisions on Questions in Law and Equity Relating to Banks, Banking and Commerce...

Vol. I

James H Monroe

Standard Decisions on Questions in Law and Equity Relating to Banks, Banking and Commerce...

Vol. I

ISBN/EAN: 9783337123659

Printed in Europe, USA, Canada, Australia, Japan

Cover: Foto ©Suzi / pixelio.de

More available books at **www.hansebooks.com**

STANDARD DECISIONS

ON

QUESTIONS IN LAW AND EQUITY

RELATING TO

BANKS, BANKING

AND

COMMERCE,

RENDERED IN THE

HIGHER COURTS

OF THE

UNITED STATES, CANADA, ENGLAND, IRELAND
AND SCOTLAND.

By JAMES MONROE.

Vol. I.

NEW YORK:
EDWARD G. WARD,
7 COLLEGE PLACE.
1879.

PREFACE.

THE purpose of this work is to present in a convenient and concise form the most important and valuable decisions of the higher courts, especially relating to BANKS and BANKERS, to whom this book will be a guide in managing their business.

The great need of such a work has induced the author to comply with numerous requests.

It is a conflict of interests and minds which creates law-suits, and it is the mission of this work to present the law as it is interpreted in the courts.

One cannot consult his lawyer upon every occasion, neither can he be expected to always remember the rules of law governing each transaction as they may be required in his daily business; to meet these demands, and the wants of the LEGAL PROFESSION, the *Standard Decisions* are presented as sure and final authority.

STANDARD DECISIONS

ON

QUESTIONS OF LAW

RELATING TO

BANKS, BANKING AND COMMERCE.

ACCEPTANCE.

1. Acceptance.—*Verbal acceptance of an order* drawn on a party is binding on him, and his statement, when presented with the order, that he could not then pay it, but would pay the same, is equivalent to an acceptance. *St. Louis National Stock Yards* v. *O'Reilly, et al.*, 85 Ill. 546.

ACCOMMODATION.

2. Accommodation Acceptance.—*Notice.*—The fact that the drawer presents the draft to the payee, with the acceptance of the drawees on it, is out of the usual course of business, and a circumstance indicating to the payee the accommodation character of the acceptance. *Bloom* v. *Helm*, 53 Miss. 21.

ACCOUNT STATED.

3. Account Stated.—It seems that to give to an account delivered the force of an account stated, because of silence on the part of the party receiving it, the circumstances must be such as to justify an inference of assent, upon his part, to its correctness. Where he has disclaimed all liability upon the account, he is not bound to examine the items, upon its delivery to him, and his omission to object will not be taken as an admission of their correctness, and is not *prima facie* proof of the account. The mere rendering of an account does not make it an account stated, and an omission to object to it raises only a presumption of assent, which may be rebutted by circumstances tending to a contrary inference. *Guernsey* v. *Rexford*, 18 Sickels N. Y. 631.

ADMINISTRATORS.

4. Administrators.—The written acknowledgment of a debt by an administrator will not bind the succession if such debt does not really exist. An administrator cannot avail of any defect in a legal proceeding caused by his fault. *Succession of Margaret McAuley*, 29 La. 33.

ADVICE OF COUNSEL.

5. Advice of Counsel.—*As a defense.*—Where a party, in good faith, consults with a licensed attorney, and acts upon his advice in making a complaint for the arrest of another, he may show that fact in defense, and it is not incumbent on him to go further and show that such attorney was a man learned and skilled in his profession. *Horne* v. *Sullivan*, 83 Ill. 30. A party seeking the advice of counsel as to commencing a criminal prosecution must act in good faith and without gross negligence, and not withhold any information with an intent to procure an opinion that might operate to shelter and protect him against a suit. If a party culpably or negligently withholds from counsel any material fact, the advice will not protect him. But where the counsel advised with is already conversant with a material fact, by being an attorney of the party in a prior suit, it will not be necessary for the party to give him information of it. He may, in such case, presume the counsel has knowledge as to such fact, without being chargeable with bad faith. *Per Breese, J., Brown* v. *Smith,* 83 Ill. 291.

AGENT.

6. Agent.—Where an agent to loan money takes insufficient security, the principal is not bound, at his peril, to accept and discharge the agent, or to reject the security and look only to the responsibility of the agent. The principal, in such case, may take the security, and still hold the agent bound for any deficiency which, after due diligence, he suffers on it. *Guernsey* v. *Rexford,* 18 Sickels, N. Y. 631.

7. Agent.—In an action for liquors sold and delivered, to which the defence was that the goods were sold to a third person, there was evidence that the defendant told the plaintiff's agent that he had bought a billiard-saloon, and was going to put the third person in to run the place ; that the latter would want some liquors and he wished some might be sent, and ordered the liquors ; that the third person in fact ran the place and appeared to do all the business there ; there was also evidence, admitted under the defendant's exception, that afterwards the third person told the agent that the defendant had given authority to buy stock for the saloon, and asked the agent to write at once to the plaintiff to hurry up the liquors previously ordered; that the agent thereupon wrote a letter containing a copy of the order which he had previously received from the defendant, in which the defendant's name appeared as the person ordering the goods, and the letter was produced and admitted in evidence, although it had not been read by the third person. *Held,* that there was sufficient evidence that the third person was the agent of the defendant, and that the letter was admissible in evidence. *Lozier* v. *Crofts,* 123 Mass. 480.

8. Agent.—Persons who deal with an agent before notice of the recall of his powers are not affected by the recall. *Hatch* v. *Coddington*, 95 U. S. 48.

9. Agent.—B., a broker, advised A. to sell certain unregisted bonds and buy certain other bonds. A. in reply, by letter, said, "I am most anxious to get my money in registered bonds," authorized B. to sell the bonds then held by B. for him, "and invest the amount in the best paying and surest bonds that you know of." "As these bonds are all I possess, I am naturally always anxious about them, for the reason that, if lost or stolen, I could recover nothing. You will please invest the results of the sale in the I. bonds (the ones recommended), or any sure road." "I want registered bonds of which I will have no trouble in drawing the interest." "I shall be under many obligations if you will kindly make such sale and purchases of bonds as your good sense dictates." It was agreed that the bonds referred to by B. were first mortgage bonds. B. in fact bought some first-mortgage and some second-mortgage bonds, all of which were unregistered. Held, that, if he acted in good faith, it was within the scope of the authority conferred upon him by the letter of A. *Matthews* v. *Fuller*, 123 Mass. 446.

10. Agency.—One cannot act as agent for both seller and purchaser, unless both know of and assent to his undertaking such agency, and receiving commissions from both. Whether such double agency, even with consent of both principals, is consistent with public policy, is not here decided. *Meyer, et al.* v. *Hanchett*, 43 Wis. 246.

10½. Agency.—A principal who employs an agent to do a legal thing, is not liable in damages for any illegal act of the agent done in the execution of the mandate, to which the principal was not accessory, or privy. *Andreas Richoux* v. *Mayer Bros.*, 29 La. 828.

11. Agency.—It is a general rule, of almost universal application that, where a person acts by an agent, the act is his, and not that of the agent. Where the agent does not disclose the name of his principal in making a contract, the other party may, when he learns it, hold him responsible for its performance, and the principal may, on showing the agency, claim and enforce the contract, precisely as if entered into by himself. *Baher* v. *Garvey*, 83 Ill. 184.

12. Agency.—The admission of the alleged agent that he is authorized to represent a third person in a suit, does not prove the agency. The authority to represent a defendant in a suit must be shown expressly, or by irresistible implication. *Mrs. Marie E. Dawson* v. *Marie Landreaux*, 29 La. 363.

13. Agency.—The principal is bound by any contract made by his agent which is necessary to carry out the objects of the agency; and no confidential limitation of the mandate can operate to the prejudice of any innocent third person. *E. H. Farrar* v. *Stephen Duncan*, 29 La. 126.

14. Agency.—Where an agent has fraudulently sold his principal's property, and embezzled its proceeds, and the principal afterward accepts from the agent something in compensation for the embezzled proceeds, he thereby ratifies the sale made by the agent, and estops himself from any recourse against the innocent purchaser of his property. *R. N. Ogden* v. *A. Marchoud*, 29 La. 61.

15. Agency.—*Personal liability of.*—An action cannot be maintained against an agent on a contract executed by him in behalf of his principal, unless it contains apt words to charge him personally, even though he acts without authority or in excess of authority; but he may become personally liable on a contract containing apt words to bind him, and then the words descriptive of his agency will be rejected as surplusage. *Hancock* v. *Yunker, et al.*, 83 Ill. 208.

16. Agency.—Where a principal has dealt with a merchant through an agent acting under a written power of attorney, the merchant may prove by parol the correctness of his account, and any acknowledgment of its correctness, or any ratification of it by the principal, even if the agent has transgressed his mandate, or there are charges in the account which could not be legally enforced. Ratification by the principal of the unauthorized acts of an agent makes those acts binding on the principal. A power of attorney sufficiently comprehensive to authorize the agent to manage a plantation, and disburse the proceeds of its crops, will justify the factor who sells the crops to pay out their proceeds on the orders of the agent. *G. W. Sentell & Co., in liquidation* v. *Mrs. M. G. Kennedy and Husband*, 29 La. 679.

17. **Agent.**—The good faith of the agent does not exonerate him from liability to his principal, if he has been in fact negligent, or has disregarded orders. *Bank of Owensboro* v. *Western Bank*, 13 Bush, Ky. 526.

18. **Agency.**—A member of a copartnership, after the dissolution, has no *agency* growing out of the former partnership relation to create or to perpetuate a liability of his late copartner for partnership indebtedness, as against the operation of the statute of limitations. *Tate* v. *Clements*, 16 Florida, 339.

19. **Agent, and Agency.**—*Unauthorized Sale.*—Where bonds are delivered to an attorney-at-law and business agent, not a dealer in bonds, for the purpose that he should collect the amount thereof from the county in money or new bonds, or in both, but, in violation of his duty, he sells said bonds to a third person, such sale is void. *Hannon* v. *Houston*, 18 Kan. 561.

20. **Agent.**—An agent of an undisclosed principal may be treated as the principal. *Welch* v. *Goodwin*, 123 Mass. 71.

21. **Agent.**—*Authority.*—Authority by a principal to an agent to invest his money, and look after his business generally, will not enable the agent to sell his

principal's property, even such as may be acquired as the result of the investment. *Smith, et al.* v. *Stephenson, et al.*, 45 Iowa, 645.

22. Agent.—*Notice.*—Notice to an agent bound in the discharge of his duty to act upon it and to communicate it to his principal, is notice to the principal. *Philadelphia* v. *Lockhardt*, 73 Penn. 211.

23. Agent.—*Railroad Corporation.*—A railroad corporation conferred upon its president, by a by-law, authority to act as "business and financial agent" of the corporation. Thereafter such officer executed, under the corporate seal, a mortgage upon a locomotive belonging to the corporation, to secure a debt of the corporation. *Held*, that the authority of the president was confined to the ordinary business of the corporation; that the execution of the mortgage was without the scope of his authority, and that such mortgage was not a lien upon the property in question. *Luse* v. *Isthmus Transit Railway Co.*, 6 Oregon, 125.

AGREEMENTS.

24. Agreement which is forbidden by law, expressly, or by implication, or which is against public policy, will not be enforced in a court of law. Neither will an executed contract resting on such a consideration be relieved against in equity. *Ratcliffe* v. *Smith*, 13 Bush, Ky. 172.

25. Agreement.—The defendants promised to furnish to the plaintiffs sulphuric acid for their "works." Neither the terms of payment nor the time for which the arrangement should continue, was agreed upon. *Held*, that either side to the contract could terminate it at pleasure. *Cumb. Bone Co.* v. *Atwood Lead Co.*, 63 Me. 167.

26. Agreement *to pay interest upon interest at the time due and unpaid, is valid and binding.* When a debtor, upon whose obligation installments of interest which had from time to time become due remain unpaid, entered into an agreement to pay the said obligation with compound interest, the promise is met by the payment of simple interest upon the principal unpaid at the date of the agreement, and simple interest, also, upon the total arrears of interest at the time due and unpaid; it does not authorize the compounding of interest annually for the whole period, which interest has become due by the terms of the obligation. The mere rendering of an account does not make it an account stated, and an omission to object to it raises only a presumption of assent, which may be rebutted by circumstances tending to a contrary inference. *Toland v. Sprague*, 12 Pet. 330. *Guernsey, et al. v. Rexford, Adm. Apllt.*, 18 Sickels, N. Y. 631.

ASSIGNEE.

27. Assignee of Mortgage.—*In possession.*—The assignee of a mortgage, after condition broken, being in possession of real estate mortgaged and also being the holder of the note secured by the mortgage and the assignee thereof, can defend his possession under the mortgage, in ejectment brought by the mortgagor or those claiming under him. *Kilgour v. Gorkley*, 83 Ill. 109.

28. Assignee.—*Time of filing claims.*—A creditor who fails to file his claims with the assignee within three months after the first publication of the notice of assignment is not entitled to share *pro rata* in the dividends of the estate. *In the matter of the assignment of Holt*, 45 Iowa, 301.

ASSIGNMENTS.

29. Assignments.—The statute provision that blank assignments shall be taken as of a date most to the advantage of the defendant, only applies in the absence of evidence as to the date of the assignment. *Trieber v. Com. Bank of St. Louis*, 31 Ark. 128.

30. Assignment.—The surety in a bond, upon tender of the debt, is entitled under the statute to an assignment of the bond, if demanded; and a refusal to make such assignment is a discharge of the surety, *per se*, irrespective of the question whether, in consequence of such refusal, the surety has sustained injury. *Merrikan v. Godwin, et al.*, 2 Del. 236.

31. Assignment.—An assignment under seal and duly recorded, of wages, by A. to "J. B., treasurer," to secure the corporation of which J. B. was treasurer, for goods it had previously sold and might afterwards sell to A., is valid. *Giles v. Ash*, 123 Mass. 353.

32. Assignment.—*Giving preferences—when and to what extent void under bankrupt act.*—Although an assignment giving preferences is void under the bankrupt act, under the conditions therein provided, it is void only as to persons and proceedings under that act, and except as to such persons and proceedings, it is valid as ever. *Williams v. Pitts*, 55 Howard, N. Y. 331.

33. Assignment of Stock.—The assignee of stock in an insurance company, by assignment and delivery of the certificate of stock, and notice to the company, has a superior right to that of a subsequent attching creditor of the assignor, although there be a valid by-law of the company, embodied in the certificate, that the stock is only transferable on the books of the company, at their office, on surrender of the certificate, the charter containing no provision on the subject of the assignment of the stock. *State Ins. Co. v. Gennett*, 2 Tenn. Eq. 100.

ASSUMPSIT.

34. Assumpsit lies only on a claim of ownership. One who has only a mortgage lien on goods cannot bring assumpsit for their value against one who has taken them to satisfy a claim. *Randall, et al.* v. *Higbee*, 37 Mich. 40.

ATTACHMENT.

35. Attachment.—Property assigned cannot be reached on attachment based on the charge that the assignment was made to defraud creditors, if the property has changed its form. That is, moneys arising from assigned claims cannot be attached, though the claims could have been reached had the attachment been levied before they were changed into money. *Matter of Freel, assignee of Foley & Co.*, 55 Howard, N. Y. 386.

ATTORNEY.

36. Attorneys.—*General powers.*—The acts of an attorney in directing the levy upon or taking of goods upon process are in excess of his general powers as attorney, and in the absence of special authority, do not subject his client to liability. *Welsh* v. *Cochran*, 18 Sickels, N. Y. 181.

37. Attorney.—An attorney who purchases of a client a claim which is the subject of litigation, in case the propriety of such purchase is questioned, is bound to show the perfect fairness, adequacy, and equity of the transaction. *Dunn* v. *Record*, 63 Me. 17.

38. Attorney at law cannot recover for professional services, without proof of the qualifications required by statute; evidence that he is a practicing lawyer in this State is not sufficient, but he may recover disbursements. An objection, upon this ground, to his right to recover, is not too late, when taken after the argument, but before the charge of the judge. *Perkins* v. *McDuffee*, 63 Me. 181.

39. Attorney.—*Of a contingent fee.*—Where an attorney at law agrees to prosecute a suit or claim for one-half of whatever judgment is recovered, if no judgment is recovered he will be entitled to no compensation, when the failure to recover is not the fault of the client. *Fraatz* v. *Garrison, et al.*, 83 Ill. 60.

BAILEE.

40. Bailee's Relinquishment.—The voluntary relinquishment by the bailee of possession of the subject of the bailment discharges his lien unless it is consistent with the contract, the course of business, or the intention of the parties, that it should continue. *Spaulding* v. *Adams*, 32 Me. 212; also, *Danforth* v. *Pratt*, 42 Me. 52; and *Robinson* v. *Larrabee*, 63 Me. 116.

41. Bailee.—*Forfeiture of his rights.*—The forfeiture of a lien claim, when once incurred, is not waived by a subsequent arrangement between the parties, whereby the bailee resumes the custody of the subject of the bailment, unless such was the intention of the parties. When the bailee has parted with his possession, the presumption is that he has waived or abandoned his lien, unless his conduct, in so doing, is satisfactorily explained. *Robinson* v. *Larrabee*, 63 Me. 116.

BANKS AND BANKING.

42. Banks.—A depositor cannot maintain an action against a bank, without a previous demand by check or otherwise. *Doanes* v. *Phœnix Bank*, 6 Hill, N. Y. 297.

43. Banks and Banking.—Where the dealings between a bank and a customer were entered in a single account, the latter being credited therein with the proceeds of notes discounted, with drafts accepted, and moneys deposited; and when, in accordance with the uniform custom of dealing, endorsed notes of the customer discounted by the bank were charged to his account as they matured, without protest, and were thereafter surrendered to the maker, *held*, that this was a payment, and that a mortgage securing the payment of the notes was thereby discharged. *Crocker* v. *Whitney*, 71 N. Y. 161.

44. Banker.—When a banker receives a negotiable instrument for collection, it is his duty to cause it to be presented for payment at maturity, and if refused, protested, so as to charge the endorser. The failure to perform this duty will render him liable for damages thereby occasioned. In an action to recover for such damages the solvency of the endorser is a material inquiry. It is competent for the defendant in such action to prove that the endorser was, and continues to be insolvent, and that therefore no damages were occasioned by the failure to protest the note. *Steele* v. *Russell*, 5 Neb. 211.

45. Banks.—*Overdraft by an agent*, of his principal's account, with the knowledge of the cashier of the bank, the credit being extended to the principal, amounts to a simple loan of money, and does not involve moral turpitude, whether the cashier had authority to extend such accommodation or not. The authority of the cashier cannot be questioned in an action by the bank to recover money. The case of *Union Bank* v. *Mott*, 39 Barb. 180; affirmed in *Union Gold Mining Co.* v. *Rocky Mt. Nat. Bank*, 2 Colorado, 248.

BILLS OF EXCHANGE.

46. Bill of Exchange.—*Disposal of proceeds.*—A bill of exchange specially indorsed, "Pay J. C. or order on account of B. G. & S.," was indorsed generally by J. C., sent by him to his correspondents, and paid by the drawers. J. C. failed about an hour before this payment was made, in debt to his correspondents, and this failure was known about an hour after payment made. His correspondents applied the amount of the payment to reducing their claim against J. C. In an action by B. G. & S. against these correspondents to recover the amount of the payment,—*Held*, that the special indorsement showed that no consideration had been paid for the bill by J. C. ; that it was notice to all subsequent holders that J. C. held the bill in trust for B., G. & S. for collection ; that this trust followed the bill, and that neither J. C. nor his indorsees had any property in the bill. *Held*, further, that the defendants, not having paid the money over to J. C. before hearing of his failure, could not apply it to reducing the debt owed them by C. *Held*, further, that B., G. & S. were the real owners of the bill, and as such entitled to recover. A general endorsement of bills is *prima facie* evidence of property in the indorsee : but notwithstanding a general endorsement, paper sent only for collection will still remain the property of the sender as to all persons having notice. *Blaine* v. *Bourne*, 11 R. I. 119 ; also *Bank of Metropolis* v. *New England Bank*, 6 How. U. S. 212 ; *Collins* v. *Martin*, 1 B. & P. 648 ; *Wilson* v. *Smith*, 3 How. U. S. 763, 769.

47. **Bill of Exchange.**—Acceptance of a bill of exchange in these words : "Accepted. Payable after my advances are paid," may be explained by parol evidence, so far as to show what advances were meant, even including future advances. A conditional acceptance of a bill of exchange makes a new contract between the payee and acceptor, which can be enforced only on averment and proof that the condition has been performed. *Shackelford* v. *Hooper*, 54 Miss. 716.

48. **Bill of Exchange.**—The intention to assign a fund in the hands of another, founded upon sufficient consideration and expressed by a bill of exchange, operates as an equitable assignment to the payee. A., living in this State, had a certain fund to his credit in the hands of B. in New York, and on July 30th, 1861, gave to C., for sufficient consideration, a bill of exchange upon B. for the whole amount of the fund ; the bill of exchange was immediately endorsed by C. to D. (residing in New York) and mailed to his address, civil war between the States being then raging ; the bill of exchange was never received by D. nor had he notice

of it until 1866, when he was informed of the remittance by C., who had, however, then forgotten of whom he had purchased the bill; in 1865, the fund in the hands of B. was collected of him by A., in 1876, C. ascertained, by finding a memorandum upon an old check book, that the bill of exchange had been purchased from A. ; D. thereupon, in 1876, made a demand upon A. for payment to him of the fund, which A. declined to pay, and D. thereupon instituted suit against A. for the same. *Held*, that D. was entitled to recover. In such case, even if it was negligence upon the part of C. to have forwarded the bill of exchange by mail, A. was contributory to it and cannot take advantage of it. The statute of limitations did not begin to run against D., in such case, until after the demand made by him upon A. in 1876 for the amount of the fund. *Kahnweiler* v. *Anderson*, 78 N. C. 133.

49. **Bills of Exchange.**—*Drawn and accepted by the same parties—Custom—Re-exchange.*—Although bills of exchange, drawn and accepted by the same parties, may be in strictness promissory notes rather than bills, yet where the intention to give and receive such documents as instruments capable of being negotiated in the market as bills of exchange is clear, both the holders and the parties may treat them accordingly. A custom as to allowing a fixed percentage by way of liquidated damages in lieu of exchange, re-exchange, and other charges, when the bills are returned from the colonies dishonored, however valid in law, does not apply in the absence of an agreement, express or implied, to allow re-exchange. When the holders of bills drawn by P. L. & Co., in London, on P. L. & Co., in Australia, having no occasion to transfer money from *London* to *Australia*, sent them to the latter country, not for the purpose of employing the proceeds there, but of having them remitted to London, the dishonor of such bills does not entitle the holders to recover damages by way of re-exchange.

The right to "re-exchange," in the absence of express agreement, arises when the holder of a bill who has contracted for the transfer of funds from one country to another has sustained damages by its dishonor, through having to obtain funds in the country where the bill was payable. "Re-exchange" is the measure of those damages. *Willans* v. *Ayers*, 41 Eng. Law Reports, 3 Appeal Cases, 148—1878.

50. Bills of Exchange. *Accommodation drawer and endorser.—Remittitur of judgment against acceptor.—* H. drew and endorsed a bill of exchange on A. for the accommodation of the latter, who discounted it at a bank. *Held*, a *remittitur* by the bank of a judgment on the bill against A., discharged H. from liability as drawer and endorser. *Case* v. *Hawkins*, 53 Miss. 702.

51. Bills of Exchange.—*Protest, time of.*—In an appeal by the endorser of a bill of exchange who had been condemned with the makers,—*Held*, that to hold the endorser, demand of payment ought to have been made on the third day of grace, with protest and notification, and that, even when the bill was made payable at the residence of the holder himself. *Knapp, et al.* v. *The Bank of Montreal*, 1 L. C. R. 253, Q. B. 1850; 2306 *et seq.* C. C.

52. Bill of Exchange.—*Rights of Holder.* — If the holder of a bill of exchange locks it up for two years he makes it his own, and cannot have recourse to the person from whom he received it. *Rouleau* v. *Tourangeau*, 2 Rev. de Leg. 30, K. B. 1820.

53. Bill of Exchange.—*How Payable.*—Action on draft drawn in New York for goods sold and delivered there, and accepted in Montreal, the price charged being in United States currency. *Held*, that the draft was payable according to such currency. *Copcutt, et al.* v. *McMasters*, 7 L. C. J. 340; S. C. 1863.

54. Bills of Exchange.—*Damages.*—*Semble*, that in suit on a bill of exchange expressing value received, and drawn without the State by plaintiff, the holder, on defendant, who is acceptor, within this State, damages at ten per cent. are allowable, notwithstanding want of protest (Wagn. Stat. 215, 216, sec. 8). *Phillips* v. *Evans*, N. Y. 17.

55. **Bill of Exchange.**—*When the instrument is doubtful.*—G. drew upon W. requesting him to pay an amount named to himself or order. *Held*, that the instrument could be declared on either as a bill of exchange or promissory note. *Golding* v. *Waterhouse*, 3 New Brunswick, 313.

56. **Bill of Exchange.**—*Notice of drawer's effects.*—The endorser of a bill of exchange is in all cases entitled to notice whether the drawer have or have no effects in his hands, and on this ground the court nonsuited the plaintiff and refused his motion for a new trial. *Griffin* v. *Phillips*, 2 Rev. de Leg., 30 K. B. 1821, 2298 and 2319, *et seq.* C. C.

BILL TO FORECLOSE.

57. **Bill to Foreclose.**—A bill to foreclose a mortgage or deed of trust may be brought in the name of the real owner of the note secured. *Hahn* v. *Huber, et al.*, 83 Ill. 243.

BILLS OF LADING.

58. **Bill of Lading.**—The clause in a bill of lading which acknowledges the receipt of property, or declares as to its condition, may be disproved by parol proof. The holder of a bill of lading can acquire no greater rights under it than were possessed by the original consignee. *Hunt & Macaulay* v. *Mississippi Central R. R. Co.*, 29 La. 446.

59. **Bills of Lading** bound the carriers to forward the goods to their destination with the usual dispatch. To show usual time of transit, the shippers called a witness who testified thereto, but said he derived his information from a clerk in the freight office at the place of destination. *Held*, that fact being peculiarly within the knowledge of the carriers, that slight evidence

thereof on the part of the shippers was sufficient, and that the testimony was competent. *Newell, et al.* v. *Smith, et al.*, 49 Rowell, Vt. 255.

60. **Bills of Lading** imparted on its face as an absolute undertaking. On the book thereof were printed rules and regulations that modified such undertaking, but it did not appear that the shippers had knowledge thereof. *Held*, that evidence modifying such undertaking should come from the party apparently bound thereby. *Newell, et al.* v. *Smith, et al.*, 49 Rowell, Vt. 255.

BILLS AND NOTES.

61. **Bills and Notes.**—Possession of a note is *prima facie* evidence of ownership, and in an action thereon this title will be respected until denied by pleading. *Crosthwait, &c.* v. *Misener*, 13 Bush, Ky. 543.

62. **Bills and Notes.**—The alteration of a writing, after delivery, by a third person, without the knowledge or consent of the obligee, does not render the contract void, or release the obligors from liability. *Blakely* v. *Johnson*, 13 Bush, Ky. 197.

63. **Bills and Notes.**—A material alteration of a completed note by the principal obligor, after it had been signed by his surety, and without his consent or knowledge, before its delivery to the payee, renders it void as to the surety. The words "interest to be paid semi-annually," were added to the note in this case, but under such circumstances as not to entitle the surety to recover back the amount of the note and interest paid by him, without any knowledge of the fact that the note had been altered by the principal after the surety signed it. *Blakely* v. *Johnson*, 13 Bush, Ky. 192.

64. **Bills and Notes.**—If, on the transfer of negotiable paper, an endorsement is omitted through accident, mistake or fraud, a good title will pass in equity by mere delivery. *Hughes* v. *Nelson*, 29 N. J. 547.

65. **Bills and Notes.**—*Negotiability.—Indorsement.—Assignor.—Liability.*—An instrument in the following form is not a negotiable instrument: "$100. Neosho,

Mo., Aug. 29, 1874. —— after date, — promise to pay to the order of —— dollars, for value received, negotiable and payable, without defalcation or discount, with ten per cent. interest thereon from maturity, till paid; and if said interest shall remain unpaid for the time of one year from the maturity of this note, then the same to become as principal and to bear the same rate of interest as principal, and to be compounded annually; and we do each and severally waive any and all exemptions under and by virtue of any execution, exemption, homestead or stay laws of the State of Missouri, or that of any other State; and we do each further promise and agree to pay a reasonable attorney's fee for the bringing suit in collection after the same shall become due, payable at the Newton County Bank of Samstag & Stein." See *First Nat. B'k of Trenton* v. *Gav*, 63 Mo. 33. And the indorsement by the payee simply makes him liable as assignor to pay after the exercise of due diligence by the holder, and failure to collect from the maker after suit, or in case of the insolvency or non-residence of the maker, so that a suit would have have been unavailing. *Samstag, et al.* v. *Conley, et al.*, 64 Mo. 476.

66. **Bills or Notes** bearing the stamp of a bank may still be put in circulation. *Barthe* v. *Armstrong*, 5 R. L. 213; C. C. 1869.

BILLS OF SALE.

67. **Bill of Sale.**—An absolute bill of sale, executed to secure a debt, operates as a mortgage, and will be postponed to a subsequent and recorded mortgage. *Rogers* v. *Vaughan*, 31 Ark. 62.

BONDS.

68. **Bonds.**—If a negotiable city bond be stolen, and its number be altered by the thief, it will be good in the hands of a subsequent *bona fide* holder who takes it for value. *Elizabeth City* v. *Force, et al.*, 29 N. J. 587.

69. Bonds.—*Jointly and Severally.*—In debt on a writing obligatory, as follows: "Know all men by these presents that we, William J. Clark, of the city of Providence, R. I., as principal, and A. E. Burnside, Eben A. Kelly, and John Gorham, as sureties, are held and firmly bound unto the President, Directors and Company of the Commercial National Bank of the city of Providence, R. I., in the sum of ten thousand dollars; that is to say, the said William J. Clark in the whole of said sum above named, and the said A. E. Burnside, Eben A. Kelly, and John Gorham, each as surety respectively in the sum of thirty-three hundred and thirty-three and 33-100 dollars, to be paid to them, the said Commercial National Bank, their attorney, successors, or assigns, for which payment well and truly to be made, we do hereby bind ourselves, our heirs, executors, and administrators firmly by these presents." *Held*, That the obligation was several; Clark being bound in one whole sum of $10,000, and Burnside, Kelly, and Gorham, being each bound in one sum of $3,333 1-3. *Commercial National Bank v. Gorham*, 11 R. I. 162.

70. Bonds.—*Official.*—*Held*, that if the secretary was entrusted with the funds of the company, notwithstanding it was also the prescribed duty of the president to receive the money paid to the company and to deposit the same, and he was responsible for any failure of duty on his part, that did not relieve the secretary from responsibility for the faithful disposition of any funds confided to his care. That the unauthorized act of the president in entrusting funds to the secretary could not discharge the secretary from the faithful preservation thereof. That the stipulation of the bond was an undertaking for the fidelity and honesty of the secretary commensurate with the scope of his duties, and the enumeration in the 4th article of the by-laws of certain things to be performed by him, did not supersede this obligation which pervaded every department of his official functions. That the company had the right under this stipulation to insist upon indemnity for any deviation from the line of his duty to its prejudice. That in the absence of any provision to the contrary, such is the necessary import of the terms of the contract, and the sureties in executing the bond must be held as stipulating to this effect. Whilst it is an undoubted proposition, that the liability of the surety is not to be extended by implication beyond the terms of his written contract, by which his responsibility is to be measured, the bond constituting such contract must have such construction given to it as to carry out the intention of the parties thereto, and in this respect there is no difference between such contract and any other. *Engler* v. *People's Fire Ins. Co.*, 46 Md. 322.

71. **Bonds.**—A municipal corporation cannot, without legislative authority, issue bonds in aid of an extraneous object. Every person dealing in them must, at his peril, take notice of the existence and terms of the law which, it is claimed, conferred the power to issue them, no matter under what circumstances he may obtain them. *Town of South Ottawa* v. *Perkins*, 94 U. S. 260.

72. **Bonds.**—In a suit by a *bona fide* holder against a municipal corporation to recover the amount of coupons annexed to bonds issued by it, under authority conferred by law, questions of form merely, or irregularity, or fraud, or misconduct on the part of its agents, cannot be considered. *Town of East Lincoln* v. *Davenport*, 94 U. S. 801.

73. **Bonds.**—When there is a total want of authority to issue municipal bonds, there can be no *bona fide* holding of them. *Township of East Oakland* v. *Skinner*, 94 U. S. 255.

74. **Bonds.**—*Municipal.*—Every dealer in municipal bonds, which upon their face, refer to the statute under which they were issued, is bound to take notice of all its requirements. Where upon their face, the coupons refer to the bonds to which they were attached, and purport to be the semi-annual interest ac-

cruing thereon, the purchaser of them is charged with notice of all which the bonds contain. *Cromwell* v. *County of Sac*, 96 U. S. 51.

75. Bond and Mortgage *to bank—Deposit—Set-off.*—Defendant borrowed, July 5, 1875, of the New Amsterdam Savings Bank, the sum of $5,000, for which he executed his bond and mortgage. On the 20th day of September, 1876, the bank became insolvent and passed into the hands of the plaintiff as receiver. At that time there was due and owing defendant, as a depositor of the bank, the sum of $1,748.01. Held, that defendant was entitled to a set-off for the amount of his deposit. *Receiver of New Amsterdam Savings Bank* v. *Tartter*, 54 Howard, N. Y. 385.

76. Bonds of the State.—Under the provisions of the act of the Legislature authorizing an exchange of State bonds with certain railroad companies, the State was to occupy two relations to those who bought its bonds from the company. The first was that of a debtor to the holder, and the second was that of a trustee holding the bond of the company and the lien created by the act to secure payment of the party who advanced money to the company. The Legislature had no authority to create the first relation. It did have power to enact the second. *Holland* v. *T. State of Florida, et al.*, 15 Fla. 455.

77. Bond under seal, though voluntary, creates a debt, and is impeachable only for fraud. Such a bond is enforceable against the grantor and all claiming under the grantor as volunteers. *Garden, Ex'r'x* v. *Derrickson, et al.*, 2 Del. 386.

78. Bonds Stolen.—On an indictment for receiving "three bonds of the United States, each of the value of ten thousand dollars, of the property" of one S., it appeared that the bonds were, after they were stolen, and before they were received by the defendant, fraudulently altered by erasing the name of S. and inserting the name of C.; the verdict was "guilty of receiving two bonds." *Held*, that the fraudulent alteration did not take away from them the character of bonds of the United States or deprive S. of his ownership in them. *Commonwealth* v. *White*, 123 Mass. 430.

79. **Bond.**—*Surety.*—Where a party has given a bond to another to secure the faithful performance of the contract of a third person, it is the duty of the obligee to give reasonable notice to the guarantor of any defalcation on the part of the contractor. It is the prerogative of the court to define the character of the notice, and the duty of the jury to determine whether such reasonable notice has been given. *Roberts, et al.* v. *Woven Wire Mattress Co.*, 46 Md. 374.

80. Where a guaranty is subsequent to the contract between the principal and the guarantee, and forms no part of the consideration thereof, it requires a distinct consideration to give it efficacy as a collateral undertaking. But where a guaranty expressly referred to a previous agreement between the principal and the guarantee, which was executory in its character, and embraced prospective dealings between the parties; then the guaranty purports upon its face, and by necessary construction, a sufficient consideration. *Roberts, et al.* v. *Woven Wire Mattress Co.*, 46 Md. 374.

81. Where a contract of guaranty was signed by the guarantor, and delivered to the agent of the guarantee, and was in the possession of the guarantee at the time of a suit upon the contract, and was produced by him; there is sufficient *prima facie* evidence of the delivery and acceptance of the contract of guaranty, and other notice of its acceptance is unnecessary, unless there had been a stipulation to that effect. *Id.*

Where a guarantor warranted the faithful performance by his principal of certain duties stipulated in a contract, among which was the duty of making returns of sales; the failure by the guarantee to notify the guarantor of his principal's default, and permitting the principal to make returns in a manner different from the stipulated mode, cannot afford sufficient evidence of the abandonment of the contract and the substitution of another. *Id.*

BROKERS.

82. Brokers.—*Commission.*—When a real estate broker undertakes to furnish a purchaser, he is bound to act in good faith in presenting a person as such, and when one is presented the employer is not bound to accept him, or pay the commission, unless he is ready and able to perform the contract on his part according to the terms proposed. If the principal accepts the person presented, either upon the terms previously proposed or upon modified terms then agreed upon, and a valid contract is entered into between the principal and the person presented by the broker, the commission is earned. *Coleman's Ex'r* v. *Meade & Co.*, 13 Bush, Ky. 358.

CERTIFICATES.

83. Certificate of deposit given by a bank payable to order after fifteen days, and bearing interest in case the deposit should remain three months and upwards, is a promissory note. *Richer* v. *Voyer, et al.*, 5 R. L. 213, S. C. R.

84. Certificate *of deposit.*—A certificate of deposit is evidence of so high and satisfactory a character as to the sum deposited, that, to escape its effects, the maker must overcome it by clear and satisfactory evidence. Where the testimony, aside from the certificate, is balanced as to the amount deposited, the certificate will turn the scale. *First Nat. Bank of Lacon* v. *Myers*, 83 Ill. 507.

85. Certificate *of deposit.—Interest on, after due.—* When a certificate of deposit by its terms matures six months after date, and is to bear six per cent. interest from date, it will continue to bear the same rate of interest until paid. And where a bank brings up a plain case like this, the judgment will be affirmed with ten per cent. damages. *Cordell* v. *First Nat. Bank of Kansas City*, 64 Mo. 600.

86. **Certificate** *of incorporation defective.*—In a suit against a religious corporation where the certificate of incorporation was defective and insufficient to show that the defendant was a corporation. *Held*, 1st. That the fact that it held itself out as a corporation and treated with the plaintiff as such, did not estop it from denying its liability as a corporation. 2d. That the statute law of the State having expressly required certain prescribed acts to be done to constitute a corporation, the omission of those requisites cannot be supplied by the application of the doctrine of estoppel. *Boyce* v. *Trustees of the M. E. Church*, 46 Md. 359.

CHARGES ON BOOK.

87. **Charges on book.**—A person who has charged A. on his books for goods sold, may yet show that they were in fact sold on the credit of a corporation of which A. was agent, and that the corporation received the goods and gave the seller credit for them. *Northford Rivet Co.* v. *Blackman Manuf. Co.*, 44 Conn. 183.

CHATTEL MORTGAGES.

88. **Chattel Mortgage.**—Taylor mortgaged certain personal property, including a growing crop, to secure advances of goods, etc., to enable Taylor, a planter, to make and gather the crop. The mortgage debt not being paid, Paterson commenced suit to foreclose the mortgage, whereupon the mortgagor interposed that the mortgaged property had been selected and set apart to him as "exempted from forced sale under any process of law." *Held*, that the term "forced sale" as used in the Constitution, is a sale against the will of the owner, and not a sale to which he had expressly consented by giving the mortgage; that having thus for a valuable consideration, given his consent to the alienation of the property, upon his breach of the con-

dition of the mortgage, he is estopped from revoking it; and the court, in ordering a sale, does but decree a specific performance of the agreement, which agreement was not forbidden by law. *Paterson* v. *Taylor*, 15 Florida, 336.

89. Chattel Mortgage.—A chattel mortgage permitting the mortgagor to remain in possession, and to sell, and apply the proceeds, or any part of them, to his own use, is fraudulent and void in law as against creditors. While the holder of a chattel mortgage may relinquish his rights as such, and accept the chattels from the mortgagor in payment of his debt, or as a pledge, such a shifting of title must be open, express and explicit, both debtor and creditor being expressly parties to the payment or pledge, and their acts in that behalf established as expressly and satisfactory as payment or pledge in any other case. *Blakeslee* v. *Rossman*, 43 Wis. 116.

90. Chattel Mortgage.—A chattel mortgage given as continuing security to cover present and future indebtedness, is valid not only between the parties, but, when free from fraud, as to creditors. *Brown* v. *Kiefer*, 71 N. Y. 610.

91. Chattel Mortgage.—A mortgage may be fraudulent as against creditors, although founded on a valuable consideration. *Braley* v. *Byrnes*, 20 Minn. 435.

92. Chattel Mortgage, made to secure debts maturing at a future day, which conveys a stock of goods in a particular store, and any other goods which may from time to time, during the existence of the mortgage, be purchased by the grantors and put into said store to replace any part of said stock which may have been disposed of, or to increase and enlarge the stock now on hand, is void *per se*. *Phelps* v. *Murray*, 2 Tenn. Eq. 746.

93. Chattel Mortgage.—A mortgage of personal property from A. to B., expressed to be "subject to prior mortgages" to a certain amount to C., the amount and terms of which are known to B., conveys only the right to redeem the property from C.'s mortgage, and, although recorded first, does not take precedence of C.'s mortgage. *Pecker* v. *Silsby*, 123 Mass. 108.

94. Chattel Mortgage.—It is not necessary to the validity of a mortgage of chattels that it should be in writing. *McKeithen* v. *Pratt*, 53 Ala. 116.

95. Chattel Mortgage.—A. sold and delivered to B. certain machinery for the manufacture of a patent machine, the license to manufacture which was to expire at a certain date, and took in payment a note, secured by a mortgage back upon the machinery and referring to an agreement of even date between the parties, by which A. was to retain in payment of the note a part of the price of such machines as B. should make for him. When the license expired a balance was due upon the note which B. failed to pay on demand. *Held*, That A. was entitled to foreclose the mortgage for the payment of the debt secured thereby. *Avery* v. *Bushnell*, 123 Mass. 349.

96. Chattel Mortgage.—*When valid.*—In Rhode Island a mortgage of personal property to be subsequently acquired conveys no title to such property when acquired, which is valid at law against the mortgagor or his voluntary assignee, unless after acquisition possession of such property is given to the mortgagee or taken by him under the mortgage. *Cook* v. *Corthell*, 11 R. I. 482.

97. Chattel Mortgage.—*Title after delivery by and return to mortgagor.*—Although a mortgage of personal property to be subsequently acquired is in itself ineffectual to vest in the mortgagee a legal title to the property, yet if after acquisition by the mortgagor the mortgagee by delivery from, or by consent of the mortgagor, takes possession of the property under the mortgage conveyance, the title to the property both in law and equity vests in the mortgagee without further conveyance or bill of sale. *Cook* v. *Corthell*, 11 R. I. 482.

98. Chattel Mortgage.—Although the parties to a chattel mortgage neglect to make and subscribe the affidavit required by Gen. Stats., ch. 123, sec. 6, and although the mortgage is not recorded, it is nevertheless a valid mortgage as against an attaching creditor, provided possession of the mortgaged property be taken by the mortgagee. *Clark* v. *Tarbell*, 57 Hall, N. H. 328.

99. Where a mortgage is given to secure several notes held by different parties, a writ of entry to foreclose the mortgage must be in the names of all the owners of the notes. *Noyes* v. *Barnet*, 57 Hall, N. H. 605.

100. **Chattel Mortgage.**—The description in a chattel mortgage should be so explicit as to enable third persons, aided by the inquiries which the instrument itself sugggests, to identify the property covered thereby, and a mortgage mis-describing property will not affect the purchase of the same by a third party by imparting to him notice of the incumbrance. *Ivins* v. *Hines*, 45 Iowa, 73.

101. **Chattel Mortgage.**—Because a mortgagee of a chattel temporarily uses it with the assent of the mortgagor, and then returns it to him, the mortgage lien upon it is not thereby extinguished.

102. To make applicable the rule that in the absence of a specific appropriation of payments by either the debtor or creditor, the law will appropriate them, there must be some testimony tending to show that no such appropriation has been made by the parties. *Albert, Sheriff* v. *Lindau*, 46 Md. 334.

103. **Chattel Mortgage** does not protect from execution materials purchased by the execution debtor before it was given. *Held*, that this contract (chattel mortgage) of indemnity only amounted to a mortgage on the materials, and not being filed, did not protect materials that had been sold to the principal before it was executed, from seizure on execution. *Hurd* v. *Brown*, 37 Mich. 484.

104. **Chattel Mortgages.**—A chattel mortgage, as between the parties, is valid, without any acknowledg-

ment; but without the acknowledgment it has no effect upon the rights of third parties acting in good faith, and notice of such a mortgage does not prevent a creditor from subjecting the property to the payment of his debt. *McDowell, et al.* v. *Stewart*, 83 Ill. 538.

105. Chattel Mortgage.—The mortgagor of a chattel, with the verbal consent of the mortgagees, sold it to the defendant without notifying him of the existence of the mortgage; but before delivery, and before payment of the purchase-money, the mortgagees informed the defendant of the mortgage, and that they would hold him accountable to them for the price. *Held*, that the mortgagees could recover the price of the purchase in an action of assumpsit in their own names. *Bank* v. *Raymond*, 57 Hall, N. H. 144; *Huntington* v. *Knox*, 7 Cush. 373.

106. Chattel Mortgage.—*When a mortgagee of chattels upon a public sale makes reasonable and fair efforts* to sell the property for a good price, and through the acts, statements and notice of the mortgagor at the time of sale, the effect of which is to discourage bidding, and the same does not bring a full price, a court of equity will not set aside the sale on the application of the mortgagor. The effect of a public sale, upon due notice, under a chattel mortgage is to cut off the equity of redemption of a mortgagor. A mortgagee, under a chattel mortgage, may himself become a purchaser on a public sale of chattels. In order to redeem under a chattel mortgage the mortgagor must in good faith pay or tender the whole mortgage debt, and that before suit brought.

Where the plaintiff upon a trial is not found to have just ground for equitable relief, the action cannot be held to adjust rights and claims between co-defendants, not related to the cause of action set up in the complaint. *Hall* v. *Ditson*, 55 Howard, N. Y. 19.

107. Chattel Mortgage.—*Usury.—Sale under the mortgage.—Purchase by mortgagee.—Effect of sale.—Action to redeem.—Claims of co-defendants.*—Upon the loan of money to be secured by a chattel mortgage on copyrights, music plates, &c., &c., a printing contract between the parties being made at the same time, by which it was agreed that the mortgagees might print music from the plates of the mortgagor, the expense of printing and materials to be borne by the mortgagees, the profits from the music so printed to be divided equally between the parties, it appearing that the loan of the money and the printing contract were part and parcel of one general arrangement in the beginning, but were in fact made afterwards divisible, and after the mortgage was executed, and before the printing contract was made, the option was given to the mortgagors to give up the printing agreement, but they desired it to be made. *Held*, that the transaction was not usurious. *Clark* v. *Sheehan*, 47 Howard, N. Y. 188 ; also 55 Howard, N. Y. Practice Reports, 19.

108. Chattel Mortgage.—A chattel mortgage upon after-acquired goods will hold against a *bona fide* purchaser with notice. He can have no better title than his vendor. *Robson, et al.* v. *Mich. Central R. R. Co.*, 37 Mich. 70.

CHECKS.

109. Check.—*Garnishee Order.*—A garnishee order was made under Order XLV., Rule 2, attaching a debt. At the time the order was made the garnishees had given the judgment debtor a check for the amount of the debt. Upon service of the order on the garnishees they stopped payment of the check at the bank, the check not having been presented. *Held*, that upon the check being stopped it was as if it had never been given, and that there was therefore an existing debt capable of being attached, and the garnishee order was effectual. *Cohen* v. *Hale*, 3 App. Cas. (41 Victoria Law Report, Eng.) 371.

110. Check *of firm to pay individual partner's debt.*—If a partner consents that a check of the firm be applied on an individual debt of his copartner, he may, at any time before such application is in fact made, or the rights of third parties intervene, withdraw such consent, and after notice by him, not to so apply the check, it cannot be so applied. *National Bank of Jacksonville* v. *Mapes, et al.*, 85 Ill. 67.

111. Check contained this recital: "To hold as collateral for 1,000 P. T. oil, pipage paid," &c., and across its face the cashier of the bank certified "Good when properly endorsed." *Held*, that this check was not drawn in the usual course of banking business and the certificate of the cashier would not bind the bank. *Dorsey* v. *Abrams*, 85 Penn. 299.

112. Check.—The drawer of a check delivered it to the payee, intending thereby to give to the payee the fund on which the check was drawn. *Held*, that until the check was either paid or accepted, the gift was incomplete, and that in the absence of such payment or acceptance, the death of the drawer operated, as against the payee, as a revocation of the check. *Simmons* v. *Savings Society*, 31 Ohio, 457.

113. Check—Payment.—The giving of a check by the debtor with the intention of appropriating it to the debt of the plaintiffs, and the giving of a receipt therefor by the plaintiffs' agent, acting within the scope of his authority, constitute by the law of Canada an appropriation as intended. Such appropriation could only be changed by a rescission of the appropriation made by consent of all parties interested. In an action against the agent for moneys had and received on account of the plaintiffs, such rescission, being put on the footing of a contract by the Canadian law, must be specially pleaded as a defence. *Kershaw* v. *Kirkpatrick*, 41–42 Eng. Law Reports, 3 App. Cases, 345.

114. Check.—*Handed a Bank by a Depositor.*— When checks on another bank are handed by a depositor to the receiving teller of a bank, and are by the teller credited on the depositor's pass-book, they are only received for collection, and if not paid on presen-

tation, may be returned and the credit in the pass-book canceled. *National Gold Bank* v. *McDonald*, 51 Cal. 64. *Boyd* v. *Emerson*, 2 Adolphus & Ellis, 184.

115. Check.—A check is an appropriation of so much of the maker's funds in the bank upon which it is drawn as is necessary to meet it; hence the maker cannot object to any delay in presenting it, unless he can show special injury to himself arising therefrom. If the maker has withdrawn from the bank his entire deposit against which the check is drawn he is not injured by any delay in presenting it, or any lack of formal notice of its non-payment, before action brought. *Emory* v. *Hobson*, 63 Me. 32.

116. Check.—The rightful possession of a check made payable to the order of a particular person, confers no authority on the drawee to pay the same to the person having such possession, without the genuine endorsement of the payee. If the drawee relies upon false representations as to identity, for which neither the drawer nor payee are responsible, he to identity, for which neither the drawer nor payee are responsible, he makes payment to a wrong person, at his peril. *Dodge* v. *Nat. Ex. B'k*, 30 Ohio, 1.

117. Checks.—A bank which pays out money on a check, purporting to be signed by a depositor, but the signature on which is in fact forged by his clerk, is not, in the absence of evidence that the clerk has, or was supposed by the bank to have, any authority to sign the depositor's name, exempt from liability to the depositor, by proof that the forgery was committed on a blank form taken from the depositor's check-book, which was left lying about in his office during the day; that it was stamped with a hand stamp, sometimes used on his checks, and which was accessible to any one in the office; that the clerk was allowed to fill up checks, and was introduced by the depositor to the officers of the bank as the person who was authorized to receive money on the depositor's checks. *Mackintosh* v. *Eliot National Bank*, 123 Mass. 393.

118. **Checks.**—Where upon the face of a check it is apparent that it was not drawn in the usual course of business, that it was not a commercial check, a cashier has no authority to certify such a check, and such certificate is not binding upon the bank, nor can it be made so by any subsequent acts of ratification by said cashier. *Dorsey* v. *Abrams*, 85 Penn. 299.

119. **Check.**—If a customer of a bank hands the receiving teller a check drawn by another person upon the same bank, and at the same time hands him his pass-book, and the teller receives the check and enters a credit for the amount in the pass-book, but no entry is made on the books of the bank, and nothing else is said or done, and the drawer has no funds in the bank, the check may be returned to the depositor and the credit in the pass-book canceled. In such a case, a finding by the court that the check was received as a cash deposit is erroneous. *National Gold Bank* v. *McDonald*, 51 Cal. 64.

120. **Check.**—The payee of a check before it is accepted by the drawee cannot maintain an action upon it against the latter, as there is no privity of contract between them. *So held*, where a check of the Treasurer of the United States upon a national bank duly designated as a depository of the public money, having been paid upon an unauthorized endorsement of the name of the payee, suit to recover the amount of the check was brought by its owner against the bank. *First National Bank of Washington* v. *Whitman*, 94 U. S. 343.

121. The rights of the parties are not changed by the fact, on a settlement of accounts between the treasurer and the bank, the check, on the supposition that it had been properly paid, was credited to the bank. Such an error does not effect the real state of the accounts; when it is discovered, they are open to correction. *Id.*

122. Payment to a stranger upon an unauthorized indorsement does not operate as an acceptance of the check, so as to authorize an action by the real owner to recover its amount as upon an accepted check. *Id.*

123. Check.—A check was drawn to Cook; Barnes endorsed Cook's name without his authority and received the money; the bank deducted the check from the drawer's account and settled with him on that basis. —*Held*, that Cook could recover the amount of the check from the bank. The conduct of the bank was an acceptance and bound it as a certified check would. *Seventh National Bank* v. *Cook*, 73 Penn. 483.

124. Check.—*Copy.*—The protest of a dishonored check is not a written instrument which can be made the basis of an action, and in an action by the payee, against the drawer, of such check, a copy of the protest forms no part of the complaint, and cannot aid its averments.

125. If, in such action, the complaint fails to aver that the defendant has been notified of the non-payment of such instrument, or alleges no excuse for the failure to give such notice, it is sufficient on demurrer. *Griffin* v. *Kemp*, 46 Ind. 172; also *Pollard, Adm'r* v. *Bowen*, 57 Ind. 232.

126. Check.—*Diligence.*—*Presentment for payment.* —The same rule applies to checks as does to bills of exchange and endorsed promissory notes, in regard to the deligence to be used in presenting them for payment. See *Edwards on Bills and Promissory Notes*, pages 57, 389, 890 and 391; also decision in 57 Ind. 232.

127. Check.—A check given to carry out an agreement made in contravention of the provision of the Bankrupt Act (sec. 45), prohibiting officers of courts in bankruptcy from taking anything other than the fees allowed by the act for acts done under it, is not absolutely void; notwithstanding the illegality of the consideration, it is valid in the hands of a *bona fide* holder for value, taking it, before it is dishonored, without notice of its illegality. The burden of showing that the transferee had notice of the infirmity in the paper is upon the party seeking to impeach his title. *Cowing* v. *Altman*, 71 N. Y. 435.

128. Checks.—Where a bank directs checks drawn upon it to be presented for payment to another bank, if a check be there presented and payment refused, the drawer is discharged, if notice of non-payment be not given, though the check be presented to the drawees on the following day, but they had failed in the *interim*. *East River Bank* v. *Gedney*, 4 E. D. Sm. 582.

129. Check.—*Enjoined.*—If the bank on which a check is drawn, be enjoined from making any payments by an injunction out of chancery, half an hour after being opened for business, on the day following that on which it was given, the holder is excused from presentment, and may recover on the original consideration. *Lovett* v. *Cornwall*, 6 Wend. 369; S. C., 1 Hall, 56.

130. Check.—A check drawn in the ordinary form, not describing any particular fund, or using any words of transfer of the whole or any part of any amount standing to the credit of the drawer, does not operate as an assignment, equitable or otherwise, of funds of the drawer, in the hands of the drawee; and it is immaterial that the drawee is not a bank. *In re Merrill*, 71 N. Y. 325.

131. Checks.—The holder of a check, on whom it has been fraudently passed, in payment of a pre-existing debt, is not bound to present it, before bringing suit on his original cause of action. *Devoe* v. *Moffatt*, Anth. N. P. 221.

132. Check.—*Payment.*—A check, it is true, is a payment until presented and refused; but a bill is payment only if it be so agreed, and if payment by bill be part of the agreement, it must be evidenced in writing. Chitty, 681. *Mahalen* v. *The Dublin & Chapelizod Distillery Co.*, 2 Irish Reports, Common Law Series, 83.

133. Check.—A verbal agreement between the payee and the drawer of a check, contemporaneous with its execution and delivery, that the former will not present it to the drawee for payment until a certain time, is sufficient excuse for a delay until the time specified in presenting it for payment. Demand for the payment of a check, and notice of non-payment of the same, are no part of the contract between the drawer and payee, but are steps in the legal remedy of the latter. *Pollard, Adm. v. Bowen*, 57 Ind. 232.

134. Check.—*Protest.*—No protest for non-payment of a check drawn upon a bank is necessary to render the drawee liable to the payee. *Pollard v. Bowen*, 57 Ind. 232.

135. Check.—The date of a check is *prima facie* evidence of the time it was made and had its inception; and if found in the hands of the payee or third person for a considerable time (in this case fourteen months) after its date, will be deemed to be discredited. A party taking it is put upon inquiry, and, in the absence of explanation, takes subject to any defence existing as between the payee and drawer.

136. Check, however, has no inception until delivery, and for all legal purposes is to be considered as made on the day it is delivered; when the date and the time of the delivery are not the same, the latter may be shown in answer to any such defense. A party negotiating for it, who ascertains that the check was in fact delivered on the day it is offered to him, is not bound to go further and inquire as to any other objection to it; and if he takes it *bona fide*, for value, without notice of illegality or other defence, and it appears that it was in fact delivered on the day it was negotiated, he stands in no worse position than if he had first inquired and been informed of this fact. When, therefore, a check is delivered by the drawer to the payee long after its date, and is upon the same day transferred by the latter to a *bona fide* purchaser for value without notice of any defence, it is valid in his hand, notwithstanding a defect or illegality in the consideration which would be a good defense as between the drawer and payee. *Id*.

137. Accordingly, *held*, where, in pursuance of an arrangement between an assignee in bankruptcy and creditors, a check for additional compensation over and above his fees, dated on the day it was made, was deposited with a third person, to be delivered to the payee when he was discharged from his position as assignee, which check remained in the hands of the depository for fourteen months, and was then delivered upon the order of the payee, on the day the latter was discharged as assignee, to a *bona fide* purchaser from him for value, that the check had inception only on delivery, and that, in the absence of evidence of notice to the purchaser, of any defence, he, or his transferee, could, upon its being presented for payment and disdishonored, enforce it against the drawer. *Cowing* v. *Altman*, 71 N. Y. 435.

138. **Check.**—An order, check or draft, to have the effect of an equitable assignment, must be drawn on a particular, specified fund. *In re Merrill*, 71 N. Y. 325.

139. Accordingly, *held*, where an insurance company gave its check upon a trust company, in payment of a loss, the company having at the time on deposit a sum exceeding the amount of the check, but, prior to its presentation, a receiver of the company was appointed, who withdrew all the funds deposited, that the check, not having been drawn on a particular fund, did not operate as an equitable assignment *pro tanto* of the deposit; and that, the claim having been only liquidated, not paid, when the company failed and went into the hands of the receiver, whereby the rights of all the creditors became fixed by the statute, the payee of the check was not entitled to have the same paid by the receiver out of the funds, in preference to the claims of other creditors. Also, *held*, that the fact that there was a receipt on the back of the check—in-

tended for the signature of the payee—did not affect its negotiability of the particular fund. *In re Merrill*, 71 N. Y. 325.

COLLATERAL.

140. Collateral Security.—A creditor who holds railroad bonds as collateral security for a debt is not bound by an unexecuted promise to the debtor, made without consideration, to give them up. Nor does he lose his right to hold such bonds by suing the principal debtor and recovering execution, and arresting the body of the debtor thereon. *Smith* v. *Strout*, 63 Me. 205.

COLLECTIONS.

141. Collections.—When a draft is indorsed over for collection, the indorsee is not a *bona fide* holder for value, though a creditor of the indorser. *Philbrick* v. *Dallett*, 2 J. & Sp. 370; S. C., 43 How. N. Y. 409.

142. Collection Agents.—Liability for moneys collected by sub-agents. Collection agents, to whom notes are intrusted for collection, are liable for moneys received by attorneys employed by them, and which are not paid over, although the receipt given for claims when deposited for collection states: "avails are to be promptly paid over on receipt by us." *Held*, that the defendants' true relation and liability are not at all affected by this language. The money was received by them in law when collected by the sub-agent. The receipt was intended as an assurance of prompt payment over and nothing more. *Mondel, et al.* v. *Mower, et al.*, 55 Howard, N. Y. 242.

143. Collections.—An attorney at law, employed to collect a debt, may receive payment thereof in money, but has no right to accept anything else in satisfaction without express authority from his client, and if he does it will be no payment unless ratified or assented to by his client. He cannot give the debtor an acquittance of the claim by receiving payment thereof in a debt, he, the attorney, owes the debtor.

He has no right to accept notes, bonds, etc., of the debtor, as collateral security for the debt, without express authority from his client, and if he does so, his client will not be bound unless he assents to or ratifies the same. If an attorney, without the authority of his client, accept bonds, etc., of the debtor, with the understanding that he is to collect them and apply them as payment on the claim when collected, in that transaction he is the attorney of the debtor, and not the attorney of his original client. As soon, however, as he receives any money on the claims thus put in his hands for collection by the debtor, it is a payment to that extent, less his fees for collecting, upon the claim of his original client. *Wiley* v. *Mahood, et al.*, 10 West Virginia, 206.

144. Collecting Agent.—A firm in Michigan left for collection with the plaintiffs, a bank in that State, a sight draft of their own for $500, on "J. C., treasurer of the M. S. Co." a manufacturing corporation in Connecticut. The plaintiffs at once sent the draft to the defendants, a bank in Connecticut, with directions to "return at once without protest if not paid." The defendants presented the draft to the drawee, and he replied that he would look up his account with the drawers and inform the cashier with regard to payment. The drawers had also written J. C. that such a draft had been forwarded, and he wrote them in reply: "The $500 draft has been received and paid. Don't draw any more." On the receipt of this letter the drawers showed it to the plaintiffs, who, believing the draft had been duly paid, paid the drawers the $500. J. C., the drawee, was also president of the defendant bank, and this fact was known to the plaintiffs. The draft had not in fact been paid, though the drawee supposed it had, but the defendants had neglected to return it or send notice of its non-payment. If they had returned it at once it would have prevented the payment of the $500 to the drawers. Several days later the cashier returned the draft unpaid, which was his first information to the plaintiffs with regard to the matter. The plaintiffs thereupon demanded repayment of the drawers, which was refused. They were solvent, but had no visible property, and the claim could not have been collected without much difficulty. *Held*, 1. That the defendants, as agents of the plaintiffs for the collection of the draft, had been guilty of negligence in not obtaining payment of the draft or returning it at once to the plaintiffs. 2. That, although the plaintiffs paid the money to the drawers upon the statement of the drawee to the drawers that the draft had been paid, yet, as they would have been saved from loss if the defendants had performed their duty, the defendants were liable for the actual damages resulting from their neglect. 3. That these damages were to be regarded as the whole amount paid by the plaintiffs to the drawers, and that they had a right to recover this sum, although they had a right of action for the whole amount against the drawers. *Merchants and Manufacturers' Bank* v. *Stafford Bank*, 44 Conn. 564.

145. Compromise.—*Criminal Action.*—There can be no legal compromise of a criminal charge, where the person has not been arrested, nor in any way held to answer the charge. In effecting a compromise of larceny, under the statute, the person whose property has been stolen has no right to exact or receive from the person committing the larceny, anything more than the property stolen or its value, and the necessary expense of reclaiming it. *Saxon* v. *Hill*, 6 Oregon, 388.

CONFEDERATE CURRENCY.

146. Confederate Currency.—A co-surety, who discharged a judgment by paying it in Confederate money, can maintain an action for contribution against the other surety. The value of the Confederate money, at the payment, with interest, was the amount which such

payment would entitle plaintiff to recover; not the amount of the judgment discharged. *Edmonds* v. *Sheahan*, 47 Texas, 443.

147. Confederate Money.—The fact that a payment of a note was in Confederate States Treasury notes, did not prevent it from being a valid payment when made. *Long* v. *Walker*, 47 Texas, 173.

148. Confederate Currency.—*Gold.*—A sale of property, for cash, was made in Monroe County, with reference to Confederate States Treasury notes as a standard of value, on December 26, 1862. The balance of the purchase money actually paid must be reduced to its true gold value as to that date; but in ascertaining this value, the price at which gold was then selling in Confederate currency in Richmond or elsewhere in the Confederate States is not to be regarded as fixing the relative value of gold and Confederate notes. The value of Confederate notes then, as compared with gold, should be ascertained by the then average apparent appreciation in value, when sold for Confederate currency, of all kinds of property, real and personal, in Monroe County, as compared with the value of such property just before the war commenced, when gold was the currency of the country. *Bierne* v. *Brown's Adm'r*, 10 West Virginia, 748.

149. Confederate Notes.—A decree, or a judgment, when rendered upon a contract payable in Confederate Treasury notes, should be for a sum equal to the value of those notes, not in the gold coin, but in the legal-tender currency of the United States, at the time and the place where they were payable. Such notes can in no proper sense be regarded as commodities merely. *Bissell* v. *Heyward*, 96 *U. S.* 580.

CONFLICT OF LAWS.

150. Conflict of Laws.—*Of the Right and the Remedy.* —The *lex loci* governs in determining the validity, and in the construction of contracts, but in respect to the time, mode and extent of the remedy the *lex fori* governs. Statutes of limitation fixing the time within which an action may be brought, laws providing for a set-off, and statutes exempting property from levy and sale for debt, or exempting wages from garnishment, relate to the remedy only, and such laws of a State where a debt is contracted cannot be invoked where the remedy is sought to be enforced in a different State. *Mineral Point R. R. Co.* v. *Barron*, 83 Ill. 365.

151. **Conflict of Laws.**—The law of this State prohibiting an individual from doing business under a *firm* name, does not affect a person residing in another State. *Succession of Bofenschen*, 29 La. 711.

COMITY.

152. **Comity.**—In the interpretation of commercial contracts, this court will be largely influenced, and guided, by the law merchant of the United States, and the constructions of that law made by the Supreme Court of the United States. *Chaffraix & Agar* v. *Price, Hine and Tupper*, 29 La. 176.

COMMON CARRIERS.

153. **Common Carriers.**—*Agent.*—*Bill of Lading.*—*Evidence.*—*Damages.*—A carrier of freight who expressly contracts to deliver goods at a destination beyond the terminus of his own road is answerable for the negligence of any connecting road in the line of transportation. *Newall, et al.* v. *Smith, et al.*, 49 Rowell, Vt., 255.

COMMUNITY OF PROPERTY.

154. **Community Property.**—Property purchased during marriage, whether in the name of the husband or the wife, becomes community property. *Succession of Carmelite Planchet*, 29 La. 520.

155. **Community—Dissolution.**—After the dissolution of the community, the husband, as its former head, has

no power to sell, and can convey title to no greater part of the community property than his undivided half-interest in it. *W. W. Bennett* v. *J. W. Fuller*, 29 La. 663.

COMPOSITION.

156. Composition agreement *obtained by fraud.*— Where a party induced a creditor to sign a composition agreement, whereby he accepted one-half of his claim in full, upon the representation of his debtor that no person had received any other thing, etc., the fact that the debtor had given his note for $500 to induce another creditor to sign the same agreement, which note, upon suit thereon, was adjudged void, is not sufficient to avoid the contract of composition, as it worked no injury to the creditor. *Bartlett, et al.* v. *Blaine*, 83 Ill. 25.

CONSIDERATION.

157. Consideration.—*Adequacy.*—The waiver of a legal or equitable right is a sufficient consideration to support a promise. Where there is any consideration, the law will not inquire into its adequacy. *Buckner* v. *McIlroy*, 31 Ark. 631.

158. Consideration.—Debt barred by statute sufficient consideration for new promise. *Gammell* v. *Parramore*, 58 Ga. 54.

159. Consideration.—An agreement to forbear proceedings is a valid consideration for a promise, though the claim be doubtful. *Matthews* v. *Morris*, 31 Ark. 222.

160. Consideration.—*Failure of.*—Where a promissory note is given for a draft assigned by the payee of the note to the maker, and an agreement executed at the same time, that, in the event the maker of the note could not "collect or realize" on the draft, he was to be released from the payment of the note, no recovery can be had on the note where the maker has been unable to realize anything on the draft. And the fact that the assignee of such draft becomes indebted to the drawer, does not change the rule or show that the holder has realized anything on it, when no suit has been brought by the drawer on his demand to enable the holder to set off the draft against the same. *Hall, et al.* v. *Henderson*, 84 Ill. 611.

161. Consideration.—*To impeach.*—Although the consideration for a promise or undertaking may be expressed in a separate writing of the parties, still, parol evidence may be received to show that the real consideration was different, where the defense goes to the consideration. Where an action is brought upon a written contract, resort may be had to parol evidence for the purpose of impeaching the consideration of the agreement. *Wolf* v. *Fletemeyer*, 83 Ill. 418.

CONTRACT.

162. Contract of sale induced in part by a desire on behalf of both vendor and purchaser to cause certain promissory notes of the vendor's to be paid, on which he has forged the names of persons as indorsers, and thereby to prevent a prosecution for the forgery, is illegal and void, and leaves the property subject to attachment by the vendor's creditors. *Laing* v. *McCall*, 50 Vt. 657.

163. Contract.—A., who had bought ice of B., ceased to take it on account of dissatisfaction with B., and contracted for ice with C. Subsequently, B. bought C.'s business and delivered ice to A., without notifying him of his purchase until after the delivery and consumption of the ice. *Held*, that B. could not maintain an action for the price of the ice against A. *Boston Ice Co.* v. *Potter*, 123 Mass. 28.

164. Contract.—*License.*—A contract simply giving a right to take ore from a mine, no interest or estate being granted, merely confers a license. *Silsby* v. *Trotter*, 29 N. J. 228

165. Contract.—Courts cannot protect the rash against the consequences of imprudent contracts, if they enter into them voluntarily, and not through fraud or artifice. A deed made by a person while in a state of intoxication will be set aside if advantage has been taken of his situation, or his drunkenness was produced by the act or connivance of the person to be benefited by the deed. *O'Conner* v. *Rempt*, 29 N. J. 156.

166. Contract.—*Condition precedent.*—B. executed his promissory note to H. & D., payable January 15, 1876, in the usual form, with the addition of the following words: The above note is given upon, and for the sole consideration that the said Hawley & Dodd have agreed and promised that upon the payment of the said note at maturity (time being of the essence of the contract), they will sell and transfer to the undersigned, Bingham, the planing machine which they have this day entrusted to him. *Held*, that the promise of B. was not dependent upon the promise of H. & D. to sell and transfer the machine as a condition precedent; but that it was an independent promise to pay. *Hawley* v. *Bingham*, 6 Oregon, 76.

167. Contracts.—It *seems* that the rule in this State, that a common carrier may, by express stipulation, exempt himself from liability for negligence, will not be considered as overthrown or affected by the decision of the United States Supreme Court to the contrary. (*Lockwood* v. *R. R. Co.*, 17 Wal. 357). *Maynard* v. *S. B. & N. Y. R. R.*, 71 N. Y. 180.

168. Contract, *Execution of.*—If a written agreement which is intended to be signed by several persons or parties thereto is not signed by all, it is not completely executed and does not bind any of the parties. *Barber* v. *Burrows*, 51 Cal. 404.

169. Contract of Guaranty.—Meaning of the words, "*Value received.*"—In a guaranty written on the back of a promissory note the words *value received* impart a consideration which is *prima facie* sufficient to support the contract. Semble, that a guaranty is an original undertaking upon which the guarantor is liable in the absence of proof that the maker of the note is insolvent or that diligence was used to collect from him. *Martin* v. *The Hazard Powder Co.*, 2 Colorado, 596.

170. Contract.—*May be rescinded.*—When one party to a contract violates it, he cannot avail himself of its provisions against the other party, and such other party has a right to consider the contract rescinded. *Scheland* v. *Erpelding*, 6 Oregon, 258.

171. Contract.—*Security.*—Where E. delivered a note of H. to his son, with instructions to go to H. and buy a mule, and enter the price of the mule on the note as a credit, and the son entered into a bargain with R. to buy a horse for $125, with the understanding that if R. did not collect the amount out of the note by a certain time, he was to have his choice to take the horse back or take $125 for him; *Held*, that the legal effect of the transaction was to place the note with R. as a security for the price of the horse, and the property of the note remained in E. *Earp* v. *Richardson*, 78 N. C. 277.

172. Contract.—*Subsequent.*—Degree of proof to establish. A subsequent contract will not operate to extinguish a former one between the same parties unless it is expressly accepted by them for that purpose. The evidence must be clear and satisfactory that such was intention of the parties. *Watson* v. *Janion*, 6 Oregon, 137.

173. Contract.—*At public sale.*—A purchaser at an execution sale cannot in equity be excused from consummating his purchase because never having attended such a sale before, and not hearing the terms of the sale, he supposed himself to be buying the entire estate in question, and not the "right, title, and interest" of the judgment debtor in it. *Upham* v. *Hamill*, 11 R. I. 565.

174. Contract *for the purchase of grain.*—Where a commission merchant contracts for the purchase of grain for another, to be delivered at a future time, the principal making an advance on the purchase, which is in the merchants' name, and agrees to keep the margin good up to the time of delivery, the relation of pledger and pledgee will not be created, so as to require a notice of the time and place of a sale on failure to keep up the margins. *Cobett* v. *Underwood*, 83 Ill. 324.

175. Contracts.—Memorandum of contract as follows: "I hereby agree to sell J. K. the house and lot situated on L. Street, second lot east of C. Street, on north side of L. Street, for the sum of ($7,000) seven thousand dollars, and agree to give a satisfactory deed on or before the first day of September next, and hereby acknowledge the receipt of ten dollars on account of above sale." Signed W. E. T., J. K. In an action by W. E. T. against J. K., *Held*, that the memorandum was sufficient to bind J. K. *Thornton* v. *Kelly*, 11 R. I. 498.

176. Contracts *for future delivery.*—A contract for the sale of wheat in store, to be delivered at a future time, which requires the parties to put up margins as security, and provides that, if either party fails, on notice, to put up further margins according to the market price, the other may treat the contract as filled immediately, and recover the difference between the contract and market price, without offering to perform on his part, or showing an ability to perform, is illegal and void, as having a pernicious tendency. *Lyon & Co.* v. *Culbertson, Blair & Co.*, 83 Ill. 33.

177. Contracts *made on 'Change.*—All contracts for sale made on 'Change by members of the board of trade to another member, with reference to the by-laws and rules of the board, must be construed as if those rules were expressly made a part of the contract; but members of that board may, by contract on 'Change or elsewhere, bind themselves beyond and independent of these rules. Where the sale is made at its rooms, in the absence of proof to the contrary, it will be presumed to have been made with reference to these rules. *Thorne, et al.* v. *Prentiss*, 83 Ill. 99.

178. Contract.—S. residing in Indiana, received from

W., a commission merchant of Cincinnati, $6,000, advanced on account of pork, to be thereafter cut and shipped by S., for sale on commission. In pursuance of the contract, S. shipped by rail a car-load of the pork, consigned to W., at Cincinnati, to whom he also sent an invoice of the shipment, with a letter of advice, stating: "We deliver this load on our indebtedness." The value of the shipment was less than the amount of such indebtedness. The bill of lading was taken by S. in his own name, and was not forwarded to the consignee. *Held*, under these circumstances the delivery of the pork by S. to the carrier was equivalent to a delivery to the consignee, and that after such delivery S. retained no such interest in the pork as could subject to attachment at the suit of a creditor. *Strauss* v. *Wessel*, 30 Ohio, 211.

179. Contract.—In case of a mistake in the drafting of a contract, if the parties subsequently settle upon a basis of the contract as it should have been written, and a promise is made to pay or allow the balance thus found due, such promise will be enforced. A written agreement may be waived, varied or annulled, by a subsequent oral agreement of the parties.

180. In *Goss* v. *Lord Nugent*, 5 Barn. and Ad. 65, Eng., Lord Denman states the law on this subject thus: "After the agreement has been reduced into writing, it is competent to the parties, at any time before breach of it, by a new contract not in writing, either altogether to waive, dissolve, or annul the former agreement, or in any measure to add to, or subtract from, or vary or qualify the terms of it, and thus to make a new contract, which is to be proved partly by the written agreement, and partly by the subsequent verbal terms engrafted upon what will thus be left of the written agreement." Approved in *Wiggin* v. *Godwin*, 63 Me. 389.

181. Contracts.—The agreement by which a creditor, who has bought his debtor's property, stipulates to reconvey it to the debtor on condition that the latter pays a certain price within a certain time, is a valid contract, and if the debtor fails to pay the price, in accordance with the terms of said contract, his right of redemption will be forfeited, and the title of the property will vest absolutely in the purchaser. *Soulie* v. *Ranson*, 29 La. 161.

182. Contracts.—*Sunday*.—Contracts made on Sunday in this State are void, not at common law, but because they are in violation of a penal statute of this State. So an action by the payee, against the maker on a promissory note, and answer, alleging the signing and delivery of the same on Sunday to a third person or to a co-maker, and averring it to be therefore void, is sufficient. Such signing and delivery on Sunday carry with it no implied authority to the person to whom it is entrusted, to deliver the same to the payee. Such signing and delivery on Sunday render the instrument void, though then entrusted to another with instructions to deliver it to the payee on a business day. *Davis* v. *Barger*, 57 Ind. 54.

183 4. Contract.—Twelve persons entered into the following obligation under seal: Whereas, P. S. is employed by the Baltimore County Brewing, Malting and Distilling Company, as the manager of said company; and whereas, the said P. S. is employed and authorized to purchase the malt and hops for said brewery; and whereas, each of the directors of said company have agreed to become individually responsible in the sum of twenty-five hundred dollars each for malt and hops which the said manager shall purchase for the use of the said brewery, during the space of one year from the date hereof. Now, therefore, these presents witness, that in consideration that said P. S. will undertake said authority and employment, and that dealers in hops and malt will sell to him upon the faith of this bond, we bind ourselves and each of us, our and each of our heirs, executors and administrators, in the sum of twenty-five hundred dollars each, making in all the sum of thirty thousand dollars, for the payment of hops and malt, which the said P. S. may purchase for the use of said brewery, during the space of one year from the date thereof; and we, and each of us agree and promise, that we will pay such hops and malt bills, in total not exceeding the sum of thirty thousand dollars, or twenty-five hundred dollars each, in the manner and at the time the said P. S. shall agree to pay them. In an action against all of said obligors, it was *Held*, 1st. That in the construction of said paper, as in the construction of all written instruments, the cardinal rule to be observed, was to ascertain the intention of the parties as expressed on the face of the paper. 2nd. That the said instrument construed all together and in all its parts, was a contract by which each of the obligors had bound himself severally for $2,500 only. *Boyd, et al.* v. *Kienzle, et al.*, 46 Md. 294.

185. Contract.—*Equity* can no more enforce a void contract than can a court at law. *Reed* v. *Reeves, Adm'r.*, 13 Bush, Ky. 447.

186. Contract.—To establish a contract by acceptance of a proposition, it must appear that the one making it was notified of the acceptance. *Goss's Appeal*, 73 Penn. 39.

187. Contract between creditor and principal, or creditor and surety, without the concurrence of co-sureties, whereby the latter are subjected to an increased risk, operates as a discharge of such sureties. The release of one or more sureties without the assent of the co-sureties will operate *at law* to discharge the latter. In equity, however, the rule is different, and the release of one or more sureties will not be construed to have this effect, unless it subjects the co-sureties to an increased risk or liability. *Smith, et al.* v. *State, use of County Commiss'rs of Baltimore Co.*, 46 Md. 617.

188. Contracts.—*Verbal.*—Although the parties may be longer than a year in the performance of a contract, still, if that performance may be completed within a year, and such performance is entirely in accordance

with the intention and understanding of the parties, such contract is not within the statute, and need not be in writing, in order to maintain an action upon it. Although a cause of action may relate to the subject-matter of a patent right, it is within the jurisdiction of State courts, if it does not involve the validity of the patent right. *Blakeney* v. *Goode*, 30 Ohio, 350.

189. Contract.—*Fraud.— Consideration Performed. —Rescission.—Restitutio in integrum.*—On a treaty of marriage, a promissory note was given in consideration of the marriage, which was afterwards solemnized, and an action was subsequently brought by the indorsee against the two joint and several makers of the note,— *Held* (reversing the decision of the Common Pleas), that as the marriage, the consideration for the note, could not be undone, it was not competent to the defendants to avoid the note upon the ground of fraud practised during the marriage treaty.

190. That when a party exercises his option to rescind for fraud, he must be in a state to rescind—that is, he must be in such a situation as to be able to put the parties into their original state before the contract. *Hogan* v. *Daniel and Thos. Healy*, Irish Reports, Common Law Series, vol. 11, p. 119.

191. Contracts.—*Forfeiture.*—Where a party to a contract, who is entitled to a forfeiture in case of non-performance by the other party of a condition therein, by his own act induces such other party to omit strict performance within the time limited, he cannot exact the forfeiture, if the party in technical default with reasonable diligence thereafter performs or offers to perform. *Leslie* v. *Knickerbocker Life Ins. Co.*, 18 Sickels, N. Y. 27.

CONVEYANCES.

192. Conveyances.—A deed recorded after fifteen days is notice to purchasers, mortgagees and judgment creditors subsequent to such record. *Sanborn* v. *Adair*, 29 N. J. 338.

A deed not recorded in fifteen days is void as to a subsequent deed for a valuable consideration, without notice, and cannot regain its priority by being placed on record before such subsequent deed is recorded. *Id.*

193. Such subsequent deed cannot lose its priority over the earlier deed by not being put on record, but is, in its turn, if not recorded in fifteen days, subject to be postponed to a later deed, taken without notice for a valuable consideration. *Id.*

194. Conveyance.—If a grantee in a deed be a *bona fide* purchaser for a valuable consideration, his or her title is unassailable, whatever may have been the motives or intentions of the grantor in executing the deed. It is absolutely essential that both parties shall concur in the fraud to invalidate the deed. Fraud cannot be presumed; it must be proved by clear and satisfactory evidence. *Herring, et al. v. Wickham & Wife, et al.*, 29 Grattan, Va. 628.

195. Conveyance.—A voluntary conveyance is void as against creditors holding debts previously contracted. *Russel, et al. v. Thatcher, et al.*, 1 Del. 320.

A voluntary conveyance, though without a fraudulent intent, is void, as against creditors, under the statute of 13 Elizabeth. *Logan, et al. v. Brick, et al.* 2 Del. 206.

196. Conveyances.—Withholding a deed from the records for several years may, as an element in the proof fraud, be explained so as to rebut any presumption of fraud arising from it. *Thouron v. Pearson*, 29 N. J. 487.

197. Conveyance *made by a man before his marriage in fraud of the dower rights of his intended wife.—Evidence of fraud.—Trustee.—Cestui que trust.—* A voluntary conveyance of real estate made by a husband, just before his marriage, to his mother, without any valuable consideration, and kept a secret until years after the marriage, is fraudulent and void as against the wife's claim of dower.

Although a trustee may become a purchaser from a *cestui que trust* upon fair principles and proper comsideration, yet where the transaction has no pecuniary consideration to uphold it, it is liable to the closest scrutiny due from courts in such transactions.

To afford complete protection to the trustee who deals with a *cestui que trust*, such statement and information should be given by the trustee to the *cestui que trust* as to the extent and value of his interest in the estate, so that a court may see that the proposed dealing is fair, and that the act was entered upon with as much knowledge, on the part of the *cestui que trust*, as was possessed by the trustee in respect to the trust property. *Pomeroy* v. *Pomeroy*, 54 Howard, N. Y.

198. Conveyance.—*Voluntary*—is void *if it tends to hinder and delay creditors*, although it may not otherwise injure them. A conveyance being held fraudulent and void as against creditors, certain mortgages of the property conveyed, taken by the vendor by way of consideration, were nevertheless held good in the hands of an assignee for value without notice. *Logan, et al.* v. *Brick, et al.*, 2 Del. 206.

199. Conveyances.—He who buys any part of the avails of a scheme to defraud creditors, in order to keep what he gets, must not only pay for it, but he must be innocent of any purpose to further the fraud. *De Witt* v. *Van Sickle*, 29 N. J. 209.

200. Conveyances.—Property conveyed in fraud of creditors will be reclaimed for the benefit of creditors, no matter who may happen to hold it, if reclamation can be effected without injustice to innocent third persons. *De Witt* v. *Van Sickle*, 29 N. J. 209.

201. Conveyances.—*Fraudulent.*—If the grantee of property conveyed in fraud of creditors dispose of it before proceedings are instituted to reach it, he will be held answerable for its value. *Post* v. *Stiger*, 29 N. J. 554.

202. Conveyances by a solvent father to his two sons, in consideration of services rendered by them for many years, made openly, the deeds being recorded soon afterwards, and the sons remaining in continuous

possession thereafter, are good against creditors of the father. *Horton* v. *Castner*, 29 N. J. 536.

CORPORATIONS.

203. Corporations.—If a corporation, in excess of its powers conferred by its charter, receives a sum of money on condition that it will return it, if an additional sum is not raised within a given time, and the condition is broken, an action may be maintained against the corporation on an implied promise to return the money, and a demand for its return may be submitted to arbitration. *Morville* v. *American Tract Society*, 123 Mass. 129.

204. Corporations.—*Officers.*—The superintendent of a mining company has no authority by virtue of his office to borrow money on the credit of the corporation. The president of the corporation has no authority, as such, to undertake, in the corporate name, for the repayment of such an unauthorized loan. *Union Gold Mining Co.* v. *Rocky Mt. Nat. Bank*, 2 Colorado, 565.

205. One for whom another has, without authority, assumed to act, must not only disavow and repudiate what has been done but must also give notice of such repudiation to those to be affected thereby, if he would avoid the inference of assent, which the jury are otherwise at liberty to indulge. *Id.*

206. Corporation.—*Officers.* — *Statute of Frauds.*— Where goods are sold, and credit given to a corporation, an officer and stockholder cannot be held personally liable for the debts thus created, upon a promise to pay or see them paid, unless such promise be in writing. *Searight* v. *Payne*, 2 Tenn. Eq. 175.

207. Corporation.—*Certificate of Stock.*—If a certificate of shares in the capital stock of a corporation is taken without the owner's knowledge, and, together with forged power of attorney, is delivered to an auctioneer for sale, to whom the corporation issues a new

certificate in the name of the auctioneer, who delivers it to an innocent purchaser for value, to whom, in turn, on its presentation, the corporation issues a new certificate, the owner is entitled, on a bill in equity against the corporation and purchaser, to a decree to compel the corporation to issue to him a certificate for his shares and to pay him the dividends thereon, but not to a decree against the purchaser; and, upon such bill, the court cannot decide, unless by consent, whether the corporation is liable to the purchaser. *Pratt* v. *Taunton Copper Co.*, 123 Mass. 110.

208. Corporations.— *Officer's Liability.*— An officer and stockholder of a corporation who states to a creditor that the corporation is, in his opinion, solvent, does not thereby make himself liable to the creditors, if the statement was made in good faith, although the corporation was, in fact, at that time insolvent. *Searight* v. *Payne*, 2 Tenn. Eq. 175.

209. Corporation Bonds, payable to bearer or order, and the coupons annexed thereto, are now recognized as possessing all the ordinary properties of negotiable instruments. Such bonds or coupons, although stolen, are collectible in the hands of a *bona fide* holder, who took them for value, in the usual course of business, before maturity and without notice. *Spooner* v. *Holmes*, 102 Mass. 503; *Evertson* v. *Nat. Bank of Newport*, 6 N. J. 14; *Carpenter* v. *Rommel*, 5 Phila. Pa. 34.

210. Where an instrument is incomplete, as if any essential part is in blank, and is afterwards filled up by the thief, or holder through the thief, no recovery can be had. The place of payment was left in blank, and before it was filled up by the president, the bonds were stolen. *Held*, that a *bona fide* holder could not, by inserting the name of a place in the blank, recover. *Maas* v. *Missouri R. R. Co.*, 11 Hun, N. Y. 8, also *Jackson* v. *Vicksburg Co.*, 2 Woods, 141. The thief's insertion of the name of a payee in the blank left for that purpose is not such an alteration as will avoid the

bond. For the fact of the bond not being payable to a particular person does not render it non-negotiable. Same rule applies to a coupon. *Dutchess Co. Ins. Co.* v. *Hachfield,* 1 Hun, N. Y. 675; *Smith* v. *County,* 54 Mo. 58; *Boyd* v. *Kennedy,* 9 Vt. 1846.

211. The *status* of a corporation doing business in a State other than that in which it was incorporated was clearly defined by the Supreme Court of the United States in the case of the *Bank of Augusta* v. *Earle,* 13 Peters, 538. *Held,* "That it exists only in contemplation of law and by force of the law, and when that law ceases to operate, and is no longer obligatory, the corporation can have no existence. It must dwell in the place of its creator, and cannot emigrate to another sovereignty."

212. Corporation.—*Action against trustees for injuries caused by fradulent acts or misapplication of corporate funds.*—*Corporation, necessary party.*— An action for injuries caused by the fraudulent acts, or for misapplication or waste of corporate funds, by an officer of a corporation, must be brought in the name of the corporation, unless such corporation or its officers refuse to bring such action. In that contingency, and then only, can a stockholder bring an action for the benefit of himself and others similarly situated, and in such case the corporation must be a party defendant. *Greaves* v. *Gouge,* 54 Howard, N. Y. 272.

213. Corporations.—*Pre-emptions under contract.*— The charter of a corporation provides that no "stockholder in said corporation shall have the right to transfer his shares therein, without first giving ten days' notice in writing of such intention, and ten days' refusal thereof to said corporation, at the lowest price at which he will sell to any other person, and if in such case said corporation elect to purchase said shares at said lowest price, such stockholder shall, on the price being offered to him, convey said shares to said corporation." A stockholder offered to the corporation a certain number of shares at a gross price, and subsequently sold to a third party a smaller number of shares at a given price per share. *Held*, that the offer to the corporation did not comply with provisions of the charter, and that the corporation could not be compelled to allow the transfer of the stock sold upon its books. *Sweetland* v. *Quidnick Co.*, 11 R. I. 328.

214. Corporation.—*Suit*.—In case a corporation on request refuses or neglects to bring suit against a defaulting officer, such suit may be brought by a stockholder for himself and his co-stockholders, making the corporation a party respondent. *Hazard* v. *Durant*, 11 R. I. 195.

A corporation cannot gratuitously condone or release the fraud of a defaulting officer, unless by a unnanimous vote of its stockholders. *Trenton Mutual Life Insurance Co.* v. *Johnston*, 24 N. J.; also, 98 Mass. 381; approved, *Clark* v. *Allen*, 11 R. I. 205.

215. Corporations.—*Stock Subscriptions*.—Where the charter does not require the payment of a certain amount at the time of subscribing for stock, but the agreement of subscription does, the failure to make such payment does not vitiate the subscription. *Water Valley Manufacturing Co.* v. *Seaman*, 53 Miss. 655.

216. Corporations.—*President of Bank.—Authority to contract*.—The president of a bank may contract, on sufficient consideration, with the defendant in a judgment in favor of the bank, to enter a *remittitur* of the judgment. *Case* v. *Hawkins*, 53 Miss. 702.

217. Corporations.—A bank which issues bills for circulation as money is a public corporation; but a bank, which beyond a power to contract in its corporate name, has no power beyond those which every other person possesses, must be deemed a *private* corporation. *Attorney-General* v. *Simonton*, 78 N. C. 57.

218. Coupons.—*The Title to Interest*.—Coupons pass from hand to hand by mere delivery. A transfer of possession is presumptively a transfer of title, but does not impart a guaranty of payment. *Ketchum* v. *Duncan*, 96 U. S. 659.

DAMAGES.

219. Damage.—In a suit upon the first of several promissory notes given for the price of a chattel sold by plaintiff to defendant, where it does not appear that the notes were received *as payment*, nor in whose hands the remaining notes are, defendant cannot recover any excess of his damages, from breach of warranty of the chattel, over the amount due on the note in suit. *Reuter, et al.* v. *St. Louis, et al.*, 43 Wis. 693.

220. Damages.—*Measure of, under Count for Goods Sold.*—If a plaintiff surrenders a note given for the price of goods sold, and proceeds under the common counts, he can only recover their real value upon the defendants showing a warranty, its breach, and the difference in the goods as warranted and as they really were. *Wilson, et al.* v. *King*, 83 Ill. 232.

221. Damages.—The rule of damages for negligence or delay in the transportation of goods by common carriers, is the difference between the market value of the goods at the time they should have arrived at the place of delivery and the time they did arrive there, with interest thereon, *as damages*, from that time. *Newell, et al.* v. *Smith, et al.*, 49 Rowell, 255.

DEBTOR AND CREDITOR.

222. Debtor and Creditor.—B. gave a mortgage to secure a note of $5,200. He afterwards gave to the mortgagees another note for $5,500, with the privilege of two renewals upon making part payments at each renewal. B. did not request any renewal of the note. After its maturity he paid $1,500 without any direction as to its appropriation, and the mortgagees applied it to the note of $5,200. *Held*, on foreclosure of the mortgage, that as against a purchaser of the mortgaged premises under a judgment against B., he could not question such appropriation. *Paterson Sav. Inst.* v. *Brush*, 29 N. J. 119.

223. **Debts, Priority of.**—A debt claimed by a wife against her husband, and first put in writing when his debts begin to jeopardize his future, must always be regarded with suspicion, and when attempted to be enforced against his creditors, must be rejected unless proved very clearly. *Post* v. *Stiger*, 29 N. J. 554.

224. **Debtor and Creditor.**—*Release. — Concealment.*— Where the defendant's creditors signed a paper in the words: "We the undersigned agree, in consideration of one dollar paid us, to discharge H. Schulting from the legal payment of the money loaned to him, February, 1866; said Schulting giving his moral obligation to refund the money, in part or whole, as his means will allow in the future,"—*Held*, that the agreement was not an absolute discharge of the debt, but that, if the debtor acquired means in the future, and he refused to recognize the moral duty to repay the money, he would be liable in an action for the amount. The paper may be regarded as an agreement on the part of the creditors not to enforce their legal claims, so long as the debtor was without the means to pay. Where, after a creditor had signed such agreement, the debtor paid the creditor a portion of the original debt, and received a release from all claims and demands,—*Held*, that, notwithstanding such release, the creditor might maintain an action for the balance of the original loan if the debtor, at the time of obtaining release, concealed facts in regard to the value of his interest in certain property, which was of large value, but which, before the release, he had stated to the creditor was of little or no value, it appearing that when the action was commenced the debtor had means to pay his debts. *Dambman* v. *Schulting*, 54 Howard, N. Y. 289.

DEEDS.

225. Deed.—*Construction.*—*Distances and Areas.*— Where the distances and areas in the description of a deed do not correspond so as to describe the same quantity of land, the terms describing the distances will control that describing the area, and measure the quantity conveyed, in the absence of words indicating that the latter is to prevail. *Sanders, et al.* v. *Gooding, et al.*, 45 Iowa, 463.

226. Deeds.—*Description in, by words and figures, which shall govern.*—In deeds as well as notes, where words and figures are used to describe the same thing, and are contradictory, the description by words will govern. Thus, where a deed conveyed "lot number (142), one hundred twenty-four (124)," the lot conveyed was held to be 124 and not 142. *Bradshaw, et al.* v. *Bradbury*, 64 Mo. 334.

227. Deed.—*Title.*—No title passes by a deed for lands, without it has been delivered. A deed for land without the name of a grantee, when it is acknowledged and delivered, is invalid. There must be in every grant a grantor, a grantee, and a thing granted; and a deed wanting in either essential, is absolutely void. *Whitaker* v. *Miller, et al.*, 83 Ill. 381.

DEED OF TRUST.

228. Deed of Trust.—*Legal effect of.*—A deed of trust executed for the purpose of securing a debt, and to be void upon payment of the debt, and containing a power of sale upon default, is in legal effect a mortgage. The grantor retains an equity of redemption, which is subject to seizure and sale under execution as other equitable estates are under the statute. But where the grantor parts with his title absolutely, conveying it to the trustee to sell for the purpose of raising a fund to pay debts, it is properly a deed of trust, and no interest, legal or equitable, remains in the grantor. This opinion is held in Sumner, 533 ; Story's Eq., sec. 1017 ; 20 Ohio, 469 ; *Id.* 572 ; 2 Devarou, 555 ; *Eaton* v. *Whitney*, 3 Pick, 484 ; *Bloom* v. *Rensselaer*, 15 Ill. 505. Approved in *Turner* v. *Watkins, et al.*, 31 Ark. 429.

229. Deed of Trust.—It is now finally and definitely settled by this court, that a deed of trust to secure the payment of a debt does not operate as an absolute transfer of the property on which it is executed to the trustee, upon the trust mentioned in the deed, defeasible upon conditions therein stipulated ; but that such instrument is, in legal effect, a mere mortgage, with a power to sell. *McLane* v. *Paschal*, 47 Texas, 365.

230. Deed of Trust.—An actual delivery of a trust deed to the trustee therein named, who has no interest in the trust, is not required, but a delivery to the *cestui que trust*, together with the notes secured by it, will fully answer the requirements of the law. *Groeker, et al.* v. *Lowenthal, et al.*, 83 Ill. 579.

231. Deed of Trust, *as security for future advances.* —The parties to notes secured by deed of trust have the right, in their mutual dealings, to treat them as unpaid, and as standing as security for future advances, and they will be good for such advances as between the parties and all others not prejudiced thereby. *Darst* v. *Gale, et al.*, 83 Ill. 136.

232. Deed of Trust, *sale under.*—*When no money need be paid.*—Where the holder of notes secured by a deed of trust, becomes the purchaser of property at the trustees' sale, a mere endorsement of the amount of his bid on the notes will be a sufficient compliance with the power and terms of sale requiring it to be for cash. *Jacobs* v. *Turpin*, 83 Ill. 424.

DEFENCE.

233. Defences.—Where a party is induced to enter into an executory contract for the purchase of lands by means of false representations on the part of the vendor, if, after discovery of the fraud, he accept a conveyance, he cannot set up the fraud as a defence in an action for the purchase money. *Vernol* v. *Vernol,* 18 Sickels, N. Y. 45.

234. Defences.—Where a corporation has fully performed a contract on its part to manufacture and deliver certain articles, it is no defence to an action brought to recover the purchase-price, that the contract was not within or incidental to its chartered powers, and privileges or the purposes for which it was created. *Whitney Arms Co* v. *Barlow, et al.*, 18 Sickels, N. Y. 62.

DEMAND.

235. Demand.—Where, by the terms of a contract between vendor and vendee, the purchase-price of merchandise was to be paid in cash or the notes of third parties, at the option of the vendee, the indebtedness of the vendee accrued upon the delivery of the merchandise, and a demand for the notes need not be shown to entitle the vendor to a right of action thereon. *The Davis Sewing Machine Co.* v. *McGinnis, et al.*, 45 Iowa, 538.

DEPOSITS.

236. Deposits.—The fact that the principal in a note payable to a bank has funds on deposit in the bank after the maturity of the note, and before suit on the note, exceeding the sum due thereon, and the bank does not appropriate the same to its payment, does not discharge the surety. *Voss* v. *The German-American Bank of Chicago*, 83 Ill. 599.

237. Deposits.—Special deposits withdrawn by person having authority, though bank acted without knowledge of that fact, not liable to answer for. Where deposits consist of stocks and bonds, written authority indorsed on certificate, to pay out the dividends and coupons, no authority to surrender stock and bonds. *Chat. Nat. Bank* v. *Schley, Guardian*, 58 Ga. 369.

238. Deposit.—*Receipt.*—*Endorsement and delivery of.*—*Payment to dorsee after death of depositor.*—

M., shortly before his death, indorsed a bank deposit-receipt and delivered it to S., stating that it was for his (M.'s) niece, K.; S. indorsed the document, and, after M.'s death, presented it to the bank, who transferred the amount to S. against the bank. *Held*, that the deposit-receipt was not a negotiable instrument passing by indorsement; that there was no equitable assignment of it; that if the transaction constituted S. an agent of M., his authority was revoked by M.'s death; that the transaction did not amount to a *donatio mortis causâ*. *Adm'r of D. R. Moore* v. *Ulster Banking Co.*, 2 Irish Reports, Common Law Series, 512.

DISCOUNT.

239. Discount.—The discount of a draft, at legal interest, is not rendered usurious, by reason of any intended lawful use of the paper by the party discounting, though he may thus realize more than legal interest. *Farmers' & Mechanics' B'k* v. *Parker*, 37 N. Y. 148.

240. Discount.—Discounting a note at the rate of seven per cent. is not usury. *Manhattan Co.* v. *Osgood*, 15 Johns. 162; *Bank of Utica* v. *Phillips*, 3 Wend. 408; *Utica Ins. Co.* v. *Bloodgood*, 4 Wend. 652; *Kent* v. *Walton*, 7 Wend.; *Anderson* v. *Schenck*, 1 N. Y. Leg. Obs. 107; *Marvine* v. *Hymers*, 12 N. Y. 223.

241. Discount.—In taking interest in advance, in discounting a note, it is lawful to include the three days of grace in the computation. *Bank of Utica* v. *Wager*, 2 Cow. 712.

242. Discount. If a bank, on discounting a bill, at the request of the party, give a certificate of deposit, payable at a future day, it is not usury. *Knox* v. *Goodwin*, 25 Wend. 643; *Cayuga County Bank* v. *Hunt*, 2 Hill, 635.

243. Discount. If a person give his creditor a note for part of the debt, which is discounted at more than legal interest, he cannot plead usury to an action on it. *Handy* v. *Empie*, 1 How. Pr. 46.

244. Discount. The purchase of one's note at a discount is not usurious. *Staley* v. *Kneeland*, Clarke, Ch. 30.

245. Discount. Ante-dating a note, bearing interest, as of a date when the money was due on the contract, does not render the note usurious. *Powell* v. *Jones*, 44 Barb. 521.

DIVIDENDS PLEDGED.

246. Dividend pledged *pledged to the bank.*—A bank has the right to hold a cash dividend as pledged for the indebtedness of the shareholder to the bank. A bank had sued an overdue note of a stockholder, discounted by the bank, and attached his shares. During the pendency of this action, the stockholder demanded payment of the dividends declared upon the attached shares, which was refused. He subsequently settled that suit, and then without renewing his demand brought the present action for his dividend. *Held*, that it could not be maintained. *Hagar* v. *Union Nat. Bank*, 63 Me. 509.

DUTIES.

247. Duties *of an office.*—A contract to perform the duties of an office is implied by the party accepting. *Commonwealth* v. *Evans*, 74 Penn. St. 124.

ENDORSEMENTS.

248. Endorsement.—The general rule in this State and elsewhere is, that the endorsement of a negotiable note or bill before maturity by the payee, creates an absolute warranty to the immediate and subsequent endorsement; among other things, that the maker or acceptor will pay it on due presentment when it is due, but that if he does not, the endorser will pay it if due notice is given him of such dishonor; and evidence of a contemporaneous or subsequent parol contract varying or contradicting such endorsement as to any of its terms is not admissible. *First Nat. Bank of St. Paul* v. *Nat. Marine Bank of St. Paul*, 20 Minn. 63.

249. Indorsement.—An indorsement on a promissory note, "assigned to" A., made in the name of the payee, is one upon which the latter is liable *prima facie*, as endorser. *Henderson* v. *Ackelmire*, 59 Ind. 540.

250. Endorser.—Where the endorser of a note was released from liability by the fact that the note was not protested, but afterwards went to the lawyer of the holder and promised to pay it, and again subsequently sent a letter to the same effect, which was destroyed,— *Held*, on action brought, that his promise to the lawyer was as binding as if made to the holder, and, moreover, could be proved by parol evidence. *Johnson* v. *Geoffrion*, 7 L. C. J. 125; 13 L. C. R. 161; C. C. 1863.

251. Endorser.—The fact of an endorser having been appointed to a temporary office in a place where he went alone, leaving his family for some time afterward in the domicile occupied by him at the time of his appointment, did not effect a change of domicile, and notice of protest left at such domicile was good and sufficient to render him liable for the payment of the note. *Ryan, et al.* v. *Malo*, 12 L. C. R. 8 Q. B. 1861; 82 & 2328 C. C.

252. Endorser.—If the endorser desires the benefit of any security held by the creditor, he must first pay the paper, assert his right of subrogation, and himself enforce the security. *First Nat. Bank* v. *Wood*, 71 N. Y. 405.

The fact that other parties occupy the same position, and are interested with him in enforcing the security, is immaterial. He is only entitled to such benefit as is conferred by the security as it is, and beyond this, has no valid claim for protection. *Id.*

253. Endorser.—*Liability of.*—The holder of a note to order under protest, who has received an account from the maker and another note as security for the first, does not lose his recourse against the endorsers of the first note who have given their assent to the transaction, notwithstanding the insolvency of the maker of the first note. *Woodbury* v. *Garth*, 9 L. C. R. 438, Q. B. 1858.

254. Endorser.—When the last endorser has paid the amount of a judgment on the note, with interest and costs obtained at the suit of the holder,—*Held*, such payment being made subsequently to the institution of another action on the same note by the same holder against the maker and payee, such endorser has a right to intervene in the latter action, and obtain a judgment in his own favor against the maker and payee of a note. *Mitchell, et al.* v. *Brown, et al. & Baillie*, 15 L. C. R. 425, C. C. 1865.

255. Endorser.—An accommodation endorser of promissory notes discounted by a bank cannot, in the absence of any special equities, require the bank first, to resort to a mortgage on real estate held by its collateral before maintaining an action upon the endorsement. The fact that the avails of the note are passed to the credit of the maker to take up other paper, does not affect the rights of the bank in this particular. *First Nat. Bank* v. *Wood*, 71 N. Y. 405.

256. Endorser.—When an endorser of a promissory note, who has been discharged from liability by failure of the holder to make demand and give notice of non-payment, with full notice of the laches of the holder, unequivocally assents to continue his liability as though due protest had been made, he waives his right to object, and stands in the same position as if the proper steps had been taken to charge him. *Ross* v. *Hurd*, 71 N. Y. 14.

257. Endorser.—*Accommodation.*—In an action by the bearer, who was also the maker, against an endorser, the latter pleaded that he endorsed the note simply as an accommodation, and on the understanding that the plaintiff should place his name above his (the defendant's) as second endorser. On appeal from a judgment against the defendant,—*Held*, reversing the judgment of the court below, that the order of signature by endorsement of a note was a mere presumption of the undertaking of the endorsers with respect to one another, and that this presumption could be destroyed by proof of a contrary understanding, and that, accordingly, in the case submitted, the endorsement made by one of the endorsers, with the express condition that such endorsement would be preceded by the endorsement of a third party, who was made acquainted by the bearer of the note with the conditions of the endorsement, could not give to such third party a right of action against the endorser, the bearer of a note being considered in such case the agent of the endorser. *Day v. Sculthorpe*, 11 L. C. R. 269, Q. B. 1861.

269. Endorser and Endorsee.—*Protest.*—A bill of exchange drawn in England and payable in Spain, was endorsed in England by the defendant to the plaintiff, who endorsed it to M., residing in Spain. Acceptance having been refused, a delay of twelve days occurred before M. wrote to inform the plaintiff of the dishonor. On receipt from M. of the notice of dishonor, the plaintiff gave immediate notice to the defendant. No notice of dishonor by non-acceptance is required by the law of Spain. *Held*, that the plaintiff was entitled to recover the amount of the bill. *Horne v. Rouquette*, 3 Eng Law Rep., Queen's Bench Div. C. A. 514.

259. Endorser of a promissory note after its maturity and his liability on it has become fixed, joined with the maker of the note in a bond giving further time, at his request. *Held*, that he was surety on the bond and not a principal. *Merriken v. Godwin, et al.*, 2 Del. 236.

260. Endorser.—In an action against an endorser, who was a banker, plaintiff's evidence was to the effect, that, prior to the maturity of the note, plaintiff and defendant had some conversation in regard to extension of time, but no arrangement was made ; after the discharge of the defendant by failure of demand and notice, plaintiff and K., the maker, went to defendant's bank to arrange an extension of time. K. asked plaintiff if he desired a new note. Plaintiff replied that if the parties agreed he would let the note stand; defendant said, "then I waive protest," and plaintiff thereupon agreed to an extension. *Held*, that the evidence was sufficient to authorize a finding that the defendant, with knowledge, assented to continue his liability; and that a nonsuit was error. *Ross* v. *Hurd*, 71 N. Y. 14.

261. **Endorser.**—*Rights of.*—In an action against an endorser,—*Held*, that the defendant had a right to set up in compensation against the holder all sums of money, which the holder had been paid, by, or in which he had become indebted to the maker since the protest of the note, and that the salary of a bank officer paid by quarterly instalments, ought in this way be set up against the bank by an accommodation endorser. *The Quebec Bank* v. *Molson*, 1 L. C. R. 116, 1851.

262. **Endorsement.**—*Mortgage.*—The transfer of a note by endorsement carries with it the mortgage and frees the mortgage in the hands of a good faith holder, like the note, of any equities between the original parties. *Updegraft* v. *Edwards, et al.*, 45 Iowa, 513.

263. **Endorser.**—Waiver of demand and notice may be made by parol. *Smith* v. *Lownsdale*, 6 Oregon, 78.

264. **Endorser** *on Promissory Notes.*—The endorsee cannot maintain suit against the endorser or assignor of paper not commercial, where the amount exceeds fifty dollars, without averring and proving suit against the maker to the first term, prosecuted to judgment and return of "no property," or some sufficient excuse for not having done so. All contracts for payment of money, except instruments governed by the commercial law, are subject in the hands of the assignee to all payments, discounts, and set-off made or had prior to notice of assignment, and to any defence which could have been made against the assignor or endorser. *Cook* v. *Citizens' Mutual Ins. Co.*, 53 Ala. 37.

265. **Endorser**—*Promise by, after failure to protest.*—A promise to pay, made after maturity, with knowledge that demand and notice of non-payment had not

been made, removes the effect of any negligence in making demand or in giving notice. An endorser who has taken sufficient security to protect himself against possible loss waives his legal right to require proof of demand and notice. *Smith* v. *Lownsdale*, 6 Oregon, 78.

266. Endorser of a promissory note is a competent witness to prove an agreement in writing made with its holder at the time of his endorsement, that he shall not be held liable thereon, where the paper has not afterwards been put into circulation, but is held by the party to whom the endorsement was made. *Davis* v. *Brown*, 94 U. S. 423. *Bank of United States* v. *Dunn*, 6 Pet. 51, explained and qualified.

267. Endorser *on Promissory Notes.*—Delay granted to the maker of a promissory note by the holder, without the knowledge of the endorser, does not discharge the latter. *Massue* v. *Crebassa*, 7 L. C. J. 211, S. C.; 1961 C. C.

268. Endorser *of promissory note.*—If the endorser of a promissory note, after it falls due, promises to pay the same, with a knowledge that the holder has failed to give notice of non-payment and make demand of payment, the promise dispenses with the necessity of demand and notice. A statement made by the endorser of a promissory note, after it falls due, to the holder, that he is responsible for the note, is in effect a promise to pay it. If the payee of a promissory note endorses it in blank, and delivers it to another, the note becomes payable to the transferee, not as endorsee, but as bearer The fact that the payee endorses a note in blank, and delivers it to a person who afterwards reassigns it to him without recourse, and that the payee then delivers it to another person, do not change the rule. *Curtis* v. *Sprague*, 51 Cal. 239.

269. Endorsers.—*Rights.*—*Liabilities.*—Whenever a negotiable promissory note is drawn up and is signed by the maker, and is then endorsed in blank, first by the payee and then by a third person, and the note is then delivered by the maker for a sufficient consideration to still another person, who thereby becomes the holder thereof, the presumption in such case should be, and is, that the payee and said third person intended to assume, and did assume, all the rights and privileges, as well as all the obligations and liabilities, usually assumed by endorsers of negotiable instruments. When a note is executed, endorsed and delivered in the foregoing manner, the endorser will be discharged unless due demand of payment is made, and due notice of non-payment given to the endorsers. *Bradford* v. *Pauly, et al.*, 18 Kansas, 216.

270. **Endorsements.**—A stranger who endorses negotiable paper at the time it is made, is *prima facie* liable to the payee as original promissor or as guarantor, as the payee may at any time elect. But it may be shown by parol evidence that he intended to bind himself only as guarantor, or even as second endorser; and if so shown by such evidence, he can only be held bound according to the original understanding. *Burton & Co.* v. *Hansford, et al.*, 10 West Va. 470.

279. **Endorsement.**—After a note under seal from Frow to Wilson was due, at the request of Frow, Wilson agreed to continue it, if Frow would give security. Belford agreed with Wilson to become surety, and there being no room at the bottom of the note to sign his name, Belford said it would do to sign on the back, and in signing thus, said to Wilson, he understood he was "going on the note as security." *Held*, this was within the Statute of Frauds, and Belford was not liable. The endorsement, the testimony being parol, did not take it out of the statute. Endorsement in blank of notes not negotiable is not evidence of a written promise to pay under the statute. *Wilson* v. *Martin*, 74 Penn. St. 159.

EXEMPTIONS.

272. Exemptions.—*Partnership Property.*—The members of a firm are neither severally nor jointly entitled to partnership assets, exempted to heads of families under section 11 of the statute touching exemptions. *State ex rel. Billingsley* v. *Spencer*, 64 Mo. 355; *Pond* v. *Kimball*, 101 Mass. 105; *In re Handlin*, 3 Dill. 290; *Bonsall* v. *Conley*, 44 Penn. St. 447; *Guptil* v. *McFee*, 9 Kas. 30. The courts of New York, Wisconsin and North Carolina hold otherwise.

EVIDENCE.

273. Evidence.—*Extrinsic.—To vary written contract.—Sale.—Sale upon approval.*—A written contract having no latent ambiguity can neither be qualified nor controlled, enlarged nor diminished, by evidence of a contemporaneous parol understanding. Thus where defendant addressed plaintiff by writing signed by him and plaintiff's agent, requesting them to send him a set of patent milk-pans, and saying, "I agree to pay you . . . . if satisfied with the pans," it was *Held*, that evidence of an agreement between defendant and said agent as to manner in which the pans should be tested, entered into at the time the written contract was drawn, and as part of the same agreement, was inadmissible. If one order goods, agreeing to pay if satisfied therewith, he must, in ascertaining whether he is satisfied or not, act honestly, and in accordance with the reasonable expectations of the seller as implied from the contract, its subject matter and surrounding circumstances. His dissatisfaction must be real and not pretended, to be available as a defence to an action for the contract price. *Daggett, et al.* v. *Johnson*, 49 Rowell, Vt. 345.

FAIR DEALING.

274. Fair Dealing.—*Presumptions in favor of.*—When any transaction is equally susceptible of two explanations, one of which is that it is fraudulent, and the other is consistent with good faith and fair dealing, that explanation will be preferred which is consistent with good faith and fair dealing. Parol evidence is admissible for the purpose of showing that a deed absolute on its face was in fact intended as a mortgage. *Hurford* v. *Harned*, 6 Oregon, 362.

FALSE PRETENCES.

275. False Pretences.—An action of deceit will not lie upon false representations either as to what a patent-right cost the vendor ; or was sold for by him ; or as to offers made for it, or profits that could be derived from it ; or for any mere expressions of opinion of any kind about the property sold. *Bishop* v. *Small*, 63 Me. 12.

Where the testimony does not exhibit any want of ordinary care on the part of the plaintiff in an action of deceit, but the reverse, the jury may properly be instructed that it will not relieve the defendant from liability to come into court now, and say to the plaintiff, "If you had exercised more diligence and circumspection it would have frustrated my plan for deceiving you, and therefore you cannot recover." *Roberts* v. *Plaisted*, 63 Me. 335.

276. False Representations.—*Will not avoid contract, when.*—False representations made by one party to another to induce him to enter into a contract, will not avoid the contract, unless it is shown that the party complaining relied upon such representations, and was thereby misled and induced to make said contract. *Dunning* v. *Cresson*, 6 Oregon, 241.

FIXTURES.

277. Fixtures.—A mortgage of a building covers an engine and boiler, a steam gauge, a water tank, a steam pump connected therewith, and the shafting therein, intended to permanently increase the value of the building for occupation ; but not machines which are incidental merely to the particular business carried on in the building at the time, although some of them are attached to the building by nails or bolts. *McConnell* v. *Blood*, 123 Mass. 47.

278. Foreign Corporations.—Section 8 of the act of the Legislative Assembly of Oregon, entitled "An act to regulate and tax foreign insurance, banking, express and exchange corporations or associations doing business in the State," approved October 21, 1864, is an indirect prohibition against such corporations transacting business in the State until they shall have executed and recorded the power of attorney required by that section. A contract made by such corporation in this State before it shall have complied with the provisions of said section 8 is as to third parties void, and cannot be enforced by the corporation. *Bank of British Columbia* v. *Page*, 6 Oregon, 431.

FORECLOSURE.

279. Foreclosure.—*Promissory note.*—The payee of certain promissory notes, having assigned the same to another by a blank endorsement, executed to the assignee, to secure the payment of such notes, a mortgage on certain real estate, conditioned that if the payee "shall pay said notes according to their tenor and effect, or cause the same to be paid, this mortgage shall be void," etc. *Held*, in an action upon such notes, and to foreclose such mortgage, by the assignee, against the maker and payee, that the plaintiff is entitled to personal judgment against both defendants for the amounts due on such notes, the foreclosure of such mortgage against the payee and execution over against the maker for any part of such judgment remaining unsatisfied by the sale of the mortgaged premises. *Held*, also, that the liability of such payee is primary, and not merely that of an endorser. *Robertson* v. *Cauble*, 57 Ind. 420; also, *Zekind* v. *Newkirk*, 12 Ind. 544; *Burnham* v. *Gullentine*, 11 Ind. 295; *Watson* v. *Beabout*, 18 Ind. 281.

FIXTURES.

280. Fixtures.—Actual annexation to the realty or something appurtenant thereto, is the condition upon which property, ordinarily regarded as personal, become a fixture and part of the realty. The intention to make a chattel a part of the realty, is only important upon the question whether the owner intended to make the chattel so fixed a temporary or a permanent accession to the freehold. Having once been a part of the realty, a removal temporarily, without intent to sever permanently, will not reconvert the chattel into personalty and destroy its character as a fixture. *Williamson* v. *New Jersey R. R. Co.*, 29 N. J. 311.

FRAUDS.

281. Fraud.—The rule is universal, whatever fraud creates justice will destroy. Where fraud is committed in the name of a corporation, by persons having the right to speak for it, for their personal benefit, they will be made to answer personally for the injury inflicted by their fraud. *Jewell* v. *Bowman*, 29 N. J. 171.

282. Fraud is never presumed, and to justify a court of equity in setting aside or in any manner interfering with a judgment on this ground the fraud must be clearly and conclusively established. The burden of proof is on the complainant to prove his case as it is alleged by the bill, and circumstances of mere suspicion will not warrant the conclusion of fraud. *Hill* v. *Reefsnider, et al.*, 46 Md. 555.

283. Frauds.—*Statute of.*—D. & Co. sued B. upon the following agreement, signed by B. and others, but not under seal: "We, the undersigned, take pleasure in recommending S. to D. & Co. We also severally agree to become responsible for $350 to said D. & Co., to be forthcoming in thirty days after the final delivery of the work. *Held*, 1. That the consideration for this guaranty could not be collected, or implied with *certainty* from the *instrument itself* without recourse to parol proof, or to other papers unconnected with it save by such proof. 2. That parol testimony for the purpose of showing that the guaranty did refer to a contract between S. & D. & Co., and thus make out a consideration for it, was wholly inadmissible if objected to. *Deutsche, et al., use of Kanders* v. *Bond*, 46 Md. 164.

283½. **Fraud Contract.**—A contract for the purchase of goods on credit, made with intent, on the part of the purchaser, not to pay for them, is fraudulent, and if the purchaser has no reasonable expectations of being able to pay, it is equivalent to an intention not to pay. But where the purchaser intends to pay, and has reasonable expectations of being able to do so, the contract is not fraudulent, although the purchaser knows himself to be insolvent, and does not disclose it to the vendor, who is ignorant of the fact. *Talcott* v. *Henderson*, 31 Ohio, 163.

284. **Fraud.**—*Vendor and Vendee.*—*Intent of Vendor.*—To defeat a sale it is not necessary to establish a fraudulent intent on the part of the purchaser, but it will be sufficient if it be shown that he knew of the fraudulent intent of the seller, or had notice of such facts as would have put a man of ordinary prudence upon an inquiry which would have led to a knowledge of the fraudulent purpose of the seller. A purchaser in good faith, who has paid a part of the purchase money, is entitled to the possession of the goods, notwithstanding he may subsequently discover that the vendor sold them with intent to defraud his creditors. *Jones* v. *Hetherington, et al.*, 45 Iowa, 681.

FRAUDULENT REPRESENTATIONS.

285. **Fraudulent** *Representations — Basis of.* — An action for fraudulent representations, as a general rule, cannot be maintained without proof that defendant believed, or had reason to believe, the representations to be untrue when made, and that they were made

with fraudulent intent. *Stitt* v. *Little*, 18 Sickels, N. Y. 427.

286. Fraudulent *Representations.* — A mere fraudulent representation is not actionable *per se*. To recover, the plaintiff must not only show that the representations were made, and that they were false and fraudulent, but he must also show, affirmatively, that he has been injured thereby, that he is, in some way, placed in a worse condition than he would have been had the words been true. *Bartlett, et al.* v. *Blaine*, 83 Ill. 25.

287. Fraudulent *Representations.*—Infancy is a bar to an action on a case of false and fraudulent representations by a vendor or pledgor as to his ownership of property sold or pledged. *Doran* v. *Smith*, 49 Rowell, Vt. 353.

288. Fraudulent *Representations.* — Material representations by a vendor of matters assumed by him to be within his personal knowledge, made with intent to deceive the vendee, which are untrue and are relied upon by the vendee in making the purchase to his damage, are, in a legal sense, false and fraudulent, although the vendor did not know them to be untrue. When a vendor, in the course of the negotiations for a sale, authorizes an agent to make representations to the vendee as to the quality of the goods to be sold, and recommends the agent to the vendee as one whose statements are to be relied upon, such vendor is liable for false representations made by the agent. Although, upon a sale of property a warranty of quality is taken by the vendee, yet, if it appear that he was induced to make the purchase and to take the warranty in reliance upon representations on the part of the vendor knowingly false and fraudulent, an action *ex delicto* may be maintained. *Indianapolis, Peru & Chicago R. R. Co., Resps.* v. *Tyng, Appell.*, 18 Sickels, N. Y. 653.

GUARANTEE.

289. Guarantee.—*Construction of documents*.—In an action on a guarantee, alleged to be contained in a letter and telegram in which there were no words of doubtful trade meaning, and the extrinsic facts not being in controversy,—*Held*, that the question whether the words used amounted to a contract of guarantee was for the determination of the court alone. The following words were *held* not to constitute a contract to guarantee: "Our friends H. and M. have purchased a cargo from G. Last year there was delay and trouble owing to bills of lading coming in different lots, and through more than one source, and without insurance being perfected. If you will obviate a repetition of this now you will oblige us. On presentation of cash order, and all documents at Union Bank, payment will be promptly made. Excuse this trouble." *The Bank of Montreal* v. *Munster Bank*, Irish Reports, Common Law Series, vol. 11, 47.

GUARANTY.

290. Guaranty.—*What constitutes*.—In response to an order for goods, plaintiffs replied that they would not deliver them unless the purchaser would procure some one to guarantee payment for them; the purchaser answered, stating that defendant had offered to assist him, and defendant endorsed upon the letter his agreement to the proposition. *Held*, that he was liable as guarantor. *Westphal, Hinds & Co.* v. *Moulton*, 45 Iowa, 163.

290½. Guaranty.—Where the guarantor undertook to insure the payment of all indebtedness of his principal to the guarantee, whether consisting of accounts, notes, endorsement of notes or otherwise, the guarantor was held to be liable upon notes which his principal transferred to the guarantee, with no other endorsement than simple words of guaranty. If, under the contract of guaranty, the guarantee took other or different notes than those provided for in the contract, or gave additional time for payment to the principal, or waived any material condition on which payment was to be made, the guarantor was released from liability. *The Davis Sewing Machine Co.* v. *McGinnis, et al.*, 45 Iowa, 538.

291. Guaranty.—If a promissory note in the hands of the payee has upon its back the signature in blank of a third person, the presumption, in the absence of proof, is that such person indorsed as a guarantor, but this presumption may be rebutted by clear and satisfactory proof of a different intention. Proof that the indorser's name was put upon the note for the purpose of becoming liable as security that the maker should be responsible for the payment of the note, and that the indorser refused to sign as maker, will not rebut the presumption of a contract of guaranty. *Id.* 120. No legal proceedings against the maker of a note are needed to fix the liability of a guarantor, nor is it necessary to show the insolvency of the maker, or to prove demand or notice of non-payment, or to use diligence against the maker. *Stowell* v. *Raymond*, 83 Ill. 120.

292. Guaranty.—Where assignor of order for money agreed, if not paid by party to whom addressed in a certain time, to pay its face value, notice to assignor of non-payment not necessary to recovery by assignee. *Gammell* v. *Parramore*, 58 Ga. 54.

293. Guaranty.—The sufficiency of a complaint founded upon a "special promise to answer for the debt or doings of another," considered and determined. Parol evidence is admissible to show the circumstances under which such a promise was given. The objection that the consideration for such a promise is not stated, does not apply to a guaranty of a note where the written promise of the debtor sets forth a consideration and is made and delivered at the same time therewith. *Wilson S. M. Co.* v. *Schnell*, 20 Minn. 40.

HOMESTEAD.

294. Homestead.—*Incumbrance Upon.*—Under the Code of 1851 and Revision of 1860, the homestead could be sold only to supply a deficiency existing after exhausting the other property of the debtor liable to execution, whether the debt existed before the purchase of the homestead, or was contracted afterward and secured by mortgage on the homestead. A mortgage upon the homestead was of no validity unless both husband and wife united in the execution and the record of it, therefore, imported no notice to a subsequent purchaser. *Higley & Co.* v. *Millard, et al.*, 45 Iowa, 586.

295. Homestead.—A mortgage on property exempt under the homestead act cannot be enforced ; and the owner of such property may sell the same *free from the mortgage* he has imposed on it. *Jacob C. Van Wickle* v. *Acée Landry*, 29 La. 330.

296. Homestead.—A deed in ordinary form, executed by husband and wife, which contains no waiver of the homestead right, is sufficient to pass the title of the grantors to lands occupied by them as a homestead under the act to provide homesteads in Colorado (R. S. 285). *Drake* v. *Root*, 2 Colo. 685.

297. Homestead Exemption.—A claim for homestead exemption, in order to avail against a debt, must rest upon a deed executed anterior to the creation of the debt. (Wagn. Stat. 698, sec. 7). *Lincoln* v. *Rowe*, 64 Mo. 138.

298. Homestead.—Unless one abandons his homestead right in a house, he does not lose it by living temporarily in a rented house, especially if he has left part of his furniture in it. So *held*, where the owner was absent on business for two years and kept his family with him. The duration of a man's absence from his own house does not of itself supply a conclusive presumption that he has abandoned it as a homestead. *Bunker* v. *Paquette*, 37 Mich. 79.

HUSBAND AND WIFE.

299. Husband and Wife.—When a wife executing a mortgage at the instance and upon the representations of her husband, will not be permitted to avoid the same on the ground of deception, or mistake. It is the right of the wife to demand that every paper presented to her for her signature be fully read and explained to her; and if she omits to claim or exercise such right, and executes the paper solely upon the representations of her husband, she does so at her peril. *Roach* v. *Karr*, 18 Kan. 529.

300. Husband and Wife.—A husband, having reduced to his possession funds to which he became entitled in right of his wife, cannot subject them to a voluntary trust for the wife to the prejudice of his creditors. *Russell, et al.* v. *Thatcher, et al.*, 2 Del. 320.

301. Husband and Wife.—The husband becomes the absolute owner of the wife's legacy, and may dispose of it. *Jacks* v. *Adair*, 31 Ark. 616.

301½. Husband and Wife. A husband cannot loan money to his wife, both being insolvent. All property is held subject to the payment of the debts of the owner, except in so far and to the extent only that it has been specifically exempted. The income derived from a homestead is not likewise exempt from liability for the owner's debts, and all acquisitions of property derived from such income are subject to sale under execution against the debtor; and the same is true of the natural increase of personal property set apart to the debtor as exempt from sale under execution. The homestead law does not vest in the owner any new rights of property; it only imposes a restriction upon the creditor that in seeking satisfaction of his debts, he should leave to the debtor untouched five hundred dollars of his personal and one thousand dollars of his real estate. *Citizens' Nat. Bank* v. *Green*, 78 N. C. 247.

302. Husband and Wife. A bill was filed against a *fême* *covert* and her trustee for the purpose of charging her separate estate with a lien for materials furnished by the complainants for the improvement of the same; the bill did not aver that there was any contract by her to bind her separate estate, or any intention on her part to create a charge or specific lien thereon for the payment of the complainant's claim. On demurrer to the bill, it was *held*, that the bill stated no case entitling the complainants to relief in equity, and that the demurrer be sustained. In order to charge the debts contracted by a married woman upon her separate estate as a lien in equity, it is necessary that it should affirmatively appear, that her contract was made with direct reference to her separate estate, and that it was her intention to charge the same. *Wilson & Hunting* v. *Jones, et al.*, 46 Md. 349.

302½. **Husband and Wife.**—Property conveyed to the wife, for which payment was made out of the husband's property is not liable to be taken under the provisions of R. S. c. 61, sec. 1, upon an execution recovered against the husband upon several debts, some of which accrued before and some after the conveyance. When a creditor unites two classes of claims against his debtor in one suit, and obtains judgment therein upon them, he reduces that in which his rights are superior to the level of that in which they are inferior. *Reed* v. *Woodman*, 4 Me. 400; also *Usher* v. *Hazeltine*, 5 Me. 471; *Miller* v. *Miller*, 23 Me. 22; *Quimby* v. *Dill*, 40 Me. 538; *Holmes* v. *Farris*, 63 Me. 318.

303. **Husband and Wife.**—The other creditors of a husband cannot complain that he prefers to discharge a debt to his wife rather than those to them, nor will the relation of the parties, nor the fact that her claim is barred by the statute of limitations, be conclusive evidence of bad faith. *French* v. *Motley*, 63 Me. 326.

304. **Husband and Wife.**—In an action against husband and wife for necessaries furnished on the credit of the wife, the plaintiff, in order to recover judgment, need not prove that the husband has no property or is insol-

vent or refuses to support his family. To recover judgment against the husband, it is necessary only to prove that the debt was contracted by the wife for necessries for the support of the family of the husband and wife. *Rigoney* v. *Nieman*, 73 Penn. 330.

304½.—A wife may mortgage her estate to secure future as well as present indebtedness of her husband. *Haffey* v. *Carey*, 73 Penn. 431.

305. Husband and Wife.—*Contracts between, Void.*—Husband and wife are incapable of contracting with each other. *Pillow* v. *Wade and wife, et al.*, 31 Ark. 678.

306. Husband and wife.—*Conveyance of land by husband to wife.*—A voluntary conveyance of land made by a husband to his wife, through the intervention of a trustee, will not be held void as to future creditors on the mere ground that the husband subsequently became insolvent. Such conveyance will be set aside at the suit of a subsequent creditor, only on proof that it was made with intent on the part of the grantor thereby to defraud such subsequent creditor or creditors. One having a valid cause of action, sounding in tort, against such grantor at the time of such conveyance upon which an action was subsequently brought and judgment recovered, is to be regarded as a *subsequent creditor*. *Evans* v. *Lewis*, 30 Ohio, 11.

INDEMNITY.

307. Indemnity.—*Subsequent circumstance.*—Where the owner of real estate, in consideration of the agreement of another to become an endorser, to a specified amount, of negotiable paper of the former, executes to the latter a mortgage on such real estate, to indemnify him against loss, not only from such future endorsements, but also from similar endorsements already made, such future endorsements, when made, relate back to the execution of such mortgage, and are valid liens against encumbrances placed upon the mort-

gaged property subsequently to the execution of such mortgage, by persons having either actual or constructive notice thereof, though such endorsements be made by the mortgagee subsequent to the placing of such encumbrances and with notice thereof. *Brinkmeyer* v. *Helbling*, 57 Ind. 435.

INNOCENT HOLDERS AND PURCHASERS.

308. Innocent Purchasers.—An unrecorded deed passes the title of the grantor to the grantee, but to be valid against creditors and purchasers without notice, it should be acknowledged or proved, and lodged for record within the time prescribed by law. The protection of innocent purchasers in such cases, prior to the passage of the act of February 10, 1858, applied to purchasers from the grantor himself, but did not apply to purchasers from his heirs or devisee. *Dozier & Co.* v. *Barnett & Co.*, 13 Bush, Ky. 457.

309. Innocent Holders.—*Negotiable Paper.*—The judgment bonds of a county in the hands of innocent holders for value, with notice of their illegality for any cause, cannot be defeated by showing that the judgments were rendered upon warrants issued in excess of the constitutional limitation of five per cent., and that the board of supervisors fraudulently omitted to interpose the defense when the warrants were sued upon. *The S. C. & St. P. R. R. Co.* v. *The County of Osceola, et al.*, 45 Iowa, 168, Beck, J., dissenting.

INSURANCE.

310. Insurance.—A policy of insurance should be construed most strongly against the insurer, and liberally in favor of the assured. *Brick & Co.* v. *Merchants' and Mechanics' Ins. Co.*, 49 Rowell, Vt. 442.

311. Insurance.—*Life.*—When a policy of life insurance contains a clause declaring it void on failure of the assured to pay the annual premium on the day it falls due, to work forfeiture, it is not necessary for the insurer to give notice of intention to claim it, but on failure to pay at the time stipulated the policy becomes void because of the non-payment. Such conditions in a policy are not unreasonable or against public policy. *Roehner* v. *Knickerbocker Life Ins. Co.*, 18 Sickels, N. Y. 160.

312. Insurance.—*Marine.*—One who has the control of property, either as owner, consignee or agent, may effect an insurance thereon in his own name, on account of whom it may concern, loss payable to him; and, in case of loss, may maintain an action thereon. An over-valuation does not *per se* render a valued marine policy void; in the absence of fraud, accident or mistake, the valuation agreed upon is binding and conclusive, however largely in excess of the true value. *Sturne* v. *At. M. Ins. Co.*, 18 Sickels, N. Y. 78.

INTEREST.

313. Interest.—To an action for money loaned, and for interest upon money loaned and upon an account stated, a plea that the several promises were to pay interest at a greater rate than ten per cent. per annum, and that such promises were not in writing, is bad. If upon payment of the principal sum due on a promissory note, the maker promises to pay interest due on the same note at a future day, and the payee thereupon cancels the note, and deliver it to the maker, to enable the latter to show it to other parties with whom he has dealings, an action may be maintained upon such promise. *Hall* v. *King*, 2 Colorado, 711.

314. Interest.—When both parties lived in Virginia during the war, the creditor is entitled to war interest. *Johnston, Trustee, &c.* v. *Wilson's Adm'r, et al.*, 29 Grattan (Va.) 379.

315. Interest.—*Sureties liable* for interest as damages in an action upon an official bond. Interest upon the balance due from the principal was properly allowed from the date when he rendered his account. *Jenness* v. *City of Blackhawk*. 2 Colorado, 578.

316. Interest.—Ten per cent. interest for discounts on loans can be taken under the general banking law of Michigan (Comp. L. sec. 2185). *Cameron, et al.* v. *Merchants' & Manufacturers' Bank*, 37 Mich. 240.

317. Where ten per cent. interest is exacted, the rate need not be expressly stated in writing; it is enough if the contract clearly expresses the sum to be paid. The statutory requirement that stipulations for ten per cent. interest shall be in writing was meant to prevent ambiguity as to what interest was to be paid, and to conform to the rule rejecting parol explanations of writings. *Id.*

318. Interest.—A promissory note was made in 1872, with interest payable semi-annually at the rate of eight per cent. per annum, which was then legal. The note was given for a loan made by a corporation, and was intended to run for several years. In 1875 an act was passed limiting the rate of interest in Connecticut for money loaned to seven per cent. *Held*, that eight per cent. continued to be the legal rate of interest upon the note, after the act was passed, and until the note was paid.

The note was given by a husband and wife and secured by a mortgage of her land. The husband at the same time signed a paper agreeing to an increase of interest so long as any interest remained unpaid, and to a foreclosure if it remained unpaid sixty days after due. *Held*, that this paper was admissible for the purpose of showing that a permanent loan was intended. *Seymour* v. *Continental Life Ins. Co.*, 44 Conn. 300.

319. Interest.—The act of April, 1873, Code of 1873, ch. 173, sec. 14, p. 1120, which authorizes the abatement of war interest upon debts contracted before the 10th of April, 1865, is unconstitutional and void; and a creditor residing in Virginia during the war is entitled to have interest upon his debt. *Pretlow* v. *Bailey's Ex'r, et al.*, 29 Grattan (Va.) 212.

320. Interest.—An allowance for the failure to pay at

maturity money due by contract, is regarded as damages for the breach of contract, not as interest on the money due. The measure of such damages is the value of the use of the money during the time for which it has been withheld. The stipulation of the parties as to the rate of interest after maturity may be accepted as the measure of damages, provided they adhere to what may be reasonably sufficient to compensate the loss arising from the breach of contract.

If, however, the rate of interest specified in the contract greatly exceeds the real value of the money, it is to be regarded as a penalty for non-payment of the principal sum, rather than a just recompense for detaining it.

In the absence of evidence as to the current rate of interest at the time the contract was made, the rate specified in the contract may be accepted as the true measure of damages. *Browne* v. *Steck*, 2 Colorado, 70.

321. **Interest.**—*Compound Interest* is never allowed, except in special cases; as, where there has been a settlement of accounts, after interest has become due; or there has been an agreement for that purpose, subsequently to the original contract; or a master's report, computing principal and interest, has been confirmed. *Connecticut* v. *Jackson*, 1 Johns. Ch. 13; *Stoughton* v. *Lynch*, 2 Johns. 209.

322. **Interest.**—C. and P. executed their single bill, dated October 18, 1871, whereby they promised "six months after date to pay to H. or order the sum of seven thousand dollars, with interest at the rate of 12 *per centum per annum* from date." *Held*, 1. The contract for interest at the rate of 12 *per cent. per annum*, was legal under the constitutional provision in force at the time of the contract, and is not affected by the subsequent abolition of that provision. 2. The obligors in the bond are bound to pay interest after the rate of 12 *per cent. per annum*, not only up to the maturity of the bond, but after maturity and until the

payment thereof. *Cecil & Perry* v. *Hicks*, 29 Grattan (Va.) 1.

323. Interest.—*Compound.*—An agreement, made at the time of the original loan, that interest shall be compounded, in case of default in paying it when due, is not valid. *Van Benschooten* v. *Lawson*, 6 Johns. Ch. 313; also *Van Rensselaer* v. *Jones*, 2 Barb. N. Y. 643.

324. Interest.—Where a promise is made to pay in labor and material in annual payments, interest does not begin to run until the year is completed in which any given payment is to be made, and the debtor is in default. *Fredenburg, Adm.* v. *Turner, et al.*, 37 Mich. 402.

324½. Interest.—When interest is made payable annually upon a fixed date, the fact that the first installment falls due *within* a year is not a departure from the terms. *Griffin, et al.* v. *Johnson, et al.*, 37 Mich. 87.

325. Interest.—Upon a guaranty endorsed upon a promissory note, the interest specified in the note, as well as the principal sum, may be recovered. *Martin* v. *Hazard Powder Co.*, 2 Colorado, 569.

326. Interest.—A promise to pay on demand £200, with interest, is a promise to pay interest from the date of the note. *Baxter* v. *Robinson*, 2 Rev. de Leg. 439, K. B. 1816.

327. Intereest.—A note which contains the following as to the interest, viz.: "With interest at the rate of sixteen per cent. per annum from date," bears the legal and not the conventional rate of interest, after maturity. *Newton* v. *Kennerly*, 31 Ark. 626.

328. Interest.—*On Accounts.*—By the statute of 1869-70, p. 699, accounts draw interest only from the day on which they are settled, and a balance is ascertained. *Bank of California* v. *Northam*, 51 Cal. 387.

329. Interest.—A depositor in a national bank, when it suspends payment, and a receiver is appointed, is entitled, from the date of his demand, to interest upon his deposit. The interest being a liquidated sum

at the time of the payment of the deposit, an action lies to recover it, and interest thereon. *National Bank of the Commonwealth* v. *Mechanics' National Bank*, 94 U. S. 437.

INTERLINEATIONS.

330. Interlineations.—It was said in *Stanberry* v. *Moore*, 56 Ill. 472, that the practice of making amendments by erasures and interlineations is a bad one, and ought not to be tolerated: that a paper thus disfigured ought to be stricken from the files. This, however, was not necessary to be said, as that matter was not a point of the case. The remark was only intended to indicate a better practice. *Garrity* v. *Wilcox, et al.*, 83 Ill. 159.

330. Interest.—A judgment to bear interest at ten per cent. per annum until paid was proper on a note bearing interest at the rate of ten per cent. per annum "from date until paid," the statute authorizing ten per cent. interest when the note was executed. *Crosthwait & Co.* v. *Misener*, 13 Bush, Ky. 543.

331. Interest.—When at the place of contract the rate of interest differs from that at the place of payment, the parties may stipulate for either rate, and the contract will govern. *Cromwell* v. *County of Sac*, 96 U. S. 51.

332. Interest *on interest.*—The bonds of a railway company were made payable on the first day of January, 1861, with interest, "at the rate of six per cent. per annum, payable half-yearly, at said treasurer's office, on the first days of July and January of each year after the first day of January, 1851, upon the surrender of the corresponding warrants hereto annexed." *Held*, that interest after maturity and the payment of all the coupons was recoverable by way of damages for the detention of money due, and should be computed at six per cent., without semi-annual or other rests. *Ashuelot R. R. Co.* v. *Elliot*, 57 Hall, N. Y. 397.

333. Interest.—By the act of 1872 it was provided

"that no greater rate of interest than six per centum per annum shall be recovered in any action except where the agreement to pay such greater rate of interest is in writing." The agreement in the note to pay eight per cent. should not be construed to extend beyond its maturity, especially in face of the stipulation, where the interest after maturity is treated as a penalty, not covered by the contract, and liable to be raised on a contingency. *Fisher* v. *Bidwell*, 27 Conn. 363. *Brewster* v. *Wakefield*, 22 How. 118; *Ludwick* v. *Huntzinger*, 5 Watts & Serg. 51.

334. Interest Coupons.—Upon the bonds of a railroad corporation received, by one who has advanced the money with which they were taken up, under an agreement that they were to be delivered to him uncanceled as security for the advances, as against the corporation are valid securities in the hands of the holder, and a mortgage upon the corporate property given to pay the bonds may be enforced for his benefit. *Union Trust Co. of N. Y.* v. *Monticello and Port Jervis R. R. Co.*, 18 Sickels, N. Y. 311.

335. Interest.—Where the contract does not fix the rate of interest to be paid after the maturity of the date, the law fixes the rate at six per cent. *Evans* v. *Chapel*, 13 Bush, Ky. 121.

IRREGULARITY.

337. Irregularity.—A party consenting to a proceeding which he might prevent by resisting it on account of irregularity, thereby waives all exception to such irregularity. *Patton* v. *Hughesdale*, 11 R. I. 188.

LAPSE OF TIME.

338. Lapse of Time.—Trustee and *cestui que trust.*—Lapse of time does not bar a *direct* trust as between the trustee and *cestui que trust.* Otherwise as to *constructive* trusts. *Castwell, Adm'r* v. *Perkins*, 2 Del. 102.

LIENS.

339. Lien.—A lien is neither property nor a debt, but a right to have satisfaction for a debt and of property, and is not the subject of sale or assignment. *Roberts, et al.*, v. *Jacks*, 31 Ark. 597.

340. Lien.—*Transfer, Release.*—While the holder of a debt, secured by a lien, cannot transfer the lien to a stranger, without also assigning the debt, he may release it on claiming an interest, or a junior lien on the property. *Buckner* v. *McIlroy*, 31 Ark. 631.

341. Lien—*Change of.*—In exchanging one form of security for another for the same debt, no other lien can intervene and become paramount thereto. *Thorpe Brothers* v. *Durbon, et al.*, 45 Iowa, 192.

LIFE POLICY.

342. Life Policy *is a Chose in Action.*—The sale and assignment of a life policy, outstanding and valid, and containing no prohibition of such alienation, is good in Rhode Island, though made to one who has no interest in the life insured, provided such sale and assignment is a *bonâ fide* business transaction, and not a device to evade law. *Clark* v. *Allen*, 11 R. I.; also *Trenton Mut. Life Ins. Co.* v. *Johnston*, 24 N. J. Law, 576; *Campbell* v. *Mut. Life Ins. Co.*, 98 Mass. 381.

MARRIED WOMEN.

343. Married Women.—*Husband's Consent may be Implied.*—Where a husband left this State for California, leaving his wife in charge of his farm, and to manage the same, and during his absence the wife sold a horse, taking a note, payable to herself, for the price, and endorsed the same to a creditor of the husband in payment of his debt, and the husband, on his return, approved the same, it was *held*, that the wife's endorsement could be sustained on two grounds: an implied authority from her husband, and his subsequent ratification. *Mudge* v. *Bullock, Adm'r*, 83 Ill. 22.

344. Married Women.—*Endorsing for her Husband.*—An answer of a married woman, made to an action by the endorser of a promissory note to charge her separate estate, on her endorsement thereof, which denies that she intended to charge her separate estate, and avers that she endorsed the same through the influence and persuasion of her husband, and not of her own free will, and that she received no part of the money paid for said note, but the same was used for the sole benefit of her husband, states a good defense to such action. The endorsement by a married woman of a promissory note, solely for the accommodation of her husband, and as surety thereon, in order to enable him to dispose of the same, is, of itself, not sufficient to warrant a court of equity in presuming that she intended to charge her separate real estate with the payment of the same. *Levi* v. *Earl*, 30 Ohio, 147.

345. Married Woman.—A married woman cannot bind herself by contract, under Gen. Stats. ch. 164, sec. 13, unless such contract is in respect to property held by her in her own right. *Blake* v. *Hall*, 57 Hall, N. H. 373. A contract by a married woman, for groceries sold to her upon her promise to pay for the same out of wages to be earned by her under a subsisting contract with a third party, is not a contract made by her in her own right, and therefore is not within the provisions of Gen. Stats. ch. 164, sec. 13. *Muzzey* v. *Reardon*, 57 Hall, N. H. 378.

346. Married Woman.—A promissory note given by a married woman and her husband for property purchased by her as sole trader, is valid in law, and the amount of such note may be recovered against the husband and wife in an action of assumpsit. *Barnes* v. *De France*, 2 Colorado, 294.

347. Married Women.—*Debts of husband.*—The sale or mortgage by a married woman of her separate property for the payment of her husband's debts may be enforced. *Moore* v. *Fuller*, 6 Oregon, 272.

348. Married Woman.—At common law, the promissory note of a married woman is void. The constitution and statute of this State make no change in this respect. Neither at law nor in equity can she bind herself so as to authorize a personal judgment against her. *Dollner, Potter & Co.* v. *Snow, et als.*, 16 Florida, 86.

349. Married Woman.—Where money is lent to a married woman, upon an agreement that it shall be applied to the use of her husband or his firm, she is not liable on a note given by her therefor prior to the St. of 1874, c. 184. *Nourse* v. *Henshaw*, 123 Mass. 96.

MARSHALLING SECURITIES.

350. Marshalling Securities.—The assignee of certain mortgages, having a collateral security for money advanced upon the mortgages, was required for the benfit of junior creditors against the mortgaged property, first to exhaust his remedy upon the collateral security. A creditor having the security of two funds out of which he can satisfy his debt, upon one of which only another creditor has a junior lien, will be compelled in equity to resort first to the fund which the junior creditor cannot reach. *Logan, et al.* v. *Brick, et al.*, 2 Del. 206.

351. Marshalling of Securities.—A. held a mortgage on two tracts of land, B. also held a mortgage on one of the tracts; in a proceeding by A. to foreclose, B. sought to compel him to exhaust the tract not embraced in his mortgage first. The widow of the mortgagor, who was also a party, claimed a homestead in the latter tract. *Held*, that by reason of the widow's equity, the securities should not be marshalled. Where one creditor has a security upon two funds, another, having a security on one of them, may, if necessary to the protection of his security, compel the other to resort to the fund embraced in it, if it can be done without prejudice to the other creditors or injustice to the common debtor or third persons having an interest in the fund. *Marr* v. *Lewis*, 31 Ark. 203.

MERGER.

352. Merger.—A conveyance of the fee to a mortgagee will not merge his mortgage, where such intention on his part does not exist, and no detriment to other encumbrancers shown. *Andrus* v. *Vreeland*, 29 N. J. 394.

MISTAKES.

353. Mistakes in Payment of Money.—Money paid under a mistake of a material fact may be recovered back although there was negligence on the part of the person making the payment, unless the position of the party receiving it has been changed in consequence thereof, and it would be inequitable to allow a recovery. If circumstances exist taking the case out of the general rule allowing a recovery, the burden of proving them rests upon the party resisting the repayment. *Mayer* v. *The Mayor*, 18 Sickels, N. Y. 455.

354. Mistake is recognized as a sufficient ground upon which to decree the reform of a deed, but the courts exercise their power in this respect with great caution, and only upon very clear and satisfactory proof. *Mendenhall* v. *Steckell*, 47 Md. 453.

355. Mistake. Question of Payment.—The endorser, upon receiving notice of protest, sent the money to take up the bill. The holder, under an honest mistake, informed him that it was taken up; in consequence of which he was prevented from taking up the bill and collecting it from the drawer, who became insolvent. *Held*, that the holder could not afterwards recover from the endorser. He was estopped. That he made the misstatement in good faith makes no difference. The estoppel applies, not on the ground of willful fraud in making the representation, but that showing the representation, to be true, to the prejudice of the endorser, would be a fraud. *Kingsley* v. *Vernon*, N. Y. Superior Court, 4 Sandf. 361.

356. Mistake.—The defendant having several contracts, produced one of them, supposing it to be a different one, and settled with plaintiffs, under this mistake. *Held*, that under the circumstances he was not estopped from proving the truth of the case. *Young* v. *Bushnell*, 8 Bosw., N. Y. Superior Ct. 1850, 1.

357. Mistake.—Although a party to a lease may be misnamed in the body of the writing, yet if he signs it it is his contract, no matter by what name he is called in the body of the instrument. *Montanye* v. *Wallahan*, 84 Ill. 355.

358. Mistake, to avoid an agreement, must be a mistake, not of *law* but of fact, and it must be a plain mistake, clearly made out by satisfactory proof—not resting upon evidence loose, equivocal or contradictory. *Pickering* v. *Day*, 2 Del. 333.

359. Mistake.—It *seems* that a mere inadvertent mistake, made by a bankrupt in stating the amount of a debt, will not avoid, as to the creditor, a composition made under and in pursuance of the act of Congress of June, 1874 (sec. 17), amending the Bankrupt Act. *Beebe* v. *Pyle*, 71 N. Y. 20.

360. Mistake.—*Deed may be corrected, how far.*—In a suit to reform a deed, lands which were not included in the deed, but omitted by mistake, may be inserted in the deed as reformed. *Loomis* v. *Ramsey*, 6 Oregon, 368.

361. Mistake.—*Degree of proof required to reform instrument on the ground of.*—In order to warrant a court of equity in reforming an instrument on the ground of mutual mistake, the proof of the mistake and that it was mutual must be clear. Where the complaint alleges mistake and asks relief on that ground alone, the court will not reform the instrument on the ground that one of the parties to it was guilty of a fraud in executing it. The complaint should point out the mistake and show in terms what the tenor of the instrument ought to be. It is not sufficient to say that it was the intention of the parties to make an instrument that would accomplish a certain object, and then ask the court to make a writing that will accomplish that object. The complaint should show the true contract in its terms. *Stephens* v. *Murton*, 6 Oregon, 193.

MORTGAGES.

362. Mortgage.—A. made a promissory note payable to the order of B., and executed to him a mortgage of land as security therefor, which was duly recorded. B. endorsed the note to C., and afterwards assigned the mortgage to D., and delivered to him another note similar in terms, and each paid a valuable consideration to B. *Held*, that C. was entitled in equity to an assignment of the mortgage from D. *Morris* v. *Bacon*, 123 Mass. 58.

363. Mortgagee's *Right of Entry.*—The mortgagee after condition ,broken, may, without notice, enter upon the mortgaged premises and take possession thereof, if he can do so peaceable and unresisted.

364. About January 1, 1874, the plaintiff went away on a visit, and left his son, a lad, in care of the premises; that on January 3, the defendant went to the premises and enquired of the boy for the plaintiff, stepped upon the door-step, and proclaimed that he took possession of the premises as owner, went quietly into the house, which was unfastened, the boy neither resisting nor consenting, removed the plaintiff's goods therefrom to an open shed, and left them there in the custody of the boy, and fastened up the house, and forbade the boy to enter. *Fuller* v. *Eddy*, 49 Rowell, Vt. 11.

365. Mortgage.—In a writ of entry brought by a mortgagee against the heirs of the mortgagor, to foreclose a mortgage of land, it is a good defence that the mortgage was given without consideration; and parol evidence is admissible to show that no debt ever existed between the parties to the mortgage. *Hannan* v. *Hannan*, 123 Mass. 441.

366. Mortgage.—A mortgagee who makes an absolute assignment of a mortgage to her agent, can claim no relief as against a *bona fide* holder to whom the agent assigned it as security for his own debt. *Grocers' B'k* v. *Neet*, 29 N. J. 449.

367. Mortgages.—A mortgagee's power to sell only continues as long as the debt exists. When the debt is extinguished, the power to sell ceases, and an attempt to exercise it is, therefore, *ultra vires*, and transfers no title, unless the mortgagor so acts as to estop him from showing the facts. *Lycoming Fire Ins. Co.* v. *Jackson*, 83 Ill. 302.

368. Mortgage *or Sale.*—A bill of sale of a vessel, like a deed absolute on its face, may be shown by parol to be, in fact, a mortgage only, or a mere security for a debt. *National Ins. Co.* v. *Webster*, 83 Ill. 470.

369. Mortgage.—Where a party sells *one* of a series of notes, secured by mortgage on certain property, without warranty, and reserving to any holder of any other of said notes equal rights, it will not debar him from subsequently proceeding on another of said notes, and subjecting said property to the ratable satisfaction of each of said notes. *Howard* v. *Schmidt*, 29 La. 129.

370. Mortgages.—An equitable mortgage may arise from non-payment of purchase-money, a deposit of title deeds, or an unsuccessful attempt to make a valid mortgage deed. *Gale* v. *Morris*, 29 N. J. 222.

371. Mortgage.—*Foreclosure.*—Where a senior mortgagee forecloses his mortgages without making a junior mortgagee of the same premises a party to his action for the foreclosure, the rights of the junior mortgagee remain unaffected, and are not prejudiced by such foreclosure. *Stewart* v. *Johnson*, 30 Ohio, 24.

372. Mortgage.—*Deed.*—Where one person advances money for another with which to purchase the title to land, taking the conveyance in his own name, as a security for the money so advanced, with interest, his deed will be treated as a mortgage, and on repayment he will be required to convey to the person for whom he so purchased. *Strong, et al.* v. *Shea, et al.*, 83 Ill. 575.

373. **Mortgage.**—The holder of a mortgage, given by a wife with her husband's authority, on her separate property, without the authorization of the judge under the Act of 1855, must prove that the debt which the mortgage was given to secure inured to the wife's separate benefit, before he can hold her liable. A wife separated in property is liable for her proportion of the household expenses, and for the whole of such expenses, if her husband is without means. *Mrs. Mary L. Hardin* v. *Wolf & Cerf*, 29 La. 333.

374. **Mortgages.**—An instrument of conveyance that on its face purports to be given to secure a payment, is merely a mortgage. *Cowles* v. *Marble*, 37 Mich. 158.

375. **Mortgage.**—*Sale of by a mortgagee.*—A sale by a mortgagee has the same effect as a sale by the mortgaging debtor. A mortgagee's sale relates back to the date of the mortgage, so far as to cut off redemption rights under titles or liens subsequent to the date of the mortgage, and to substitute for such redemption rights the pecuniary surplus from sale, which surplus is treated as the realty would have been. *De Wolf* v. *Murphy*, 11 R. I. 630 ; *Denton* v. *Nauny*, 8 Barb. S. C., N. Y. 618 ; also, *Mills* v. *Van Voorhis*, 23 Barb., 20 N. Y. 412.

376. **Mortgage.**—A grantee executed, at the same time and place, two mortgages on the same lands, one a purchase-money mortgage to his grantor, the other a mortgage to secure a bond given by himself and three sureties to W., for $2,000, which were paid at the same time to the grantor. *Held*, that W. could not, by having his mortgage registered first, acquire a priority over the purchase-money mortgage ; and that W.'s assignee held it subject to the same equity. *Brasted* v. *Sutton*, 29 N. J. 513.

377. Mortgage.—Besides a mortgage on lands, a chattel mortgage, covering the fixtures thereon, was executed at the same time and to secure the same debt, consisting of several bonds. *Held*, that one bondholder could not, by obtaining a judgment on his bond and levying on such fixtures, acquire a preference over the other bondholders, even if those fixtures were not a part of the realty, and the chattel mortgage had not been re-filed within the time required. *Fish* v. *New York Water Proof Paper Co.*, 29 N. J. 16.

378. Mortgage.—A lien or mortgage, securing a negotiable note, passes as an incident to the note, to the assignee or endorser, free from the equities between the original parties. *Duncan* v. *Louisville, &c.*, 13 Bush, Ky. 378.

379. Mortgage.—An assumption of a mortgage contained in a deed and to a married woman, without her knowledge or consent, and never delivered to her, does not bind her. *Culver* v. *Badger*, 29 N. J. 74.

380. Mortgage.—A. executed a deed or mortgage of land containing the condition "that if, on demand, there shall be paid" $1,000 on a certain promissory note, signed by A. as indorser, then the deed shall be void. The note was signed by A.'s son, as principal, and was for more than $1,000, and was given on account of a defalcation of his, and upon the giving of which the son was taken back into the promisee's employ, upon an agreement that a part of his wages should be applied in payment of the debt; under which arrangement more than $1,000 was received by the promisee, out of the son's wages, leaving more than $1,000 due on the note. *Held*, on a bill in equity by A. to redeem the mortgage, that the amount received from the son's wages was not to be credited to the mortgage. *Popple* v. *Day*, 84 Ill. 520.

381. Mortgages.—An assignee of a mortgage takes it subject to all defences existing against the mortgagee in favor of the mortgagor, but free from latent equities existing in favor of third persons. *De Witt* v. *Van Sickle*, 29 N. J. 209.

382. **Mortgage.**—The grantee of a mortgagor of land cannot, because of fraud practiced by the mortgagee upon the mortgagor in obtaining the mortgage, maintain a bill in equity against an assignee of the mortgagee to restrain a sale of the mortgaged premises under a power in the mortgage, without paying the entire debt secured by the mortgage, although the mortgage was assigned to the defendant as security for a less amount. *Foster* v. *Wightman*, 123 Mass. 100.

383. **Mortgage.**—*Assignment.*—An assignment, duly recorded, by the holder of a mortgage containing a power of attorney of sale, and made to secure two notes for $1,000 and $2,000, of "the said mortgage deed, the real estate thereby conveyed, so far as the same is security for said note of $1,000, thereby secured," transfers the mortgage as security in the first place, for the payment of the whole of the note of $1,000, although the assignment contains no covenant of warranty. *Foley* v. *Rose*, 123 Mass. 557.

384. **Mortgage.**—If one who holds, by an assignment duly recorded, a mortgage and a note endorsed in blank, purporting on its face to be secured by it, "the same being collateral to" a certain note, assigns the mortgage, and afterwards endorses the note for which it was collateral, retaining the mortgage note, to another, by an assignment in like words duly recorded, he conveys a title to the mortgage debt, except as against an innocent purchaser for value without notice; and one, to whom he subsequently passes the mortgage note and fraudulently assigns the mortgage upon a separate paper as collateral security for a loan, is not such a purchaser. *Strong* v. *Jackson*, 123 Mass. 60.

385. **Mortgage.**—If a third mortgagee of land, which is subject also to a fourth mortgage, sells, under power of sale contained in his mortgage, the entire title in the land, with the assent of the prior mortgagees, for a sum

sufficient to pay off all the four mortgages, the fourth mortgagee can maintain an action against him for money had and received. *Cook* v. *Basley*, 123 Mass. 396.

396. Mortgage.—A., for the purpose of enabling B. to raise money for him, made a promissory note payable to the order of B., and executed to him a mortgage of land, as security therefor, which was duly recorded. B., without A.'s knowledge or consent, and to secure his own debt, delivered the note unendorsed to C., and afterwards assigned the mortgage and a note, procured from A. by artifice, to D. for value. *Held*, that C. was not, in the absence of fraud on the part of D., entitled in equity to an assignment of the mortgage. *Blunt* v. *Norris*, 123 Mass. 55.

387. Mortgage.—A *bona fide* assignee of a mortgage is entitled to hold it as against the original owner, who, by placing it in her agent's hands assigned in blank or for a particular purpose, gave him the opportunity to perpetrate a fraud upon her. *Putnam* v. *Clark*, 29 N. J. 412.

388. Mortgage. — *Cancellation.* — The unauthorized cancellation of a mortgage by the recorder of mortgages cannot impair any rights of the owner of the mortgage. *Mechanics' Building Association* v. *Ferguson*, 29 La. 548.

389. Mortgage.—A lessee of land became the owner of an undivided portion of it, and executed a mortgage of this undivided portion, reciting that a part of the premises was subject to a lease, and that the leased premises were included in the description and in the mortgage. The mortgagee afterwards entered to foreclose. *Held*, that, even if the lease passed by the mortgage, the lessee had the right of possession against all persons except the mortgagee, until the expiration of three years from the entry, and could maintain an action of tort, for a trespass within that time, against a third person. *Martin* v. *Tobin*, 123 Mass. 85.

390. Mortgage, *not recorded.*—The mere fact that a

mortgagee withholds a mortgage from record does not
necessarily invalidate the mortgage as against creditors; it may have effect against him after it is recorded,
unless it is impeached for fraud, and in determining
that question such withholding from record must be
considered. *Black* v. *Ruhlman,* 40 Ohio, 196.

391. **Mortgages.**—*Equity of Bank in.—Latent equity.
—Bankers' liens.*—M., one of the defendants, entered into a contract with H. in the summer of 1872 to
the effect that H. would furnish him with building materials, and M. would pay H. therefor at the market
rates, a portion by a mortgage and a balance in cash.
H. furnished the materials as they were required by
M., and at various times in August and September M.
gave H. four promissory notes for $1,000 each. Three
of the notes were endorsed by H. and delivered to the
Manufacturers' and Builders' Bank, which discounted
the same for him. The fourth note was also endorsed
by H. and offered by him to the Eleventh Ward Bank
for discount, and was by it refused, and they never
paid any sum to him on the credit thereof; but when
applied to by H. said bank refused to surrender the
note, but claimed to hold the same for a general balance of account owing by him to the bank, arising on
previous dealings with him. On September 25, 1872,
M. and wife executed and delivered to H. the bond
and mortgage in question to secure the sum of $7,000,
which was justly owing to H. for materials furnished,
and in final settlement of the amount for such materials a credit was given by him on account of said
mortgage for the full face thereof. H. promised to
pay the three notes discounted for him by the Manufacturers' and Builders' Bank out of the proceeds
derived from the sale of the mortgages, and also to
procure and surrender to M. the note offered to the
Eleventh Ward Bank for discount, but he was prevented from performing this promise by the bank's refusing to surrender the same. It was not intended or
agreed at the time the bond and mortgage was deliv-

ered to H. that it was to be assigned to the Manufacturers' and Builders' Bank as security for the notes held by them or for any other purpose, and the only agreement relating to said notes was as above stated. H. assigned the bond and mortgage to Daniel P. Ingraham, Jr., who assigned the same to Edward B. Stead (both assignments being for a valuable consideration), who afterwards duly assigned the same to plaintiff, who paid therefor the sum of $6,700. The plaintiff had no notice or knowledge of any claim or equity against said bond and mortgage, and as an inducement to purchase the same there was shown and delivered to him a certificate of both of the mortgagors, asserting said bond and mortgage to be valid and free from all defences and equities. In action to foreclose the mortgage, *Held*, that the bank had no right upon declining a discount to retain the note, and its action was clearly tortious. The bankers' lien does not extend to such paper.

392. *Held, further*, that even if the right to hold the note were established, the banker had no possible equity in the mortgage. Such an equity could attach, if at all, only in favor of one who had actually negotiated the note or parted with the value upon the strength of the security.

Although, as to the receiver there is, perhaps, a case of a latent equity arising out of an implied trust, such an equity is not to be preferred to that of a *bona fide assignee* for value received. Equity will not aid a *cestui que trust* against a *bona fide* purchaser (from a trustee) without notice of the trust. Where the mortgage was ultimately given to H. without reserve and with a mere understanding as *to the application of the proceeds*, no equity is raised in the security, certainly not as against the plaintiff, who has paid full value, and who could not, by any *proper enquiry*, have learned of the latent equity. *Petrie* v. *Myers, et al.*, 54 Howard, N. Y. 513.

393. **Mortgage.**—The plaintiff, being embarrassed,

upon defendant's advice conveyed to him real estate, on defendant's parol promise that he would obtain from a building association, on the security of the real estate, a loan, with which he would pay plaintiff's liabilities, repay the loan from the rents, and reconvey to plaintiff when the loan should be repaid. *Held*, that the transaction was a mortgage. The purpose not being to sell, but convey as security, it is immaterial that defendant was to procure the money at a future time and from a third person. The defendant received the deed without consideration, except his promise to raise the money for plaintiff; if it was not intended to be raised it would be a fraud, and the defendant a trustee *ex maleficio*. The plaintiff's bill charged that defendant held in trust for him; did not allege that he was mortgagee, and prayed for account and reconveyance; it was dismissed below on the ground that there was no trust. The facts set out showing it to be a mortgage, the Supreme Court sustained the bill, to reach the justice of the case, disregarding the use in the bill of inappropriate terms. *Danzeisen's Appeal*, 73 Penn. 65; *Barnet v. Dougherty*, 8 Casey, 371; *Sweetzer's Appeal*, 21 P. F. Smith, 264.

394. **Mortgage Lien.**—*Priority.*—In August, 1872, F. and H. executed a joint note to G., payable in one year. On the face of the note each appeared as principal. The note was, in fact, given for borrowed money, and the money was borrowed for F., and received and used by him. To secure this note H. gave a mortgage on certain real estate, which mortgage was duly recorded. In September, 1873, F. handed to H. the amount of the loan, and took from him a receipt therefor, in which the latter promised to pay the note, but instead of then paying it, he obtained an extension of a year, by the payment of advance interest and a bonus. In January, 1874, H. borrowed money of S., and gave a note secured by a mortgage on the same and other property. In September, 1874, F. paid to G. the amount then due on the note, and took an as-

signment without recourse. *Held*, that at the first E. was to be regarded as the principal debtor, and that a payment by him to the payee of the note, prior to September, 1873, would have discharged both note and mortgage absolutely; but that by the payment in September, 1873, from F. to H., the promise of the latter to pay the note, and the obtaining of a year's extension of the time of payment, H. became in equity the principal debtor; and that as all this took place before the note and mortgage to S., the latter's rights were in no way prejudiced; and that F. by his subsequent payment to G., and the assignment of the note, was entitled to hold that note and mortgage as a valid and prior lien upon the mortgaged premises. *Field v. Sherrill*, 18 Kansas, 365.

395. Mortgages.—A third person cannot be affected by any notice of a mortgage, except the notice conveyed to him by the inscription of the mortgage. All are third persons, except the parties. The inscription of a mortgage, after the lapse of ten years from the date of inscription, unless re-inscribed, is utterly void as to third persons, and is no longer any proof of the mortgage, even between the parties to it. *Adams & Co. v. Daunis*, 29 La. 315.

NATIONAL BANKS.

396. National Banks.—A national bank is liable to be sued in any court having jurisdiction; it is not competent for Congress to restrict the jurisdiction to any particular courts. *Cooke* v. *State Bank of Boston*, 52 N. Y. 96; S. C., 50 Barb. 339.

397. National Banks. — *Stockholders' Liability.* — A religious society purchased and held in its own name certain shares of a national bank, using for the purpose a fund which had previously been given to such society by a testator, the whole bequest being used in the purchase. The society had other funds, given by other donors, which were otherwise invested. *Held*, that the society was not to be regarded as a trustee, but as an ordinary stockholder, and was liable as such to assessment for the debts of the bank on its failure. *Davis* v. *Essex Baptist Society*, 44 Conn. 582.

398. National Banks.—Under and by the provisions of National Banking Act (secs. 8, 28), a national bank is prohibited from taking a mortgage upon real estate, except for debts contracted prior to the giving of the mortgage; and a mortgage given to secure future indebtedness is void. *Crocker* v. *Whitney*, 71 N. Y. 161.

399. National Banks.—*Special deposit.*—A special deposit of bonds was left by a customer with the cashier of a national bank for safe keeping, with the knowledge of its directors, and the cashier gave a receipt therefor. The bonds were subsequently stolen and the bank offered no satisfactory explanation of the manner of the theft. *Held*, that there was sufficient evidence of gross negligence to be submitted to the jury. *Held, further*, that a recovery could be had against the bank if the bonds were stolen through the gross negligence of its officers. *Bank* v. *Graham*, 85 Penn. 91.

400. National Banks.—It *seems* that a bank, in the absence of any restriction imposed by its charter, may take a mortgage to secure anticipated liabilities, as well as those existing at the time; but the Legislature, whose creation it is, may impose such a restriction in its charter. *Crocker* v. *Whitney*, 71 N. Y. 161.

401. National Banks.—*Special deposits.*—By habitually receiving special deposits to be kept for mere accommodation, national banks incur liability for gross negligence. *Chat. Nat. Bank* v. *Schley, guardian*, 58 Ga. 369.

402. National Banks, as Federal agencies, are only exempted from State legislation so far as it may impair their efficiency in performing the functions by which they are designed to serve the government of the United States. It is only where a State law incapacitates them from discharging these duties that it becomes unconstitutional. *Thomas, et al.*, v. *Farmer's Bank of Md.*, 46 Md. 43.

403. National Banks.—*Stockholders.*—To protect a trustee, who is a stockholder in a national bank, from personal liability, under the provisions for such exemption in the act of Congress with regard to national banks, it must appear on the books of the bank that he was such trustee. *Davis* v. *Essex Baptist Society*, 44 Conn. 582.

404. National Banks.—The omission of the officer of a national bank to exact security for moneys lent cannot be made a ground of defence to an action brought by the bank to recover such loan. *Union Gold Mining Co.* v. *Rocky Mt. Nat. Bank*, 2 Colorado, 248.

405. National Banks.—*Who are stockholders.*—In ordering an assessment for the payment of the debts of an insolvent national bank, the stock certificates and stock ledger of the bank must be taken by the comptroller of the currency, in the absence of fraud or mistake, as showing who the stockholders were at the time of the failure of the bank. *Davis* v. *Essex Baptist Society*, 44 Conn. 582.

406. National Banks.—*Suits in State courts.*—State courts have jurisdiction of suits brought by national banks, it not having been taken away by Sec. 57, No. 85, of Sts. U. S. 1863-64. *First Nat. Bank of Montpelier* v. *Hubbard, et al.*, 49 Rowell, Vt. 1.

407. National Bank.—*Special deposits.*—National banks are not responsible for the safe keeping of special deposits made according to usage, for the accommodation of depositors, and with the knowledge and acquiescence of the bank directors, but without profit to the bank—the receiving of such deposits not being authorized by the National Banking Act, under which such banks are organized. *Whitney* v. *First Nat. Bank of Attleboro'*, 50 Vt. 388.

408. National Banks.—*Stockholders' assent as security.*—The stockholder, in subscribing for or in accepting the stock, assents to becoming security to the creditors for the payment of the debts of the bank. *Davis* v. *Essex Baptist Society*, 44 Conn. 582.

409. National Banks.—*Taxation.*—A statute of Vermont is not void, which, for the purpose of taxation, requires, under a penalty for his neglect or refusal, the cashier of each national bank within the State to transmit, on or before the fifteenth day of April in each year, to the clerks of the several towns in the State in which any stock or shareholders of such bank shall reside, a true list of the names of such stock or shareholders on the books of such bank, together with the amount of money actually paid in on each share on the first day of that month. *Waite* v. *Dowley*, 94 U. S. 527.

410. National Banks.—The shares of stock of a national bank in New York should be assessed for taxation at their actual value. The ruling in *Van Allen* v. *The Assessors*, 3 Wall. 573, as to the invalidity of the act of the Legislature of New York of March 9, 1865, known as the Enabling Act, so far as it provided for the taxation of shares in a national bank, reaffirmed. *People* v. *Commissioners of Taxes and Assessments*, 94 U. S. 415.

411. National Banks. — *Depositors' Claims.* — The claims of depositors in a national bank at the time of its suspension for the amount of their deposits are, when proved to the satisfaction of the comptroller of the currency, placed upon the same footing as if they were reduced to judgments. *National Bank of the Commonwealth* v. *Mechanics' National Bank*, 94 U. S. 437.

412. National Bank.—When a national banking association is insolvent, the order of the comptroller of the currency, declaring to what extent the individual liability of the stockholders shall be enforced, is conclusive. *Kennedy* v. *Gibson, et al.*, 8 Wall. 498; cited and approved. *Casey* v. *Calli*, 94 U. S. 673.

413. When his order is to collect an amount equal to the full par value of the stock, the suit by the receiver against the stockholders must be at law, and that amount will bear interest from the date of the order. In such a suit the stockholder is estopped from denying the existence or the validity of the corporation. *Id.*

414. No authority other than that conferred by Congress is required to enable a bank existing under a special or a general State law to become a national banking association. The certificate of the comptroller is conclusive as to the completeness of the organization under the act of Congress in a suit against a stockholder to enforce his liability, or a party upon his contract with the bank. *Id.*

415. A plea is bad which sets up that the comptroller has decided to pay a large amount of claims for which the bank is not responsible, and that, aside from those claims, there are means enough to meet the just liabilities of the bank. *Id.*

416. **National Banks.**—By an act of Congress with regard to National Banks, all stockholders of such banks are liable to assessment for the debts of the banks in case of their insolvency, to the extent of the par value of their stock in addition to the amount invested in such stock; but persons holding stock as executors, administrators and trustees are not to be personally subject to any liability as stockholders, but such liability is to attach only to the property in their hands. W. died in January, 1871, being at the time a stockholder of a national bank. His estate was subsequently settled, with a limitation for the presentation of claims, a settlement of the administration account, and a final distribution. The bank failed December, 1871, and a receiver was appointed by the comptroller of the currency, and in January, 1877, a long time after the distribution of W.'s estate, the comptroller made an assessment upon those who were stockholders at the time of the failure of the bank. *Held*, in a suit brought by the receiver against W.'s administrator—1. That the stock was not to be regarded as having been, at the time of the failure of the bank, the property of the administrator, in such a sense as to constitute him the

shareholder within the meaning of the act. 2. That the provision of the act exempting executors, administrators and trustees from personal liability was not intended to affect the liability to assessment of estates in process of settlement, but only to prevent a personal liability from running against persons acting in a trust capacity, who had received the stock for the benefit of the trust estate. 3. That the fact that the assets of the estate of W. had been distributed before a demand was made for the assessment, so that the administrator had nothing in his hands, was no reason why judgment should be rendered against him, *de bonis decedentis*. 4. That the liability of W.'was in the nature of a contract, and as such was a personal liability, for which his estate was holden at his death. Under the Connecticut statute the settlement of an administration account and the distribution of an estate does not prevent the estate being subjected, if actually solvent, to the payment of a debt which accrued after the settlement of the estate. *Davis, Receiver of Ocean National Bank of N. Y.* v. *Weed*, 44 Conn. 569.

417. **National Bank.**—A defendant sued by a national bank for moneys it loaned him cannot set up as a bar that they exceeded in amount one-tenth part of its capital stock actually paid in. *Gold Mining Co.* v. *National Bank*, 96 U. S. 640.

NEGLIGENCE.

418. **Negligence.**—*Who must suffer.*—If one of two innocent persons must suffer a loss, he who contributed to it, or enabled another to commit a wrong, must bear it. If a party signs and acknowledges a deed, supposing it to be a lease, without reading the same, and thereby enables his grantee to sell the property to an innocent purchaser for a valuable consideration, the title will pass to such purchaser, and the grantor must bear the loss. *Gavagan* v. *Bryant, et al.*, 83 Ill. 376.

419. Negligence.—*Contributory and Comparative.*—The general rule, where parties are guilty of negligence that of the plaintiff must be slight when compared with that of the defendant, and his must be gross, to authorize a recovery against him. A mere preponderance of negligence on the part of the defendant is not sufficient. *Schmidt, Adm'x.* v. *Chicago & Northwestern Ry. Co., et al.*, 83 Ill. 405.

420. Negligence.—*Burden of proof.*—Before any recovery can be had by a party receiving an injury by falling into an excavation in a sidewalk not properly protected, he must show that he had observed due care for his personal safety, and the burden of proving such fact is upon him. *Kepperly* v. *Ramsden*, 83 Ill. 354.

421. Negligence.—*Who must suffer from.*—As between two innocent persons, where one of two innocent parties is to suffer loss, it must fall upon the first one in fault. If, therefore, the equitable owner of a note loses the same, and it is found and put upon the market, and comes into the hands of an innocent and *bona fide* purchaser, the loss must fall upon the loser of the note for his negligence in not taking proper care of the same. *Gavin* v. *Wiswell*, 83 Ill. 215.

NEGOTIABLE NOTES.

422. Negotiable Paper.—Defendant gave to Hevner a negotiable note in payment of a patent which defendant alleged was a fraud; plaintiff being about to discount the note, defendant told him not to buy it, that Hevner had promised when the sale was made that he would not negotiate it; that if plaintiff bought it he would buy a lawsuit; no notice was given to plaintiff that the sale was fraudulent. Plaintiff having discounted the note, *Held*, in a suit on it, that these facts were no defence, although Hevner had committed a fraud on defendant in the sale. A parol agreement, although made at the time of making negotiable paper, that the payee will not negotiate it and would renew it, &c., is admissible to vary the effect of the paper. *Heist* v. *Hart*, 73 Penn. 286.

423. Negotiable Instruments.—A negotiable instrument, payable to bearer, or endorsed in blank, produced by a transferee suing to recover its contents, is, when received in evidence, clothed with the *prima facie* presumption that he became the holder of it for value at its date, in the usual course of business, without notice of anything to impeach his title. *Collins* v. *Gilbert*, 94 U. S. 753.

424. The title of a *bona fide* holder for value of an accepted draft, endorsed in blank, is not affected by the fact that the party from whom he received it before its maturity had possession of it for certain purposes and misappropriated it. *Id.*

425. Negligence may consist in either failing to do what, under the circumstances, a reasonable and prudent man would ordinarily have done, or in doing what he would not have done. *Railroad Company* v. *Jones*, 95 U. S. 439.

426. Negotiable Notes.—A *bona fide* purchaser of negotiable paper for value, before maturity, takes it freed from all infirmities in its origin, unless it is absolutely void, for want of power in the maker to issue it, or its circulation is by law prohibited by reason of the illegality of the consideration. Municipal bonds, payable to bearer, are subject to the same rules as other negotiable paper. Though he may have notice of infirmities in its origin, a purchaser of a municipal bond from a *bona fide* holder, who obtained it for value before maturity, takes it as freed from such infirmities as it was in the hands of such holder. A purchaser of negotiable securities before their maturity, whatever may have been their original infirmity, can, unless he is personally chargeable with fraud in procuring them, recover against the maker the full amount of them, though he may have paid therefor less than their par value. *Cromwell* v. *County of Sac.*, 96 U. S. 51.

427. Negotiable Instruments.—Where the title of the

original holder of negotiable instruments, which are infected with fraud, invalidity, is destroyed, that of every subsequent holder which rests on that foundation, and no other, falls with it. *Cemmissioners of Marion County* v. *Clark*, 94 U· S. 278.

428. Where the first endorser, without notice of any prior equities between the original parties, purchases, for value, a negotiable instrument, the second indorsee, who acquires it before it is due, and for value, takes a good title, although he had notice of such equities. *Id.*

Bonds issued, pursuant to legislative authority, by a municipal corporation in aid of a railroad company, are negotiable instruments. *Id.*

429. **Negotiable Notes.**—A promissory note in the ordinary form, signed by a married woman, made payable to the order of her husband, and endorsed and presented for discount by him, is *prima facie* a nullity; to give it vitality and effect it must be made to appear by evidence *aliunde* the instrument, that it was made in her separate business or for the benefit of her separate estate. The fact that she owns separate estate is not alone sufficient to give it validity. Accordingly, *Held*, in an action upon two such notes against the maker, that a charge to the jury to the effect that defendant gave the notes to her husband with a view of having them discounted was calculated to convey the impression that she was the principal, and whatever was done was for her benefit, was an error. *Second Nat. Bank* v. *Miller*, 18 Sickels, N. Y. 634.

430. **Non-Negotiable Promissory Note.** — *Pleading.* — *Complaint.*—*Demurrer.*—*Defence.*—When it appears from the complaint that one of the two defendants made the note in suit in favor, but not to the order, of the plaintiff, the payee therein named ; that the other defendant endorsed it, and that it was thereupon delivered to the plaintiff, *Held*, that, inasmuch as such an endorsement before delivery imparts the liability of a maker, these averments, taken together, must be

deemed equivalent to an allegation that the two defendants made the promissory note, and that both are jointly liable as makers thereof. Although not negotiable, the instrument is a promissory note, and as such imparts a consideration, though none is expressed. Want of consideration is matter of defence.

A question of pleading must be determined according to the course of practice prevailing in the courts of this State, although the obligation sued upon, *i. e.*, a promissory note, was made in another State. In the absence of proof to the contrary, it will be presumed by the courts of this State that the law of another State in regard to a subject-matter before the court, is the same as the law in this State. *Paine* v. *Noelke*, 53 Howard's N. Y. 273; also 54 Id. 333.

431. Negotiable Notes.—A promissory note, in form negotiable, is not rendered non-negotiable by being made payable at one or two years after date, nor by the statement on its face that it was given for and secured by a lien on real estate. *Duncan* v. *Louisville, etc.*, 13 Bush, Ky. 378.

432. Negotiable Instruments.—Note payable one day after date becomes due on day after it was made, and cannot be sued until the day following. If such note was not made on the day of its date, it cannot be sued until the second day after it was in fact made. *Ruefle* v. *Moore, et al.*, 58 Ga. 94.

NOTARY PUBLIC.

433. Notary Public.—There is no statute conferring on notaries public a general power to administer oaths and take affidavits. Such a power is not one of the incidents of the office of notary public, under the law merchant, and as it is not, by the statutes of Texas, conferred on notaries of other States, an instrument purporting to be an affidavit executed before a notary public of another State, by an appellant, stating an inability to give bond, with security, for costs, is not an affidavit, within the meaning of the statute. *Jenks* v. *Jenks*, 47 Texas, 220.

434. Notary—Sureties.—The sureties on the official bond of a notary public are liable for any loss or damage caused by his affixing his notarial paraph to any mortgage note which he knew to be forged. And any one injured by his act has a right of action on the bond against his sureties. *Rochereau, et al.* v. *William McC. Jones*, 29 La. 82.

NOTES.

435. Notes *given for too much—Not void.*—The fact that notes are given for a larger sum than was agreed by the parties to be due for land purchased, does not render them void, but goes to the consideration, partially, and there may be a recovery *pro tanto*. *McGord* v. *Crooker*, 83 Ill. 556.

436. Note *signed by one as principal. Proof that the contract was that of surety.*—When one signs an obligation describing himself as principal, he renounces his right as surety, and parol evidence showing that his agreement was that of surety only, and that his liability was extinguished by reason of an extension granted to the principal without his knowledge, is inadmissible, as varying the terms of his written contract. And more especially is this true where he expressly stipulates in the instrument that no extension of time shall affect his liability. And it is immaterial in such case that the instrument signed is a note and not a specialty. *McMillan* v. *Parkell*, 64 Mo. 286; *Claremont Bank* v. *Wood*, 10 Vt. 582; *Picot* v. *Signiago*, 22 Mo. 587.

437. Notes.—A promissory note made payable a specified number of months after date, without grace, falls due on the same day of the month as that of its date. *Roehner* v. *Knickerbocker Life Ins. Co.*, 18 Sickels, N. Y. R. 160.

438. Notes and Bills.—*Parol evidence to change the mode of payment.*—Equity may entertain a bill to rectify a written instrument drafted, by accident, mistake, or fraud, otherwise than according to the agreement of the parties, but if a person deliberately execute a particular instrument, such as a promissory note, intending it to be what it is in reality, parol testimony is inadmissible, either at law or in equity, to change or alter its legal effect. *Bridges* v. *Robinson*, 2 Tenn. Eq. 720.

439. **Notes and Bills.**—The statute (Gen. Statutes, 343, sec. 2) which provides that any promissory note payable on demand, which remains unpaid four months from its date, shall be considered overdue and dishonored, does not affect the rights of the original parties to the note, but only those of third parties, as endorsers, guarantors or purchasers. *Seymour* v. *Continental Life Ins. Co.*, 44 Conn. 300.

NOTICE.

440. **Notice.**—An association (not incorporated) desired to raise money, individual members made notes in large sums for the purpose and placed them in the hands of Hostetter, one of the association. The amounts being too large to negotiate, he gave his individual notes in smaller sums and retained the large notes as security for himself. Evidence tending to prove the ratification of his acts by the other members of the association was admissible in a suit upon the original notes by a holder. *Held*, that Hostetter's knowledge of the circumstances, &c., of the notes was to be imputed to the firm. *McClurken* v. *Byers*, 74 Penn. St. Repts. 405.

441. **Notice** to the cashier of a bank lending on trust stocks, that the stock pledged is held in trust, is notice to the bank. *Gaston* v. *Am. Exch. Bank*, 29 N. J. 98.

442. **Notice to Sue.**—*To release a surety, under the statute*, satisfactory proof must be made, or a notice in writing, by him to the holder of the obligation, to

from its date, shall be considered over-due and dishonored, does not affect the rights of the original parties to the note, but only those of third parties, as endorsers, guarantors or purchasers. *Seymour* v. *Continental Life Ins. Co.*, 44 Conn. 300.

OFFER.

443. Offer to Endorse.—Defendant not liable thereon unless plaintiffs, within reasonable time, give notice that they had accepted the offer, or had acted on it. *Claflin & Co.* v. *Bryant*, 58 Ga. 414.

OFFICERS.

444. Officers' Sureties.—The illegal cancellation of an official bond will not release the sureties on the bond from their liability for any official delinquency of their principal. *A. Rochezeau, et al.* v. *Wm. McJones, et al.*, 29 La. 82.

445. Officers of a Bank.—The cashier of a bank is not, by reason of his official position, presumed to have power to bind it as an accommodation endorser on his individual note, and the payee who fails to prove that the cashier, as such, had authority to make the endorsement, cannot recover against the bank. *West St. Louis Savings Bank* v. *Shawnee County Bank*, 95 U. S. 557.

OVER-DUE COUPONS.

446. Over-Due Coupons *detached from railroad bonds payable to bearer are negotiable instruments.*—When a railroad corporation, through its president, borrowed money of its agent, and pledged with him mortgage bonds as security, although the agent could, as between himself and the corporation, only hold the bonds as security for the loan, on payment of which they should be surrendered to the company, yet a person in good faith purchasing the bonds from the agent could hold them for at least the amount he paid for them. The amount paid for the bonds may be taken into consideration in determining the question of good faith.

447. And where the purchaser from an agent afterwards sells the bonds to a *bona fide* purchaser, the fact that the bonds were then over-due will not preclude the last purchaser from holding on to the bonds as indemnity for the amount he paid, although in excess of the sum originally borrowed by the company upon them.

448. An honest purchaser from the agent of the company can give a good title to another, although the bonds become due before the last transfer. The question of a *bona fide* purchaser considered, as also effect of the clause making the principal due, by an omission to pay an installment of interest. Under the circumstances of this case the last party was held entitled, in an action brought against him by the company for the recovery of the bonds, to detain them as indemnity for the amount he had paid on their purchase. *Todd v. Shelbourne*, 8 Hun, 510. Decision on all the above questions in the case of *Grand Rapids and Indiana Railroad Co. v. Joshua C. Sanders*, 54 Howard's, N. Y. 214.

OWELTY.

449. **Owelty.**—*Manner of paying proceeds of sale.*—When owelty is required to equalize partition between two tenants in common, the estate of one being mortgaged, it should, if to be paid by the unincumbered owner, be paid to the mortgagee of the other and credited on the mortgage note. *Green v. Arnold*, 11 R. I. 364.

PAROL.

450. **Parol Evidence** is not admissible to vary the terms of a written contract. *Serviss v. Stockstill*, 30 Ohio, 418.

PATENT-RIGHT NOTE.

451. Patent-Right Notes.—The Michigan Statute (Comp. L., sec. 1565-6) imposing conditions on the transfer of patent-rights by requiring notes given therefor to show it, and making it a misdemeanor to take or transfer them otherwise, is unconstitutional, as impairing rights that are regulated and protected by Congress. Fraud is not to be presumed against a patent-right note, but must be proved. *Cranson* v. *Smith*, 37 Mich. 309.

PARTNERSHIP.

452. Partner surviving of a firm may assign a promissory note payable to the late firm, by endorsement, so as to vest the legal title in the assignee, as effectually as if the note had been made payable to him. *Johnson, et al.* v. *Berlizheimer*, 84 Ill. 54.

453. Partnership.—A note by a partnership to one of its members for money borrowed, may be enforced at law in the name of an endorsee not a member of the partnership, although the payee be a party defendant and the real owner of the note,—no reason appearing why a judgment at law would not do legal justice between the real parties. *Walker* v. *Wait, et al.*, 50 Vt. 668.

454. Partnership.—*Authority of Partner.*—One member of a partnership cannot bind his co-partner by a promissory note for a partnership demand, made after the dissolution of the partnership. *Curry* v. *White*, 51 Cal. 530.

455. Partnership.—In an action against A. for goods sold and delivered, to which the defence was payment by the negotiable promissory note of B. and C., it appeared that the plaintiff took the partnership note of B. and C. in payment. *Held*, that the declarations of one of the partners, to the effect that A. was a member of the firm, were admissible in evidence to show that the plaintiff took the note under a misapprehension, and that, if this were so, the action could be maintained. *Tozier* v. *Crafts*, 123 Mass. 480.

456. **Partnership.**—The holder of a claim against a partnership has a legal right to have his claim established against the estate of the deceased partner, and, in the ordinary course of administration, his claim will be paid *pari passu* with other claims of the same class, without regard to the distinction between partnership and individual claims. *Higgins* v. *Rector*, 47 Texas, 361.

457. **Partnership Obligations.**—While it is true that, after the dissolution of a partnership, the members thereof cannot create obligations which will bind the firm, or change the character or form of those already existing, still it devolves on them to give actual notice to those with whom the firm has had dealings; and any act done within the scope of the partnership, by one of the members, after its dissolution, and before actual notice of dissolution to those with whom said firm had been dealing, is binding upon all the members of such firm. Partnership notes import at law—although it is otherwise in equity—a joint, and not a joint and several obligation. *Davis* v. *Willis*, 47 Texas, 154.

458. **Partnership.**—As by operation of law a partnership is dissolved by the death of any of its members, any agreement taking the partnership out of this rule must be shown distinctly and by evidence satisfactory. *Alexander* v. *Lewis*, 47 Texas, 481.

459. **Partnership.**—A new partner, in a firm not liable for the debts of the old firm of the same name, is not responsible for money borrowed, without his knowledge or consent, by the members of the old firm, and used to pay a debt of the old firm, the lender being aware that the money was to be so applied. *Elkin* v. *Green*, 13 Bush, Ky. 612.

460. **Partnership.**—Two partners constituting an old firm could not bind the third partner who, with them, constituted a new firm of the same name, without his

knowledge or consent, by borrowing money and using it to pay debts of the old firm, or by making and delivering to themselves the notes of the new firm, when the new was not indebted to the old firm. *Elkin* v. *Green*, 13 Bush, Ky. 612.

461. Parties *in action for breach of contract.*—An action for a breach of contract must be brought by the party with whom the contract was made. *Corbett* v. *Schumacker*, 83 Ill. 403.

462. Partnerships *and partners.*—The power of one partner to bind his co-partners rests alone upon the usages of merchants, and does not amount to a rule of law in any other than commercial partnerships. In non-commercial partnerships, one who seeks to hold the firm bound upon a contract made by a single member, must be able to show either express authority, or that such is the custom and usage of the particular branch of business in which the firm is engaged, or such facts as will warrant the conclusion that the partner had been invested by his co-partners with the requisite authority.

The extent of the power of a partner to bind his firm is a question of law in commercial, and a question of fact in non-commercial partnerships. The business of a commercial partnership being ascertained, and the nature of the contract made by a single member, and the circumstances attending it being known, the court may generally determine, as matter of law, whether the contract was within the scope of the implied powers of a partner. Not so, however, in reference to a contract made by a member of a non-commercial partnership.

463. A partner in a non-commercial partnership does not generally possess power to bind the firm, and consequently the extent of his power is not fixed by the rules of law, but each case is left to be decided upon its particular facts; and in all such cases, in order to make out the liability of the firm, it ought to be made out affirmatively by the plaintiff that the partner had power to make the contract in question.

464.—A partnership engaged in the business of mining, &c., is a non-commercial partnership. A partner has no implied power to purchase land in the name of the firm in a partnership formed for the purpose of mining, &c. *Dickinson* v. *Valpy*, 10 B. & C. 125; *Levy* v. *Pyne & Richards*, 41 E. C. & L. 249; *Smith* v. *Sloan*, 37 Wis. 289. Sustained by the court in *Judge &c.* v. *Braswell & Co*, 13 Bush, Ky. 67.

465. Partnership.—On the trial of an action against B., upon an issue as to whether one W. and B. were partners, there was evidence that W. and B. were together, and had certain stock together; that B. carried a note to bank to be discounted, with a written request from W. that it should be done; that B. said that the money *was for himself and* W.; that they were *buying* stock *together*, and that the money was to be used in buying stock; that B. afterwards referred to the debt he and W. owed the bank, &c. *Held*, that the jury were warranted in finding that a partnership existed between W. and B. *Dobson* v. *Chambers*, 78 N. C. 334.

466. Partnership.—*Liability of a firm.*—Where a member of a firm of real estate brokers receives money with which to purchase land for the person advancing the same, and passes the same over to a partner, who deposits the same to the credit of the firm, and the proof fails to show that it was invested as agreed, the whole firm will be liable in assumpsit to the party so advancing, for the amount, with six per cent. interest. *Kerr, et al.* v. *Sharp*, 83 Ill. 199.

467. Partnership.—Agreement between A. and B., by which A. agreed to build five houses for B. at actual cost, to be completed, etc., and the houses and the lots whereon they were built to be sold, and the proceeds of the sale, after deducting the cost of the houses and the value of the land, rated at five cents a foot, and other expenses, to be divided between A. and B. *Held*, that if this agreement could be construed as a partnership at all, it was one for disposing of the houses and land, not for building them. *Bisbee* v. *Taft*, 11 R. I. 307.

468. Partnership.—Where one member of a firm, at its dissolution, sold all his interest in the property and accounts of the firm to his partner, who gave his note therefor, the defendant in a suit upon the note by the payee, cannot set off against such note an account due from the plaintiff to the firm at its dissolution. *Wiggin* v. *Goodwin*, 63 Me. 389; also, *Lesure* v. *Norris*, 11 Cush. 328.

469. Partnership.—*Individual debts.*—*Levy on partnership property.*—An execution creditor of an individual member of a co-partnership, having caused property of such co-partnership to be levied on by an officer, to satisfy his debt, was, together with such officer, on application of another partner, temporarily enjoined from making sale until the partnership debts had been paid, and directed to deliver such property to a receiver appointed in such proceedings to settle the partnership affairs. On appeal by such creditor alone to the Supreme Court, such injunction was reversed as to him, and the cause remanded for further proceedings. Such receiver having subsequently sold such property and reported a distribution of the proceeds of the sale to the partnership creditors, such execution creditor instituted an action against such co-partner and his surety, on the bond executed by them to procure such injunction, to recover damages resulting therefrom. *Held*, that no reversal of such injunction having been obtained as to such officer, or as to the appointment of such receiver, and such creditor having continued to be a party to such action, resulting in the sale of such property and the distribution of the proceeds thereof, the judgment therein rendered, after such reversal, the reports of such sale by the receiver, and the approval thereof by the court, were competent evidence against, and bound him. *Donellan* v. *Hardy*, 57 Ind. 393.

470. By the levy of his execution upon partnership property, the creditor of an individual partner acquires no interest whatever in the property itself, but only a lien for the share of such partner, individually, in the surplus remaining after all partnership debts and prior liens shall have been paid. *Id.*

471. Partnership.—An action at law cannot be maintained by one partner against another, involving the state of the partnership accounts. But one partner may sue another at law on a promise to pay a balance which has been ascertained and agreed upon. And a *fortiori* may an action at law be maintained on negotiable promissory notes given by one partner to another for the amount of the balance ascertained upon dissolution. And it would not be competent for the defendant to defeat such action by showing that there had been no final settlement of partnership accounts. *McSherry* v. *Brooks and Barton, Trustees,* 46 Md. 103.

472. Partnership.—*Incoming partner—Liability.*— It is not necessary that an incoming partner should do *something*, in order to *escape* liability for the previous debts and obligations of his co-partners, but on the contrary it is necessary that he should *do something* in order *to make himself liable* for such debts or obligations. *Gauss* v. *Hobbs,* 18 Kansas, 504.

473. Partnership.—One partner, without the consent, expressed or implied, of his co-partner, cannot apply a claim of the firm to the payment of his individual debt, even in order to retain for the firm its debtor's custom, and such attempted application with knowledge of the facts by such debtor, will not defeat *an action at law* upon a claim, by the firm or its assignee. *Viles* v. *Bangs,* 36 Wis. 131; also, *Cobyhausen* v. *Judd, et al.,* 43 Wis. 213.

474. Partnership.—Partners have no implied authority to confess judgment for each other. An infant cannot in his own name confess judgment. An infant's assignment is not void but only voidable, and that only by the infant or some one in his right. A judgment confessed by an infant's partner in the name of the

firm is void and will not support an attachment as against a previous assignee of the goods attached. *Soper* v. *Fry*, 37 Mich. 236.

475. Partnership.—Foresman sold out his interest in a firm to the remaining members, who covenanted jointly and severally to pay the debts, and indemnify him against them ; the remaining members continued in the same business as a partnership, took all the first firm's assets and took upon themselves the debts, without any division of Foresman's interest. Foresman paid debts of the first firm, the second firm afterwards assigned for the benefit of creditors. *Held*, that Foresman was entitled to come in as a creditor. The distribution of firms' assets is governed by the equities of the partners, not the rights of creditors. In insolvency the firm's assets go to discharge the firm's creditors before the individual property of the members can be taken. The other partner having bought Foresman out and indemnified him, he became then surety, and, having paid debts, was subrogated to the rights of the creditors. *Frow, Jacobs & Co.'s Estate*, 73 Penn. 459.

476. Partnership.—Contracts made by one partner on behalf of the firm, in the business of the firm, are binding upon the firm. *Wilson* v. *Elliott*, 57 Hall, N. H. 316.

477. Partnership.—It is a violation of good faith for any partner to stipulate clandestinely with third persons, for any private and selfish advantage and benefit to himself exclusive of the partnership ; for all the partnership property and partnership contracts should be managed for the equal benefit of all partners, according to the respective interests and shares therein. If, therefore, any one partner should so stipulate clandestinely for any private advantage or benefit of himself, to the disadvantage, or in fraud of his partners, he will in equity be compelled to divide such gains with them. *McMahon, et al.* v. *McClernan*, 10 West Va. 419.

478. Partnership.—*When general Reputation insufficient to prove Partnership.—What is not Reputation.*—Although the most conclusive proof is not required where defendants are sued as partners, there must be some proof of partnership. Where the only proof of partnership was the evidence of the plaintiff who swore they were partners because "she knew it in business," "she had heard so," "everybody knew it," "and there was a sign on the store Uhlig & Co.," "she knew only two of the defendants, never saw and did not know the name of the third one," and which of the two defendants named Uhlig was the one she did not determine. *Held*, that there was no direct evidence of defendant's co-partnership, and no proper proof of reputation to that effect, and the complaint should be dismissed for this reason. *Gulke* v. *Uhlig*, 55 Howard N. Y. 434.

479. Partnership.—A sale by a partner, in payment of his own debt, of goods which are in fact goods of the partnership, but which the partnership has so entrusted to him as to enable him to deal with as his own, and to induce the public to believe to be his, and which the creditor receives in good faith and without notice that they are the goods of the partnership, is valid against the partnership and its creditors. *Locke* v. *Lewis*, 124 Mass. 1.

480. Partnership.—A community of profit and loss is the test of a partnership, even where the dispute is between the partners. Parties casually met together, who make an agreement to buy what goods they can, either jointly or separately, and on reaching the home market to sell on joint account, and divide the proceeds among themselves *pro rata*, according to the amount each should put in the venture, become partners as to such venture. Such a partnership is a trading or commercial partnership, and one of the partners may borrow money in the name and on the credit of the firm, by note, bill, or otherwise, and all will be liable. Misappropriation of the funds by the partner borrowing the money does not relieve the firm from liability. *Howze* v. *Patterson*, 53 Ala. 205.

481. Partner and Partnership.—A debtor, being a member of an insolvent partnership, conveyed his separate estate in satisfaction of a debt due to a separate creditor. The real estate exceeded in value, to a considerable amount, the debt for the satisfaction of which it was conveyed. *Held*, that the other creditors had an interest in the excess, and that in equity the property conveyed would be held as a security, first, for the debt due to the grantee, and, as to the excess of value, for other debts. The real estate conveyed being the separate property of the co-partner, the excess of value was bound, first, for his separate debts, and only after satisfying these was it applicable to the debts of the partnership. *Bailey, et al.* v. *Kennedy, et al.* 2 Del. 12.

482. Partnership property.—An attachment of partnership property for a partnership debt will prevail over a prior attachment of the same property for a separate debt of one of the partners, or over a mortgage of one of the partners to secure his individual indebtedness. *Fargo & Co.* v. *Ames, et ux.*, 45 Iowa, 491.

PAYABLE AND PAYMENT.

483. Payable in Bank.—When a promissory note is made in this State, payable in a bank named but not located, it will be presumed, unless the contrary appear, that the bank is located in this State. *Henderson* v. *Ackelmire*, 59 Ind. 540 ; also, *Burroughs* v. *Wilson*, 59 Ind. 536.

484. Payment.—If the payee of a draft present and surrender it to the drawee, on receiving his check for the amount, which he neglects to present until the next day, the drawee is discharged. *Smith* v. *Miller*, 43 N. Y. 171.

485. Payment.—Money voluntarily paid in discharge of a claim made upon the payor, or to buy off from and quit a criminal prosecution to which he is exposed, cannot be recovered. *Comstock* v. *Tupper*, 50 Vt. 596.

486. Payment.—The payment to the sheriff of the redemption money, under foreclosure, in United States treasury notes, and national bank notes, which were received without objection, *Held*, sufficient. *Nopson* v. *Horton*, 20 Minn. 268.

487. Payments—*When there are several debts.*—Where, at the time of sending a draft, the sender was, as a member of a firm, indebted to the party whom the draft was sent, in several notes, most of which were then due and bearing interest, and also in two individual notes, not then due, and maturing some time afterwards, and which bore no interest before maturity, and the debtor, at the time of sending the draft, directed the creditor to hold the amount until advised as to its application, and stating that his partner would send a statement of matters in a few days, and such partner did afterwards write, giving a statement as to the firm notes, with their interest up to the time of sending the draft, and the other debtor made no other direction for several months after, and not until the creditor had applied the draft upon the firm notes, it was *held*, that the creditor was, under the circumstances, justified in making the application he did, and being rightfully made, it could not be repudiated by the debtor afterwards. *Lewis* v. *Pease*, 85 Ill. 31.

488. Payment.—Where a mortgagor of land is the executor of the will of the mortgagee, and charges himself with the amount of the mortgage debt, as assets in his hands as executor, this operates as a payment of the debt and a discharge of the mortgage. *Martin* v. *Smith*, 124 Mass. 111.

489. Payment.—A creditor who holds notes or other obligations for the payment of money assigned to him by his debtor as collateral security, and neglects to use reasonable diligence to collect them when due, must bear the loss thence accruing. In an action by such creditor against the debtor, the burden is upon

the latter to show that the loss upon the collaterals was caused by the creditor's negligence. *Charter Oak Life Ins. Co.* v. *Smith, et al.*, 43 Wis. 329.

490. Payment.—A stipulation in a promissory note that no credit shall be allowed on it unless endorsed upon it by the payers, will not prevent the allowance in an action upon the note, of any authorized payment actually made, but not endorsed. *Kasson, et al.* v. *Noltner*, 43 Wis. 646.

491. Payment.—Where the draft of a third party is received by a creditor from his debtor for a pre-existing debt, the presumption is that it was received as a conditional payment, unless there was an agreement that it was to be an absolute payment, and the burden then of proving such an agreement is upon the debtor. *League* v. *Waring & Co.*, 85 Penn. 244.

492. Payment.—Taking a note from the debtor or a note of a third party, is no discharge of the debt, unless it is expressly agreed between the creditor and debtor that it is in absolute payment thereof. *Dunlap's Exr.* v. *Shanklin*, 10 West Virginia, 662.

493. Payment.—A bank check given and accepted by the partners to it as payment of the balance found due upon accounting together, is such a payment as will entitle the drawer to be discharged, if summoned as trustee of the payee, in an action in which the writ is served on the day after such payment, although the check is not presented and paid at the bank on which it is drawn until the next day. *Getchell* v. *Chase*, 124 Mass. 366.

494. Payments.—Partial payments are applied when their sum equals or exceeds the interest, not before. *Houston* v. *Crutcher*, 31 Miss. 51; overruled in *Brooks* v. *Robinson*, 54 Miss. 272.

495. Payment.—When partial payments are made on a debt past due (Rev. Code, sec. 1830), they should be applied first to the extinguishment of the accrued interest, and only the residue be applied to the principal. *Coleman* v. *Smith*, 55 Ala. 369.

496. Payment.—In an action upon a promissory note money paid by the maker after the date of the note and not endorsed thereon, will not be allowed as a credit, if there is nothing in the record to show it was paid as such. *Craig* v. *Young*, 2 Colorado, 112.

497. Payments.—*Voluntary.*—A married woman owning land joined with her husband in a mortgage which was assigned to a bank; in a *scire facias* on it the verdict was for her. She sold part of the land; the purchaser paid the purchase-money to the bank in order to procure a release of the mortgage. *Held*, that she could not recover money from the bank. One who voluntarily pays money with knowledge or means of knowing of the facts, and without fraud on him, cannot recover it because he paid in ignorance of the law. *Real Estate Saving Inst.* v. *Linder*, 74 Penn. St. 371.

498. Payment.—*Option to pay in money or property.*—Where the vendee of real estate contracts to pay the purchase-money in cash or by the delivery of cotton of a specified class at a designated place, as the payments become due, at his option, the right of election is not lost by the failure to deliver the cotton at the time and place, where it is brought about by the conduct of the vendor. *Brodie & King* v. *Watkins and wife*, 31 Ark. 319.

499. Payment.—*Extension.*—A payment of part of a debt before due, is a consideration sufficient to support a contract to give time. *Hartman* v. *Danner*, 74 Penn. St. 36.

500. Payments by Mistake.—Money paid under a mutual mistake for that which has no legal existence or validity, may be recovered back as paid without consideration, where the vendor is responsible for the mistake, or represents the person so responsible. So *held*, of the *bona fide* transfer by executors of a certificate of an execution sale that turned out to be void, but which had been issued to their testator. *McGoren* v. *Avery*, 37 Mich. 120.

501. Payment.—*Tender.*—Any third person, who demands no subrogation, may tender to a creditor, either in his own name, or in that of the debtor, the debt due by the latter, in whatever species of property the debt is payable, and compel the creditor to accept the payment in that property. *State ex rel. John Klein & Co. v. Ed. Pilsbury, Adm'r of Finance, &c.*, 29 La. 787.

502. Payment.—By the law of this commonwealth, the giving of the negotiable promissory note of a third person is evidence of payment of a pre-existing debt, and sufficient where there is nothing to defeat the inference or show that such was not the intention of the parties; and in the absence of evidence to the contrary, the rule will be presumed to be the same in Maine. *Ely v. James*, 123 Mass. 36.

503. Payment, *Proof of.*—In an action brought for the purpose of establishing the payment of a promissory note between parties not traders, *Held*, reversing judgment of court below, that the question was one which must be governed by the laws of England and may be made by parole evidence. *Carden, et al. & Finlay, et al.*, 8 L. C. J. 139, and 10 L. C. R. 255, Q. B. 1860, 1233, sec. 1, and 2341 C. C.

504. Payment, *What amounts to a.*—If the holder of notes by agreement accepts of the maker policies of insurance covering property destroyed by fire, upon which there is a *prima facie* cause of action, in discharge of the notes, in the absence of fraud he will be bound by the contract, and the maker, when sued on the notes, need not show that a complete cause of action existed in his favor on the policies, to make his defence availing. *Brunswick v. Birkenbend*, 83 Ill. 413.

505. Payment, *made Voluntarily.*—*Recovery.*—If a party with full knowledge of all the facts in the case voluntarily pays money in satisfaction or discharge of a demand unjustly made upon him, he cannot afterward allege such payment to have been made by compulsion and recover back the money. *Murphy, Neal & Co., et al.* v. *Creighton,* 45 Iowa, 179.

506. Payment of Mortgage.—Where property belonging to a firm is mortgaged to secure a note executed in the firm name, a partner has a right to invest upon a foreclosure of the mortgage before a personal judgment can be rendered against him upon the note. In case the party shall pay the note executed by the firm, he then becomes subrogated to the rights of the mortgagee, and his lien will be prior to that of a mortgage executed upon the same property by a grantee of the firm. *Warren* v. *Hoyzlett,* 45 Iowa, 235.

507. Payment.—*Limitations.*—An endorsement of a partial payment on the back of a note, when the fact of the payment is controverted by the payor or his representative, is not evidence sufficient to suspend the running of the statute of limitations. The burden of proving that the payment endorsed on the note was actually made, and at the time it purports to have been made in the endorsement, when the alleged payment is controverted, is upon the holder of the note, in a case where he claims that the running of the statute of limitations was suspended by the legal payment. *Frazer's Adm'rs* v. *Frazer & Co.,* 13 Bush, Ky. 397.

508. Payment.—An action lies on a note payable by installments as soon as the first day of payment is passed, but it lies only for the amount of the first installment, each of them being considered as a separate debt. *Clarihue* v. *Morris,* 2 Rev. de Leg., 30 K. B. 1820.

509. Payment *on conditional sale of goods.*—A sale of goods upon a mere promise by the purchaser to pay for them out of the avails of their sale, and of a stock of other goods owned by the purchaser, where the transaction is understood by them to create no relation between them but that of debtor and creditor, does not give the seller a lien on the goods, after their delivery, or on the avails of their sale, that can be specifically enforced; nor does it deprive the purchaser, where he owes the seller several debts, of the right to direct, when he makes a payment to such creditor, which debt shall be paid thereby. *Stewart* v. *Hopkins*, 30 Ohio, 502.

510. Payment.—*Disposition of.*—Where a person owes another several distinct debts, he has the right to choose which debt he will pay first; and where, at the time of payment, he expressly directs what application is to be made of the payment, the creditor, if he retains the money, is bound to appropriate it as directed by the debtor. The creditor cannot divert a payment so made by his debtor, from the appropriation made by him, upon mere equitable considerations, that do not amount to an agreement between the parties, giving the creditor a right to appropriate the payment otherwise than directed by the debtor, though mere equitable considerations may control, where the payment is made without designating its application. *Stewart* v. *Hopkins*, 30 Ohio, 502.

PERSONAL.

511. Personal *covenants* in the husband's mortgage do not bind the wife, although she joined in the mortgage of her husband's property. A wife's covenant in her husband's deed is a mere nullity. *Kitchell* v. *Mudgett, et al.*, 37 Mich. 81.

512. Personal *Liability.*—Wife not liable for deficiencies on foreclosure of a mortgage from her husband and herself. *Howe, et al.* v. *Lemon, et ux.*, 37 Mich. 164.

PLEDGE.

513. Pledge.—If a certificate of stock in a corporation, pledged as collateral security, is transferred by the pledgee to a creditor of his own, the pledgor may treat this as a conversion, and the fact that the pledgee had a greater number of shares standing to his credit on the books of the corporation is immaterial. *Fay* v. *Gray*, 124 Mass. 500.

514. Pledges.—A. borrowed of a bank money on call, and deposited with it as collateral security certain mining stocks, with written authority to sell them at its discretion. The loan remaining unpaid, the bank notified him that, unless he paid it, the stock would be sold. He failed, after repeated demands. to pay it, and they were sold, for more than their market value, to three directors of the bank, and the proceeds applied to the payment of the loan. A., who was advised of the sale, and that enough had been realized to pay his indebtedness, made no objection. The stocks were transferred to the purchasers. Nearly four years after the sale, the stocks having in the meantime greatly increased in value, A. notified the bank of his desire and purpose to redeem them, and subsequently filed his bill against it, asserting his right so to redeem, and praying for general relief. *Held*, that he is entitled to no relief. *Hoyward* v. *National Bank*, 96 U. S. 611.

515. Pledge.—The subsequent bankruptcy of the pledgor of a negotiable instrument does not deprive the pledgees of their right to dispose of it upon his default. *Jerome* v. *McCarter*, 94 U. S. 734.

516. Pledge.—One who lends money on the pledge of stock held in trust, will be held to have had notice that the trustee was abusing his trust and applying the money lent to his own purposes, when the certificates of the stock pledged show on their face that the stock is held in trust (though the name of the *cestui que trust* does not appear), and when the loan was apparently for the private purposes of the borrower, and that fact would have been revealed by inquiry. *Gaston* v. *Am. Exch. Bank*, 29 N. J. 98.

517. Pledge.—To constitute a pledge, there must be a delivery and retention by the pledgee of the thing pledged. If a party receives a pledge as collateral security, and in course, or at any time after he receives it, suffers it to go back into the possession of the person by whom it was pledged, the moment that he yields up the possession of it, he yields his right, and any subsequent purchaser, or an attaching creditor, would be entitled to hold it against him. *Collins* v. *Buck*, 63 Me. 459.

518. Pledge.—*Sale by the Pledgee.*—A pledgee of a chattel may sell his interest in the same, and the owner cannot recover the same of the purchaser without tendering him the sum due thereon, and if the pledgee is suffered to retain possession after tender of the sum due, and a sale is made to an innocent purchaser, who has no notice of the fact of its being only a pledge, the latter will acquire the title, even as against the real owner. *Bradley* v. *Parks, et al.*, 83 Ill. 169.

519. Where the pledgor of a chattel, after tendering the sum due the pledgee, takes no steps to recover possession, he will authorize others to regard the pledge as still subsisting, and if purchased by another he cannot recover the same in replevin, without tendering the sum due, to such purchaser. *Id.*

520. Pledge.—Possession by the pledgee is essential to a pledge; actual possession when practicable; constructive possession when actual possession is impracticable. *Seymour* v. *Colburn*, 43 Wis. 67.

521. Pledge, *What constitutes a.*—A pledge is the lien created by the delivery of personal property by the owner to another, upon an expressed or implied agreement that it shall be retained as a security for an existing or future debt. To create a pledge, the pledgee must have the possession and control of the property. *Corbett* v. *Underwood*, 83 Ill. 324.

522. Pledge.—J. A. H. borrowed $5,000 from the Citizens' National Bank of Baltimore, and deposited as collateral security for the payment thereof a note of W. H. & Sons, and a $100 U. S. bond. Next day, he gave to the bank his individual check on himself for

the amount so borrowed, and the bank delivered to him the collaterals before deposited. Shortly afterward J. A. H. failed, and it was discovered by the bank that he had returned the note to the drawers, W. H. & Sons, who on demand refused to deliver up to the bank the note or its value. In an action by the bank to recover from W. H. & Sons the value of the note, it was *held*,

523. 1st. If a bank or other party take a negotiable bill or note before maturity, for consideration and without *mala fides*, such party acquires a good title, notwithstanding there may have been negligence ; and gross negligence, while it may be evidence of *mala fides*, will not alone be sufficient to defeat the plaintiff's title.

524. 2nd. Nothing less than proof of knowledge of facts that show the want of authority on the part of the person transferring the note, will be sufficient to defeat the plaintiff's title.

525. 3rd. The plaintiff is not bound to make inquiry, and mere negligence, however gross, not amounting to wilful and fraudulent blindness, while it would be evidence of *mala fides*, is not the same thing.

4th. It makes no difference that the bill or note is only pledged as collateral security, and is not absolutely and unconditionally transferred.

526. 5th. If the bank knew that the note was not the property of the party offering to deposit or sell it, the taking of the note by way of collateral security for money loaned imparted no title as against the real owner.

527. 6th. It is a well established principle that possession is necessary to perfect a title by pledge, and it is equally well settled that the delivery back of the possession of the thing pledged, by the act or with the consent of the pledgee, terminates his title, unless it be delivered back for a temporary purpose only or to be held by the pledgor in a new character, such as special

bailee or agent. *Hooper* v. *Citizens' National Bank*, 47 Md. 88.

528. Pledge.—Possession is of the essence of a pledge; and, without it, no privilege can exist as against third persons. This doctrine is in accordance with both the common and the civil law, the Code Napoleon (art. 2076) and the civil code of Louisiana (art. 3162). *Casey* v. *Cavaroc*, 96 U. S. S. Ct. 467.

529. The thing pledged may be in the temporary possession of the pledgor as special bailer, without defeating the legal possession of the pledgee; but where it has never been out of the pledgor's actual possession and has always been subject to his disposal by way of collection, sale, substitution, or exchange, no pledge or privilege exists as against third persons. *Id.*

530. Where it was agreed that a bank should deposit bills and notes with its president and his partner, by way of pledge, to secure a loan made by a third party, and the president delivers them back to the bank officers for collection, with power to substitute other securities therefor, it is not such a delivery and possession as is necessary to create a privilege by the law of Louisiana. *Id.*

531. The ruling in *Casey* v. *Cavaroc* (*supra*, ¶ 467), as to what constitutes a valid pledge of securities, so far as third persons are concerned, applies to this case. *Casey* v. *National Bank*, 96 U. S. S. Ct. 492.

532. Pledge.—*Evidence.*—Defendant received money of plaintiff to insure him for becoming bail for another at plaintiff's request, and gave plaintiff his accountable receipt therefor. Defendant subsequently loaned the money and received interest for its use. *Held*, that he was liable for the interest thus received, and parol evidence was admissible to show the facts that created his liability. *Gilson* v. *Martin*, 49 Rowell, Vt. 474.

533. Pledge.—Where an accommodation bill has been pledged for less than its face, and the pledgee transfers it and receives the full value, and the accommodation endorser is compelled to pay the bill, he cannot recover the surplus from the pledgee; such action can only be maintained by the pledgor. *Gregory v. Burrall,* 2 Wend. 391.

534. Pledged Property.—A pledge ceases to be operative when its object is effected, and the whole beneficial interest in the security pledged then becomes absolute in the equitable owner. *Ward v. Ward,* 37 Mich. 253.

POSSESSION.

535. Possession by a man or his tenant is notice of the title, equitable as well as legal, under which he claims the property. *Wanner v. Sisson,* 29 N. J. 141.

536. Possession.—No length of constructive possession will ripen a defective title to land into a good one; the possession must be actual and continuous. Where there is no actual occupation of land shown, the law carries the possession to the real title. A possession of land under color of title must be taken by a man himself, his servants or tenants, and by him or them continued for seven years together. *Therefore,* where in an action to recover land it appeared that the plaintiff under color of title had made occasional entries upon the land at long intervals, for the purpose at one time of cutting timber, at another of making bricks, &c. *Held,* that the plaintiff was not entitled to recover. *Williams v. Wallace,* 78 N. C. 354.

537. Possession of Land.—Where A. enters into possession of land, the property of B.'s wife, under a deed from B. alone, the possession of A. is in law the possession of the wife, and enures to her benefit. *Davis v. M. Arthur,* 78 N. C. 357.

538. Possession of a Note, Bond or Bill, unattended by circumstances which, in a reasonable mind, ought to excite suspicion or distrust, or put a party on inquiry, is *prima facie* evidence of ownership in the holder, and a purchaser from such a holder will be protected until his purchase is assailed by one who can establish a legal title to the instrument. *Garvin* v. *Wiswell*, 83 Ill. 215.

POWER.

539. Power.—A power committed to two or more persons, unless it otherwise appear from the instrument by which it is delegated, is properly executed only by the joint act of all who have accepted the trust. *Giddings* v. *Butler*, 47 Texas, 535.

540. Power *of Attorney.*—If a grantor has power to sell, and sells, his act will pass title, whether he refers to the power or not. His act would pass his own and the interest of his principal. *Hough* v. *Hill*, 47 Texas, 148.

PREFERENCE.

541. Preferring Creditor.—A sale of property by an insolvent debtor, made in good faith, to pay a particular creditor of his, to the exclusion of others, without any intention to defraud, but simply to prefer one creditor to another, although the purchaser may have had full knowledge of such intent on the part of the vendor, is a valid sale. *Avery* v. *Eastes*, 18 Kansas, 505.

542. Preferred Creditors.—A bond given by a debtor in failing circumstances, covering all his property for the benefit of preferred creditors, is contrary to the policy of the statute against fraudulent insolvency. *Comly* v. *Waters, et al.*, 2 Del. 72.

PRESUMPTIONS.

543. Presumptions.—In the absence of proof to the contrary, it will be presumed that notaries of other States have no greater powers than are possessed by those of this State. *McLear & Kendall* v. *Succession of Hunsicker*, 29 La. 539.

PRINCIPAL AND AGENT.

544. Principal and Agent.—*Fraudulent misrepresentations by an agent.—Liability of principal for moneys wrongfully received by his agent.*—S. being employed by the respondent to carry on his business, credited the respondent in an account with the appellants with the sum of 5,800 taels, which he falsely represented to have been advanced in the ordinary course of business on certain goods intended for shipment. He then drew a bill in the name of the respondent's firm on the appellants for the balance of account, and having received the proceeds of such bill, including the said 5,800 taels, appropriated them to his own use. On a special case submitting whether the respondent was liable to the appellants in the said sum with interest from date of receipt by S., *Held*, that the proceeds of the bill having been received as aforesaid by S., acting throughout within the scope of his authority, belonged to the respondent, and that he having thus been paid 5,800 taels without consideration, the appellants were entitled to recover back the same. *Barwick* v. *The English Joint Stock Bank*, Law Rep. 2 Ex. 259, and *Mackay* v. *The Commercial Bank of New Brunswick*, Law Rep. 5 P. C. 412 ; approved. *Swive* v. *Francis*, 41 Canada Law Rep. 3 P. C. 106.

545. Principal and Agent.—Where a secret gratuity is given to an agent with the intention of influencing his mind in favor of the giver of the gratuity, and the agent, on subsequently entering into a contract with such giver on behalf of his principal, is actually influenced by the gratuity in assenting to stipulations prejudicial to the interest of his principal, although the gratuity was not given directly with relation to such particular contract, the transaction is fraudulent as against the principal, and the contract is void at his option. *Smith* v. *Sorby*, 3 App. Cases, Eng. (41-42 Vic.) 552.

546. Principal and Agent.—One purchasing goods for another makes himself personally liable, if he contracts in his own name without disclosing his principal; and this, although the seller supposes the purchaser is acting as agent; it is not sufficient to clear the agent from liability that the seller has the means of ascertaining the name of the principal; he must have actual knowledge. *Cobb* v. *Knapp*, 71 N. Y. 348.

547. Also *held*, that a subsequent disclosure of the principals by defendant, and the commencement of an action against them by plaintiff was not conclusive of an election to hold them only responsible; that the fact of commencing such action, and the statements in the complaint, were proper to be considered by the jury on the question of knowledge as to the principals, but did not operate as a legal discharge. *Id.*

548. Principal and Agent.—Where agents, without express authority, assume to act for their principals, the latter will be bound, if, with knowledge of such assumptions, they acquiesce in and receive the benefit of such acts; and from a continuous course of such dealings, the public will be at liberty to deal with the agents as having original authority to perform the acts, and the principals will be estopped to try it. *Co-operative Association* v. *McConnico*, 53 Miss. 233.

549. Principal and Agent.—Ratification by a principal of his agent's acts is only binding when made on full knowledge of the facts as they actually exist, not merely as the agent believed them to exist. *Bank of Owensboro'* v. *Western Bank*, 13 Bush, Ky. 526.

PRINCIPAL AND SURETY.

550. Principal and Surety.—*Delivery Bond.*—Where the real estate of the surety has been levied upon and sold at sheriff's sale, on an execution issued upon a judgment rendered against the principal and surety in a delivery bond, in an action thereon for a breach of its conditions, the latter may, in an action against the former, recover as for money paid to his use. *Collins v. Paris*, 57 Ind. 151.

551. **Principal and Surety.**—A bond executed in *blank* by H. and sureties to enable him to raise $300, by loan from B., was filled up and delivered, without their knowledge, to C. and N. for $354.48, in payment of a debt,—*Held*, fraudulent and void as to the sureties. A bond executed in *blank*, on a specific purpose, cannot be otherwise filled up, without authority of the obligors. Such authority must be proved affirmatively, to sustain the bond. *Hastings, et al. v. Clendaniel, et al.*, 2 Del. 165.

552. **Principal and Surety.**—*Release of Surety by Cashier of a Bank.*—A cashier of a bank, by virtue of his office, is not authorized to release a surety upon a note or bill belonging to the bank without payment. *Merchants' Bank v. Rudolf*, 5 Neb. 527.

553. The fact that a bank holds other securities for the payment of a note, to which it might resort, is no ground for the release of surety. Statements made by a cashier at casual interviews, away from the bank, as to payments having been made upon its securities, are not binding upon the bank. *Ib.*

554. If the cashier, on inquiry by a surety who is not an officer of the bank, state that the note upon which he is surety has been paid by the principal, the bank is estopped from denying the truth of such statement, when to do so would entail a loss upon the surety, which he would have guarded against had it not been made. But this rule is not applicable where the surety is one of the directors of the bank, for he has the means of knowledge of the true condition of its affairs, and is conclusively presumed to know whether payment has been made or not. *Ib.*

555. And where a firm is surety, and one of its members is also a member of the board of directors of the bank, all the members of such firm are affected with the notice, which the one who is director is presumed to have. *Ib.*

556. Principal and Surety.—A release of the principal debtor, against whom, with the surety, a joint judgment has been obtained, operates as a release of the surety. *Anthony* v. *Capel*, 53 Miss. 350.

557. Principal and Surety.—An agreement between the holder and principal maker of a note that the latter may retain the sum due for a definite time, upon his promise to pay usurious interest, will discharge a surety on said note not consenting to such contract of forbearance, but in the absence of such a contract, payment of the stipulated interest will not discharge the surety, even though, because of such payment, the creditor continues his indulgence to the debtor. The agreement to forbear for a definite period, in consideration of the payment of usurious interest, releases the non-consenting surety. *Brown* v. *Prophit*, 53 Miss. 649.

558. Principal and Surety.—In an action upon an administration bond, under R. S., ch. 72, sec. 9, a judgment against the administrator, in favor of the creditor of the intestate, for whose benefit this suit is brought, does not estop the sureties from showing that, prior to the commencement of the action in which judgment was recovered, the administrator's authority had become extinguished. When the plaintiff relies upon such judgment, with a demand and refusal to pay, or to show property to pay the execution, and a return of *nulla bona* thereon, proof that the administrator's authority had become extinguished before the creditor brought his original suit will defeat the action upon the bond against the sureties. *Bourne* v. *Todd*, 63 Me. 427.

559. Principal and Surety.—A surety cannot be held on a bond which he only signed upon a condition that was not performed. A bond does not take effect from the signing, but only from delivery or filing. A bond dated and made to take effect upon a week day will protect an obligee who had no notice that it was actually signed on Sunday. *Hall, et al.* v. *Parker, et al.*; 37 Mich. 590.

560. Principal and Surety.—*Extension of notes.*—The execution of a deed of trust by a principal debtor, whereby property not subject to execution was made liable for its payment, is a good consideration for a promise to extend the time for payment of the note, and such an agreement will discharge the surety. *Semple, et al.* v. *Atkinson, et al.*, 64 Mo. 504; *Smarr* v. *Schnitter*, 38 Mo. 478.

PRIVILEGE.

561. Privilege.—If the proceeds of the movables and unmortgaged property of a succession do not suffice to pay off its privileged debts, those debts must be first preferred for payment to the proceeds of its property incumbered by the *youngest* mortgage. The vendor's privilege is only operative as to third persons from the moment of its registry. The vendor's privilege will not take rank over a mortgage recorded before its own registry, unless its own registry was made on the day of the sale. To maintain his privilege on property sold by him, as to third persons, the vendor must record the sale.

562. Seizure of property under the execution of a valid judgment, gives a lien on the property, superior to any privilege recorded against it subsequent to the seizure. *O'Hara* v. *Mrs. E. Booth and Connell*, 29 La. 817.

PROFITS.

563. Profits.—*Damages.*—Probable profits are not a proper basis upon which to estimate damages, and therefore, under the testimony as reported in this case, nominal damages only can be recovered. *Winslow* v. *Lane*, 63 Me. 161.

564. Profits.—Property purchased by a wife on the credit of her separate estate, or of her earnings in its management, is not liable for the debts of the husband. *Silvens* v. *Porter*, 74 Penn. St. 448.

PROMISE.

565. Promise.—The holders of a note demanded payment from the endorser, who replied that he "had not expected to have it to pay, and that it was impossible to pay it at present." *Held*, insufficient as a promise to pay. *Cromer* v. *Platt*, 37 Mich. 132.

566. Promise.—As long as the creditor can maintain an action on the original promise, a new promise, without additional consideration, will not support an action. *Ogden, &c.* v. *Redd*, 13 Bush, Ky. 581.

567. Promise *Made to Debtor.*—A promise made to a debtor, for a valuable consideration, to pay his debt to a third person, is not a promise to answer for the debt of another person, within the statute of frauds, which applies only to promises made to a creditor; and such promise made to the debtor need not be in writing. *Centre* v. *McQuesten*, 18 Kansas, 476.

PROMISSORY NOTES.

568. Promissory Note.—*Illegality of note made in foreign State.*—To a declaration on a promissory note, a defence that the note was made in a foreign State, upon a consideration which was void under a law of that State, should be specially pleaded, and it cannot be received under the general issue. *Held*, that the issue was immaterial. *Roop* v. *Delahaye*, 2 Colorado, 307.

569. Promissory Note.—*Will not always discharge liability.*—The plaintiffs took the individual note of B., on account of the goods, but it was not given or taken as payment of the account. *Held*, that this did not discharge the liability of the corporation. B. having gone into bankruptcy, the plaintiffs presented the note against his estate, and received a dividend upon it. *Held*, they might show that they did this under the advice of legal counsel, and upon an opinion given that it would not prejudice their claim against the corporation. *Northford Rivet Co.* v. *Blackman M'f'g Co.*, 44 Conn. 183.

510. Promissory Notes.—*Payment.*—Where a promissory note for dollars, made in Georgia, in January, 1863, is shown to have been solvable in Confederate treasury notes, the sum thereby payable in actual money must be ascertained by the value in coin or legal currency of the United States, at the time when and the place where the note was made, of such treasury notes, equal in nominal amount to the number of dollars specified. *Stewart* v. *Salamon*, 94 U. S. 434.

571. Where a payment is endorsed in the same monetary terms which are used in the note itself, the presumption is that it was intended to be credited in the same circulating medium. If the parties intended otherwise, some proof on the subject should be presented. *Id.*

572. Accordingly, where a promissory note for dollars, shown to be solvable, at the time it was made, in Confederate treasury notes, had a receipt for a specified number of dollars endorsed upon it, it was *held* that, in the absence of proof, the principal designated on the face of the note was reduced only by the amount specified in the receipt. *Id.*

573. Promissory Note.—*Written contract.*—Where, at the time of making and endorsing a promissory note, a written contract in relation thereto is entered into by the parties, parol testimony varying or contradicting its terms is not admissible. *Brown* v. *Spofford*, 95 U. S. 474.

574. Promissory Notes.—In the absence of proof to show when promissory notes were transferred by the payee, the law presumes that they were, when under-due, taken in good faith by the transferee, without notice of any infirmity attaching to them, and he is entitled to the benefit of the deed of trust given to secure them. *New Orleans Canal and Banking Co.* v. *Montgomery*, 95 U. S. 16.

575. Promissory Note.—In a suit upon a promissory note, the court below charged the jury that if the defendant, without making any statement of his intention in so doing, wrote his name on the back of the note before its delivery to the payee, he is presumed to have done so as the surety of the maker, for his accommodation, and to give him credit with the payee, and that, if such presumption is not rebutted by the evidence he is liable on the note as maker. *Held*, that the charge was not erroneous. *Good* v. *Martin*, 95 U. S. 90.

576. Promissory Note.—In action by a savings bank on a promissory note, against B., as second endorser, it appeared that the note, which purported on its face to be secured by a mortgage of real estate, was payable to A., or order; that A. borrowed money of B., endorsed the note to B.'s order, and delivered it to him with an assignment of the mortgage and note, as collateral security; that afterwards A. paid B. the money borrowed, and B. wrote his name on the back of the note under the name of A. and delivered it to him, and also executed to him an assignment of the mortgage and note; that A. thereupon, and before the maturity of the note, delivered it to the plaintiff for a valuable consideration, and executed to it an assignment, in which A. was described as mortgagee named in, and assignee of, the mortgage; that A. was then a trustee of the plaintiff bank and one of its conveyancers, but took no part in the management; that the treasurer of the bank did not notice the signature of B. when he took the note and relied on the mortgage alone as security. B. testified that he did not intend to endorse the note, but only to assign it to A. Demand was made on the maker of the note and due notice given to B. *Held*, that, on these facts, the action might be maintained; and that no fact appeared which would warrant a jury in finding for the defendant. *West Boston Savings Bank* v. *Thompson*, 124 Mass. 506.

577. Promissory Note.—In an action by the payee on a promissory note, signed on the back thereof, by the defendant before delivery, oral evidence is inadmissible to show that the payee agreed to treat him as an endorser, and not as an original promisor. *Allen* v. *Brown*, 124 Mass. 77.

578. Promissory Note.—A person, not the payee, who before the St. of 1874, c. 404, wrote his name upon the back of a negotiable promissory note at its inception, and before its delivery, is liable as an original promisor; and parol evidence is inadmissible to show that he wrote his name upon the note, not with the intention of adding his personal responsibility to its security, but merely in approval of it as the president of a company; or that the treasurer issued the note in violation of a by-law of the company; the plaintiff, the payee of the note, having no knowledge of the facts. *Gilson* v. *Stevens Machine Co.*, 124 Mass. 546.

579. Promissory Note.—*Conditional.*—If a promissory note is made payable on condition that a proceeding pending in the courts is decided in favor of the payee, and the proceeding is decided against him, the note cannot be enforced. *Frisbie* v. *Moore*, 51 Cal. 516.

580. Promissory Note.—*Interest payable quarterly.*—A note on which the interest is payable quarterly at the legal rate, is not usurious. *Mowry* v. *Shumway*, 44 Conn. 493; also, *Bridgeport* v. *Housatonic R. R. Co.*, 15 Conn. 503; and *Rose* v. *Bridgeport*, 17 Conn. 247; and *Brooks* v. *Holland*, 21 Conn. 388.

581. Promissory Notes.—A rule which would require the maker of a note to act after its maturity, and before payment, with reference to the equitable rights attaching to it in the hands of every one who may have had it by assignment, would be destructive of the negotiability of such instruments. *Long* v. *Walker*, 47 Texas, 173.

582. Promissory Note.—Payment of a note made by partners is received by an agent in Confederate currency, upon condition that if the principal refuses to receive it, it is to be returned ; and a receipt is endorsed on the note and delivered to one of the partners. The principal declines to receive it, and the agent returns the currency to another partner, who gives the partnership promise to pay the amount of the note in the new issue of Confederate notes, which the principal was willing to receive, and this is received by the principal. *Held*, 1. The delivery of this second promise and its reception by the principal is not a discharge of the note, unless it was so intended and agreed by the principal ; and this must be clearly shown by the makers of the note. *Lewis, et al.* v. *Davisson's Ex'r*, 29 Grattan (Va.) 216.

583. **Promissory Note.**—The delivery of the note by the agent to one of the partners, and its cancellation and possession by him, will not prevent an action upon it by the principal. *Id.*

584. **Promissory Note.**—In an action by a bank against an endorser of negotiable notes, which were discontinued in Alexandria, and fell due during the war, when the endorser was within the Confederate lines, to prove notice of protest to the endorser within a reasonable time after the war ceased, the plaintiff offered in evidence a resolution of the stockholders, adopted at a meeting held on the 18th of July, 1865, at which the endorser was present at a previous period of the meeting, though it did not appear he was present when the resolution was adopted, by which those notes and others paid by the maker at a branch of the plaintiff's bank within the Confederate lines, are declared still to be due to the bank. *Held*, 1. There being no proof that the endorser had any knowledge of the resolution, it was not due notice to him of the dishonor of the notes.

2. The knowledge of non-payment of a protested note is not sufficient to bind the endorser. He must have notice that he is looked to for payment.

3. The resolution having been adopted July 18th, 1865, at least two months after communication had been

opened between the bank and the endorser, it was not in time, if it had been sufficient as a notice. *Bank of Old Dominion* v. *McVeigh,* 29 Grattan (Va.) 546.

585. **Promissory Note.**—*Descriptio personæ.*—*Executor, when personally liable on.*—*Reimbursement out of estate.*—In suit on the following note, to wit. : "Three months from date promise to pay to order of A. and B. fifteen dollars, etc., etc., with interest at ten per cent. per annum, and if interest be not paid annually to become as principal," etc. (Signed) "P. H. Ammerman, executor of last will of James Johnson, deceased," it was *held* that, as the instrument contained no words showing an intention to charge the estate, the terms "executor," etc., should be treated merely as descriptio personæ ; that the fact of payment to be made at a future day, with the interest named, might of itself be sufficient to show a personal undertaking of the executor ; that the note of itself imported a consideration, and that it devolved on the maker and competent for him, if he designed to set up that defence, to show that as his individual contract it was without consideration, and that the payee agreed to look only on the estate. And in such case, where the consideration of the note accrued after the death of the testator, the administrator will in the first instance be liable *de bonis propriis*, but he may reimburse himself out of the assets of the deceased. An administrator can maintain an action in his own name on a note made payable to him as administrator or executor, the official words being treated as mere surplusage or as descriptio personæ. *Rittenhouse* v. *Ammerman,* 64 Mo. 197.

586. **Promissory Notes.**—An instrument in the form of a promissory note, beginning, "We as trustees, but not individually, promise to pay," and signed "A., B. and C., trustees," purported on its face to be secured by mortgage of real estate. A., B. and C. were trustees of a land association, and purchased of the promisee a parcel of land, the deed of which ran to them as

trustees of the association, and set forth their powers. They mortgaged the land to the grantor, and gave the above instrument, secured by the mortgage, in part payment of the purchase money. *Held*, in an action against the makers of the instrument, by an endorsee, who took it after maturity, that they were not personally liable thereon. *Shoe & Leather National Bank* v. *Dix*, 123 Mass. 148.

587. **Promissory Notes.**—It is a good consideration for a promissory note that the promisor gave it at the request and for the benefit of his son, who was in the employ of the promisee, to be applied by the latter towards the payment of a defalcation of the son, the note being so credited to the son on the books of the promisee. *Popple* v. *Day*, 123 Mass. 520.

588. **Promissory Note.**—It is a good consideration for a promissory note given by the promisor, who was an assignee of a bankrupt, towards the payment of moneys received and misused by him, that the promisee, who was his co-assignee, refrained from pressing proceedings against him instituted to protect the interests of the creditors. *Abbott* v. *Fisher*, 124 Mass. 414.

589. **Promissory Notes.**—*Pleading.*—In assumpsit on a promissory note by the bearer against the maker, it appeared that it was drawn payable to the wardens and vestry of a certain church, or bearer, and there was evidence tending to show that after it was executed and delivered to the corporation, and before it passed into plaintiff's possession, the corporation became in fact extinct by the removal of its officers and members. It did not appear that the corporation ever parted with the title to the note, and plaintiff showed no title beyond mere possession. *Held*, that if the corporation did become extinct, the defendant was not thereby discharged from his liability on the note, but that title thereto vested somewhere, and that plaintiff, having, so far as it appeared, lawful possession of the note, might maintain an action thereon in his own name, and

recover for the benefit of the holder of the legal title. *Hyde* v. *Lawrence*, 49 Rowell, Vt. 361.

590. **Promissory Note.**—A person who receives two promissory notes upon an agreement to release a demand upon their payment at maturity, is not debarred from his original cause of action, by having one note discounted and taking it up when protested for nonpayment, and by prosecuting the other to judgment in the name of a friend, but for his own benefit, nothing being received by him upon either note, and the discounted note and an assignment of the judgment being tendered by him in court. *Lord* v. *Bigelow*, 124 Mass. 185.

591. **Promissory Note.**—If a promissory note, payable to the order of A., is given by him to the maker, it is not essential to the validity of the gift that the payee should endorse it. *Hale* v. *Rice*, 124 Mass. 292.

592. **Promissory Note.**—In an action on a joint and several note, signed by one person as principal and another as surety, and payable to the order of a bank, upon which was the memorandum, "F. & L. bonds as collateral," "F. & L. notes," being in fact deposited as security, it appeared that the treasurer of the bank, in reply to an inquiry by the surety, "if the F. & L. bonds were deposited with the note?" replied that they were. *Held*, that the surety was not discharged. *Fitchburg Savings Bank* v. *Rice*, 124 Mass. 72.

593. **Promissory Note.**—If land mortgaged to secure a promissory note is sold under a power contained in the mortgage, and brings less than the amount of the note, an action may be maintained on the note for the balance due. *Wing* v. *Hayford*, 124 Mass. 249.

594. **Promissory Notes.**—The alteration of a promissory note by one of the makers, by increasing the amount for which it was made, by the insertion of words and figures in blank spaces left in the printed form on which it was written, avoids the note as to such makers as do not consent thereto, even in the hands of a *bona fide* holder for a valuable considera-

tion. *Greenfield Savings Bank* v. *Stowell*, 123 Mass. 196.

595. Promissory Notes.—A negotiable promissory note is, under the act of April, 1873, governed by the law merchant, and an endorsee for value before maturity in due course of business, without notice, takes it free from any set-off in favor of the maker, or against the assignor. The provision of sec. 570, Gantt's Digest, that all blank assignments shall be taken to have been made on such a day as shall be most to the advantage of the defendant, merely changes the former rule of presumption to be applied in the absence of evidence, and it is competent for the plaintiff to prove the actual date of the assignment. *Clendenin* v. *Southerland*, 31 Ark. 20.

596. Promissory Notes.—A waiver of demand and notice upon a promissory note is as effectual after as before the maturity of the note. *Rindge* v. *Kimball*, 124 Mass. 209.

597. Promissory Note.—In an action against a surety on a promissory note, it is no defence that the holder delayed enforcing the note against the maker, and that the surety was thereby injured. *Allen* v. *Brown*, 124 Mass. 77.

598. Promissory Note.—A memorandum of "F. & L. bonds as collateral," on a joint and several note, signed by one person as principal and another as surety, is not notice to the payee of any agreement between them that the principal would pledge the bonds named, nor a condition precedent to the liability of the surety that the payee should receive the bonds named as security. *Fitchburg Savings Bank* v. *Rice*, 124 Mass. 72.

599. Promissory Notes.—A., through fraud, obtained from B. a promissory note signed by B. and payable to the order of C., forged the endorsement of C. and got the note discounted at a bank. On the maturity of the note B. paid it to the bank. *Held*, that B. could maintain an action against the bank for money had and received, although the bank acted in good faith in taking the note. *Carpenter* v. *Northborough National Bank*, 123 Mass. 66.

600. Promissory Notes.—When a promissory note, based on an insufficient consideration, has been obtained from a person under the influence of liquor at the time of its execution, and enfeebled in mind and body by long continued disease and drunkenness, a presumption of fraud arises, which must be countervailed by proof of a fair consideration, and fair and honest dealing on the part of him who seeks to enforce payment of the note. *Holland* v. *Barnes*, 53 Ala. 83.

601. Promissory Notes.—*Principal and surety.*—Defendant signed a note with L., as it appeared from the force of it as a principal with, but in fact as security for him. In order to procure it to be discounted, L. took the note to plaintiff, and asked him "if he would sign it with him, and defendant," and plaintiff signed it, adding to his signature the word surety, supposing from the manner in which he was asked to sign it, and from its appearance, that he was signing as surety for both L. and defendant, and regarded them as principals. The note was discounted, and, upon its maturity, L., having negotiated with the bank for renewal, drew another like it, procured defendant's signature thereto as before, and sent it to plaintiff, requesting him to sign and deliver it to the bank, and take up the former note, which he did, adding to his signature, as before, the word surety. *Held*, that plaintiff was surety for, and not co-surety with defendant. *Sherman* v. *Black*, 49 Rowell, Vt. 198.

602. Promissory Note.—One who puts his name on the back of a note at the time it is made and before it comes to the hand of the payee, there being nothing to show with what intention, is liable as maker. The opinion of the court at the former term in this cause, on this point, re-examined and affirmed. *Good* v. *Martin*, 2 Colorado, 218.

603. *The ground of his Liability.*—In an action on a promissory note against one who is charged as maker, upon the ground that he endorsed the note at the time it was made, and before it was delivered to the payee, the circumstance that he did not participate in the consideration, does not tend to explain or rebut his liability as maker. *Id.*

604. Promissory Note is secured by a chattel mortgage, executed by the maker of the note; in the absence of a demand, or any proceeding by the payee equivalent to a demand, the maker is entitled to the whole of the business hours of the last day of grace to pay the note, and is not in default until the expiration of that time. *Daly v. Proetz,* 20 Minn. 411.

605. Promissory Note.—*Principal and Surety.—Liability of Co-sureties.— Want of Consideration.*—Plaintiff and defendant were endorsers of a promissory note whereof M. was payee. The makers became bankrupt, and plaintiff paid the note, which M. had procured to be discounted. The makers compounded with their creditor, and plaintiff received his *pro rata* portion, and with the advice and consent of defendant, and upon his agreement that his liability should not be thereby affected, discharged the makers from further liability. *Held,* that the liability of the endorser was fixed by the insolvency of the makers; that when plaintiff paid the note, defendant became liable to contribute a moiety; and that defendant was estopped from questioning the agreement that induced the discharge. *Hutchinson v. Thacher,* 49 Rowell, Vt. 486.

606. Promissory Notes.—If a promissory note, not negotiable, is given to a married woman by a third person in consideration of her husband's giving up to him a like note, and she transfers the note, with her husband's consent, to a creditor of his, in fraud of other creditors, the maker, in an action upon it in her name, cannot take advantage of that fact. *Harding v. Colon,* 123 Mass. 299.

607. Promissory Note was executed on Sunday, but bore date the following day, and was endorsed before maturity, for value. *Held*, that the endorsee was not affected by the original invalidity of the instrument. *Trieber* v. *Com. Bank of St. Louis*, 31 Ark. 128.

608. Promissory Note made payable on a day named, "or before, if made out of the sale of J. B. Drake's horse hay-fork and hay-carrier, with use," is payable at all events on the day named, with six per cent. per annum interest from date. *Cisne* v. *Chidester*, 85 Ill. 523.

609. Promissory Note.—*Dishonor*.—The mere fact of cancelling the signature of the makers of a dishonored promissory note and writing "paid" on the note, corrected before the note is sent back to the plaintiffs by a memorandum thereon "cancelled in error," cannot be effectual to charge a bank with the receipt of the money. Where a promissory note is dishonored to the plaintiffs, the amount thereof having been transmitted by transfer drafts and entries in the bank's books, from the branch where the same was made payable to the branch where the plaintiffs paid the same in, such transfer and entries not being communicated to the plaintiffs, *Held*, that the bank could not be charged with the receipt of the money. The position of branch banks is, that in principle and in fact they are agencies of one principal banking corporation or firm, notwithstanding that they may be regarded as distinct for special purposes; *e. g.*, that of estimating the time at which notice of dishonor should be given; or of entitling a banker to refuse payment of a customer's check except at that branch where he keeps his account. *Prince, et al.* v. *Oriental Bank*, 41–42 Eng. Law Reports, 3 Appeal Cases, 1878, page 325.

610. Promissory Note, made payable to the order of the maker, has no validity until it is endorsed and transferred by him. *Payser* v. *Hall, Admr.*, 85 Ill. 511.

611. Promissory Notes.—The law in force when a promissory note is made and endorsed, regulates and defines the liabilities of the parties. *Cook* v. *Citizens' Mutual Ins. Co.*, 53 Ala. 37.

612. Promissory Note.—*Accommodation paper.*— Where, on the sale of a note, it is represented as business paper, the fact that it was in reality an accommodation note, ought to be clearly proved ; if the law be not violated, the intent of the purchaser is wholly immaterial. *Smith* v. *Paton*, 6 Bos. 145 ; S. C., 31 N. Y. 66.

613. Promissory Note must be certain as to day of payment. A promise to pay a sum of money upon the condition that a railroad should be built to a place named on or before 20th of February, 1871, is not a promissory note, and is not negotiable as such. *Eldred* v. *Malloy*, 2 Colorado, 320.

614. Promissory Note.—*When without consideration.* —A promissory note given in consideration of services, already rendered the maker, for which the payee had already received the amount mutually agreed on between them, is a mere gratuity and without consideration. *Holland* v. *Barnes*, 53 Ala. 83.

615. Promissory Notes.—In an action on a promissory note by the administrator of the payee there was evidence that, on the death of the payee, the note, in a division of the personal property made before the appointment of the administrator, fell to a daughter, who by an agent demanded of the principal maker payment of the note ; that the maker replied that it was not convenient for him to pay it, but agreed to pay interest at eight per cent. ; that the agent thereupon wrote the words "at eight per cent." on the note in the presence and with the assent of the maker ; that a surety on the note, when told of the maker's agreement, after his death, and when shown the note so altered, paid the interest at eight per cent. *Held*, that the legal title to the note was in the administrator, and that he could maintain an action upon it. *Held, also,* that the evidence would warrant the jury in finding that both the maker and the surety assented to and ratified the note in its altered form, and thereby agreed to pay the same to the lawful holder for the sufficient consideration of an agreement to forbear, and an actual forbearance, by those who apparently had the actual control of the note and the equitable interest therein. *Prouty* v. *Wilson*, 123 Mass. 279.

616. Promissory Notes.—*Authority of an agent or attorney to execute a promissory note.*—Where a petition alleges that "the defendant, by P. and A., her attorneys in fact, made and delivered to one T., her promissory note of that date, and thereby promised to pay to said T. or order," etc., and a copy of said note is attached to said petition as a part thereof, which is signed as follows: "Eliza C. Abeel, by Charles A. Phillip and John T. Abell" (Eliza C. Abeel being the defendant, and the sufficiency of the petition not being in any manner attacked until after judgment),—*Held*, that the allegations of the petition, with regard to the execution of the note, are sufficient to charge defendant. *Abell* v. *Harrington*, 18 Kansas, 243.

617. Promissory Notes.—*Forged signature.*—If a person pays a promissory note through mistake, supposing the signature upon the note to be his genuine signature, he may, on discovering it to be forged, maintain an action to recover back the money paid, if he is not guilty of laches, whereby the situation of the other party is changed to his injury. *Welch* v. *Goodwin*, 123 Mass. 71.

618. Promissory Notes.— *Variance.* — *Estoppel.* — A note payable *on or before* six months from date, was declared upon as payable six months from date. *Held*, no variance. B. was interested with the plaintiff, his son, in the note in suit, which purported to be signed by defendant as surety for his son, the principal. The testimony tended to show that B., having heard rumors unfavorable to the principal's solvency, went to defendant and told him he held a note against him,

and as he signed it as surety, and it was over-due, he thought he would let him know about it; that defendant, therefore, looked at the note, and at his name thereon, and said: "It is all right;" that about ten days thereafter, defendant asked B. what interest his (defendant's) son was paying on the note, and was told, and thereupon said that that was better than they could do at the bank; and that therefore B. supposed "everything was all right," and made no attempt to collect the note, nor to press payment thereof, until about a year and a half afterwards, though the principal continued in business about six months thereafter as before. *Held*, that the testimony tended to show all that was necessary to estop defendant from denying that he signed the note. *Bates* v. *Leclair*, 49 Rowell, Vt. 229.

619. **Promissory Notes.**—A note otherwise negotiable, is not rendered non-negotiable by the addition of a stipulation to pay costs of collecting, including reasonable attorney fees, if suit be instituted thereon. *Seaton* v. *Scovill*, 18 Kansas, 433.

620. **Promissory Note.**—*When Time of Payment is not Stated.*—When no time of payment is expressed in a note, the law adjudges it to be due and payable immediately. *Dodd* v. *Denny*, 6 Oregon, 156.

621. **Promissory Notes.**—*Forged.*—The situation of a person, to whom money is paid by mistake on a forged note, is not changed to his injury by the fact that, on payment, he transfers to the payer a mortgage which he received as collateral security for the note, and which, with the note, he took in good faith, supposing the note to be genuine, the mortgage having been given as security for another note, of which the forged note was a copy. *Welch* v. *Godwin*, 123 Mass. 71.

622. **Promissory Notes.**—*Transferred without Endorsement.*—Minear, being indebted to the Bank of Idaho upon his promissory note, in consideration of an extension of time thereon to Minear. Miller executed his promissory note to the bank for the sum of Minear's

note, with the understanding that both notes should be
delivered up when either was paid. Moore, a stockholder in the bank, received both notes, with notice
of all the facts, as a part of his share of the bank assets.
The Miller note was regularly endorsed to him; the
other was delivered without endorsement. *Held*, 1.
That Miller's liability was not that of an endorser upon
the Minear note, but that it grew out of an independent
contract to pay a certain sum at a fixed time, upon
conditions expressed in the agreement. 2. That Moore
became the owner of the Minear note without endorsement, and that he had the right to maintain his action
upon the Miller note. *Moore* v. *Miller*, 6 Oregon,
254.

623. **Promissory Note.**—A parol agreement, by which
the purchase-money notes were to be deposited with
an attorney, and from the proceeds of such notes outstanding liens against the land deeded to the maker
of the notes were to be taken up and discharged, may
be shown, in defence of an action upon such notes.
Such an agreement is so far distinct from and collateral to that part of the contract reduced to writing
as to allow of its establishment by parol evidence.
Thomas v. *Hammond*, 47 Texas, 43.

624. **Promissory Note** *secured by Deed of Trust.*—
Where a note, taken in renewal of the balance due on
another, secured by a deed of trust, is negotiated by
the payee, the purchaser of the new note is entitled to
enforce the deed of trust to secure payment thereof.
Giving a new note for the balance due on an old one,
will not operate to discharge the security, unless it is
apparent that the parties intended to extinguish the lien
of the deed of trust. *Gleason* v. *Wright*, 53 Miss. 247.

625. **Promissory Notes.**—M., the payee of a promissory
note, asked defendant to endorse it, which he refused
to do unless the plaintiff would endorse it. M. promised to procure plaintiff to endorse it, whereupon defendant endorsed it. Plaintiff, on being asked to endorse it refused to do so unless M. would procure

defendant to sign with him a note for a like sum, payable to plaintiff as security therefor, which M. agreed to do, whereupon plaintiff endorsed it. M. afterward procured defendant to sign the second note as agreed, and delivered it to plaintiff. *Held*, that as the second note was given without any new consideration, for the purpose of indemnifying plaintiff for endorsing the first note, on which plaintiff and defendant were made co-sureties, the second note was, as between the parties, *nudum pactum* and invalid. *Hutchinson* v. *Thacker*, 49 Rowell, Vt. 486.

626. Promissory Note.—*Purchaser.*—A *bona fide* holder of a note, who purchased it for value before it fell due, and without notice of payments made on it, can collect the face of the note and interest. The assignee of a promissory note, who purchases it in good faith before it falls due, without knowledge that payments have been made on it, and receives a covenant from the payee that the sum he pays for it is due, cannot maintain an action on the covenant if such amount is not due, for he sustains no loss, as the payer is liable to him for the face of the note. *Small* v. *Clarke*, 51 Cal. 227.

627. Promissory Notes.—When at the time of the execution of a promissory note, a contract in writing is made between the payer and payee upon a separate piece of paper, which describes the note and clearly refers to it, the note is to be read in connection with the contract as though it had been incorporated into it, and, in an action on the note brought by the payee, the payer may introduce evidence that the payee has broken the stipulations of the contract. *Goodwin* v. *Nicherson*, 51 Cal. 166.

628. Promissory Notes.—Circuit Court rule 79 excuses the plaintiff on a promissory note from proving its execution, if the defendant omits to file an affidavit denying it. *Held*, that the only object of this rule is to enable the plaintiff to make out a *prima facie* case, not a conclusive one, and that it would not preclude a defendant from introducing any defence on the merits that did not contradict the execution of the note. It would not prevent an endorser from showing that he had signed without consideration, and after the note had been delivered. *Enright, et al.* v. *Ellison,* 37 Mich. 459.

The execution of a note is only its actual making and delivery. *Id.*

629. It seems that where the considerations of a note is open to inquiry at all, it is as much so in behalf of any one of the defendants as of all. *Id.*

630. In action on partnership paper given *mala fide*, but binding one partner, evidence is admissible to exonerate a co-partner. *Id.*

631. Contemporaneous and subsequent guarantees have the same contract force, and differ only as to what considerations sustain them. *Id.*

632. Subsequent endorsement does not make the endorser jointly liable with his principal, and joint liability is not presumed when the endorsement is not dated; it is shown by independent proof of contemporaneous execution. *Id.*

The production of a note in evidence under the common counts without objection,. will not preclude raising the objection that it varies from a special count. *Id.*

633. Promissory Note.—In an action on a note by a holder who received it after it became due, and who in fact was a mere agent and *nom de plume* in the matter. *Held*, that the defendant might plead in such action all matters which might have been pleaded to the owner of the note, and also obtain a reduction of the usurious interest included in the note and of payments made on account thereof. *Brooks, et al.* v. *Clegg,* 12 L. C. R. 461 ; Q. B. 1862 ; 2287 C. C.

634. Promissory Note.—*Void ab initio.*—A note given to the new firm formed after the dissolution of the old, in satisfaction of a guarantee given to the old for advances made by them, was *held*, reversing court be-

low, to have been given in error and without consideration, and was therefore void. *Henault* v. *Thomas, et al.*, 1 L. R. 706, Q. B. 1868.

635. Promissory Note.—*Where made.*—The evidence of the plaintiff in an action on a note is admissible to prove that the note, though dated at Montreal, was made at Quebec. *Gault, et al.* v. *Wright, et al.*, 13 L. C. J. 60; S. C. 1868.

636. Promissory Notes. — *Endorsement.—Protest.*—A demand and notice are not necessary as against an endorser who at the date of the maturity of the note has sufficient property of the maker in his possession held as security against his liability. *Beard* v. *Westerman*, 32 Ohio St. 29.

637. If the endorsee of a note has protected himself against loss by taking collateral security of the maker, it is a waiver of his legal right to require proof of demand on the maker and notice to himself of non-payment. *Mead* v. *Small*, 2 Greenleaf, 297.

638. Promissory Note—*Endorser.*—If the endorser has security in his own hands fully equal to his liability he can suffer no loss by the want of demand and notice, therefore he has been held liable in such a case without proof of those facts. *Marshall* v. *Mitchell*, 35 Maine, 221.

639. If the endorser receives security to meet a particular endorsement, he waives a demand and notice in respect to that endorsement but not as to any other. *Prentiss* v. *Danielson*, 5 Conn. 175.

640. A bond and mortgage were assigned to a third party in trust to secure the endorser if the maker should fail to pay the note, and the endorser was held notwithstanding a defective notice. *Barrett* v. *Charleston Bank*, 2 McMullen, 191.

641. The endorser being indemnified by a mortgage he was held responsible although the demand was made a day too late. *Wart* v. *Mitchell*, 6 How. Miss. 131.

642. The second endorser on a note who had received

ample security from the first endorser, thereon, was held, although the security he held had afterward become doubtful. *Id.*

643. **Promissory Notes.**—*Value received.*—The want of the words "for value received," does not prevent a plaintiff from recovering on a note if it be in evidence that value was given therefor. *Duchesney* v. *Evarts*, 2 Rev. de Leg. 31, K. B. 1821, 2285 C. C.

644. Promissory note under £50, drawn to order, may be validly transferred for value received by him to whose order it is made without endorsation, and parol evidence is admissible to prove such transfer. *Dupuis* v. *Marron*, 17 L. C. J. 42, C. C. 1873; 1233 & 2341 C. C.

645. **Promissory Notes.**—*Renewal.*—Action was brought on a note and open account, and defendant pleaded that he had sent in a renewal note to the plaintiffs which they retained in their possession and which had not yet matured, and the plaintiffs replied that they had never agreed to renew. *Held*, that defendant was bound, unless on acceptance by plaintiffs, to call and take away the renewal note, and the mere fact of plaintiffs not returning it could not be construed into an agreement to renew. *Lyman, et al.* v. *Chamard*, 1 L. C. J., 285 S. C. 1857.

646. **Promissory Notes.**—Where certain notes were nearly out of date, the defendant was called on by the holder of them, and notified that unless something was done suit would be brought upon them. Whereupon the defendant signed the following endorsement upon each of the notes: "Paid Dec. 16th, 1872, $500 on acct. of this note to revive the same." *Held*, that if the parol evidence of the agreement relied on by him as a defence, was otherwise admissible, the defendant had effectually precluded himself from the resort to such defence by said endorsement upon the notes. *Held*, further, that if there were any question of the plaintiff's right to recover on the notes as specially declared on, there could be none whatever of their right to recover on them with the defendant's endorsement

thereon, under the count on an account stated. *Mc-Sherry* v. *Brooks and Barton, Trustees,* 46 Md. 103.

647. Promissory Note *of Married Woman.* — Action was brought on a note signed by a married woman separate as to property, without the authority of her husband. *Held,* confirming court below, that as the defendant was at the time of making the note in question a *merchande publique,* that the authorization of her husband was unnecessary. *Beaubien & Husson,* 12 L. C. R. 47, Q. B. 1862 ; 179, C. C.

648. Promisory Note signed with an X in presence of a witness is good and valid. *Collins* v. *Bradshaw,* 10 L. C. R. 366, C. C. 1860. Defendant was sued on a note signed with a cross, and pleaded, denying the signature, and plaintiff failed to prove the signing. *Held,* that the action must be dismissed. *Coupal* v. *Coupal,* 5 R. L. 465, S. C. R. 1873.

649. Promissory Note.—A promissory note not yet due, endorsed by a party who has since become bankrupt, does not entitle the holder to be paid *au mare la livre* concurrently with the other creditors of the bankrupt, the term for payment not having expired. *Mailloux Audet & Mailloux & Carrier,* 14 L. C. R. 207, C. C. 1864.

650. Promissory Note.—Where a note is executed by a married woman authorized by her husband, for property bought by her, during marriage, and it is not shown that she is separate in property, nor that she administered her paraphernal property, nor that she was a public merchant, nor that the property inured to her separate benefit, she cannot be held liable on the note. Such note is a debt of the community, inasmuch as the property, the consideration of the note, belongs to the community. For such a debt a wife, such as is sued herein, is incapable of binding herself. The husband is liable. *Mr. M. W. Graham* v. *Mrs. Z. A. Thayer,* 29 La. 75.

651. Promissory Note.—*Joint.*—Stewart lent to Sterling and Cooper $250 each and took their joint note for

$500; Sterling was liable for half the note as principal and half as surety. Stewart told Sterling that if he would pay half the note he would give him a receipt in full for his half; Sterling paid the half and the receipt given. *Held*, that this did not release him from the other half. *Sterling* v. *Stewart*, 74 Penn. St. Repts. p. 445.

652. Promissory Note *for Patent-right.*—The act of May 4, 1869 (66 Ohio, L. 93), making it a penal offence to take a "promissory note or other negotiable instrument" not containing the words "given for a patent-right," knowing the consideration thereof to be a patented invention, does not include in such offence the taking of notes or instruments not negotiable. An indictment which does not show that the note or instrument on which it is founded was negotiable, does not show an offence under the act, and may be met by demurrer. *State* v. *Brower*, 30 Ohio, 101.

653. Promissory Notes.—*Witness.*—The maker of a promissory note, after judgment recorded against the endorser, not a competent witness for the endorser in a suit in equity to restrain the collection of the judgment. *McDowell* v. *Bank of Wilmington and Brandywine*, Bates, 2 Delaware, 1.

654. Promissory Note.—A bank being the holder of a promissory note protested for non-payment, has not the right to credit it with deposits made by the debtor to his account as a justice of the peace; and its omission to do so does not discharge the endorser. *Id.*

655. An agreement by the bank to credit the note with such fees as the debtor might earn as a notary public in protesting bills and notes for the bank does not discharge the endorser, though made without his privity. *Id. Philpot* v. *Bryant*, 4 Bing. R. 721, also 13 Eng. Com. Law, 128.

656. An agreement between the creditor and the principal debtor, in order to discharge the surety, must be such as gives time to the debtor; and it must be for a consideration. *Id.*

657. Promissory Note.—The endorser of a promissory note due the 11th February, gave to the holder a memorandum, as follows : "My note, becoming due the 10th instant, good for ten days after date." The note to which he referred became due the 11th, there was no other note, and it was presented the 24th February. *Held*, the endorser was liable. *Burnett* v. *Monaghan, et al.*, 3 R. L. 448 ; L. C. R. 1871, 2324 C. C.

658. Promissory Note.—A mere memorandum made by a party on a note, or obligation, in his possession, cannot, when the fact it purports to establish is denied, be admitted as testimony sufficient to create or continue the liability. In this case the statute of limitations was pleaded, and the fact that the payment endorsed on the note was actually made, was controverted by the personal representative of the payer. The judgment of the circuit court, sustaining the plea of the statute of limitations, is affirmed. *Frazer's Adm'rs* v. *Frazer, et al.*, 13 Bush, Ky. 397.

659. Promissory Notes, payable at and discounted by an incorporated bank, are placed, by the law of this State, upon the footing of foreign bills of exchange. *Duncan* v. *Louisville, &c.*, 13 Bush, Ky. 378.

660. Promissory Notes.—Alterations, erasures, or mutilations of a paper upon which a liability is sought to be established against those who are originally bound, must be explained by the holder, when the fact of alteration, erasure or mutilations is raised in the pleading, and established by the proof. *Frazer's Adm'rs* v. *Frazer, &c.*, 13 Bush, Ky. 397.

661. Promissory Note.—*Minors.*—The defendant was sued on a note signed while he was yet a minor, which fact he pleaded simply as a defence to the action. *Held*, that the plea was insufficient, on the ground that the defendant should have pleaded lesion and asked to be released from the obligation. *Cartier* v. *Pelletier*, 1 R. L. 46 ; S. C., 986 and 1002 C. C.

662. Promissory Notes.—The taking of a promissory note for an antecedent debt imposes upon the creditor an obligation to wait for his pay till the note matures, without any special agreement to that effect, or any understanding that the debt shall be thereby extinguished; and the delay thus obtained is a sufficient consideration for the note. Therefore, the note of a married woman, given for the antecedent debt of her husband, is not void for want of consideration, if it is made payable at a future day. The court is not satisfied that, at the time of the giving of the note in suit, the defendant did not have an intelligent understanding of what she was doing, nor that there was any such fraud or imposition practiced upon her as ought to avoid the note. *Thompson* v. *Gray*, 63 Me. 228; also *York* v. *Pierson*, 63 Me. 587.

663. Promissory Note *to Agent.*—A note promising to pay A., or his order, £20 on account of B., enables the endorser of A. to recover the amount. *Newton* v. *Allen*, 2 Rev. de Leg., 29 K. B.; and *Moir* v. *Allen*, *Id.* 1817. And on such a note payment must be made to A. or A.'s order, and not to B. *Clarke* v. *Esson*, 2 Rev. de Leg., 30 K. B. 1820.

664. Promissory Notes.—When the maker of the note has, himself, by careless execution of the instrument, left room for any alteration to be made, either by insertion or erasure, without defacing it or exciting the suspicions of a careful man, he will be liable upon it to any *bona fide* holder without notice, when the opportunity which he has afforded has been embraced, and the instrument filled up with a larger amount or different terms than those which it bore at the time he signed it. Daniel on Negotiable Instruments, sec. 1405, sustained in *Blakey* v. *Johnson*, 13 Bush, Ky. 197.

665. Promissory Note.—*Partner's Liability.*—R. held the promissory note of the firm of T. G. & Co. After it was given, some members of the firm retired, leaving assets sufficient to pay all debts, and taking the obligations of the succeeding new firm, to pay all debts and save the retiring partners harmless. *Held*, that unless R., by some valid contract, expressed or implied, had made himself a party to this new arrangement, or had so acted as to be estopped, his rights on the note against all the members of the old firm remained unchanged; that while, as between the partners themselves, the relation of principal and surety existed, yet, as to the payee of the note, all were principals and joint debtors, although notice of such obligation was brought home to him. Where the payee of such note has received from the new firm a chattel mortgage of the partnership property sufficient, if applied, to satisfy the debt, he may, with the assent of the retiring partners, release the mortgage, and return the property or its avails to the new firm, without impairing his rights against all the joint obligors on the note, even though he had such notice of the subsequent contract between the parties. *Rawson* v. *Taylor*, 30 Ohio, 389.

666. **Promissory Note.**—*Signed by procuration.*—Proof of the due execution of such procuration must be made to entitle the plaintiff to recover judgment in an *ex parte suit* on the note. *Ettrier & Thomas*, 15 L. C. J. 225, Q. B. 1873. And even where the defendant is in default to appear. *Id.* 17 L. C. J. 79, Q. B.

667. Promissory note of hand executed by the maker's mark if endorsed gives no action to the endorsee against the maker, but the endorser is answerable for money had and received. *Jones* v. *Hart*, 2 Rev. de Leg. 29, K. B. 1819.

668. **Promissory Note.**—*Transfer of after maturity.*—A note of hand was transferred after the time appointed for payment, and there was fraud proved in the transaction. *Held*, that on slight grounds the law would presume that the endorser had knowledge of the fraud, if it appear that he omitted to satisfy himself as to the validity of the note. *Hunt* v. *Lee*, 2 Rev. de Leg. 28 K. B. 1813.

669. A firm issued paper with accommodation endorsements, and protected the endorsers by a mortgage executed by the partners. Subsequently one of the partners retired, and the remaining partners formed a new firm, which issued paper in renewal of some of that issued by the old firm. This new paper was endorsed by one of the former endorsers, and a new mortgage, executed by all the members of the old firm, covering the estate previously mortgaged, with other property, protected this endorser: After voluntary assignment by the new firm, the retired member of the old firm, and the last named endorser. *Held*, that the new paper was a mere renewal of the old, and that holders of the new paper were entitled equally with holders of the old to the fund furnished by the first. *Held*, further, that no inference of the absolute payment of the old paper by the new could be drawn either from the fact that the new mortgage was given, or from the fact that the old paper was surrendered or cancelled on the issue of the new. *Held*, further, that an agreement to discharge a retiring partner will not be inferred from the mere acceptance of the note of the continuing partners for the joint debt. *Nightingale* v. *Chafee*, 11 R. I. 609 ; see *Wilbur* v. *Jernegan*, 11 R. I. 113.

670. Promissory Note made by defendant in favor of another. The note was not paid or protested at maturity, but some time afterwards the payee endorsed it over to plaintiff, in part payment of things purchased from him. In an action on the note, want of protest was raised by the defendant. *Held*, that the note might be transferred after maturity, but the maker could raise all the questions which might have arisen in the mean time between himself and the payee. *Duguay* v. *Sénécal*, 1 L. C. L. J. 26, S. C. R. 1865.

671. Promissory Notes given by insolvents a few days before the insolvency, to secure parties to whom they were indebted on accommodation paper, and on these notes being transferred the transferees claimed to rank on the estate of the insolvents for their value. *Held*, that such notes were null and void *ab initio*, even in the hands of an innocent holder for value before maturity. *Davis, et al. in re, and Muir & Chamberlin, et al.*, 13 L. C. J. 184, S. C. 1869, 1032 *et seq.* C. C., & Ins. Act, 1875, secs. 130-133.

672. Defendant pleaded that the note sued on had been obtained from him by surprise and false representations, and for insufficient consideration. *Held*, that he was not bound to produce with such plea an affidavit under C. S. L. C. cap. 83, sec. 86. *McCarthy, et al.* v. *Barthe*, 6 L. C. J. 130, S. C. 1862.

673. **Where Maker Absconds.**—Before a note of hand payable *á terme* becomes due action may be maintained for the amount against the drawer if he absconds. *Shepherd* v. *Henrickson*, 2 Rev. de Leg., 31 K. B. 1819.

674. **Promissory Note** for £100 was given by an insolvent to one of his creditors in settlement of a claim of the creditor against another party for whom the insolvent was surety, the creditor refusing to sign the composition deed of the insolvent unless such settlement were made. *Held*, that as the settlement was in no way prejudicial to the other creditors who received the composition to which they agreed, that the note was good, and the action on it must be maintained. *Greenshields* v. *Plamondon*, 8 L. C. J. 192, 10 L. C. R. 251, Q. B. 1860, reversing 3 L. C. J. 240, S. C. Ins. Act, 1875, secs. 55 & 56.

675. Defendant pleaded want of notice of protest, but produced no affidavit in support of such plea. *Held*, that the action would be maintained, notwithstanding the protest produced contained no certificate that notice of such protest had been given. *The Bank of Upper Canada & Turcotte*, 15 L. C. R. 276, S. C. 1865, 145 C. C. P.

676. **Promissory Note** payable in this country must be made in money current in this country, and that notwithstanding the note in question may have been made

in a foreign country. *Chapman* v. *McFie, et al.*, 1 R. L. 192, S. C. R. 1869.

677. Sureties' Rights.—The holder of a promissory note being requested by a surety to proceed against the principal maker, and failing to do so, if the principal maker afterward becomes insolvent the surety is exonerated. *Pain* v. *Packard*, 13 Johns., affirmed in *Martin* v. *Skehan*, 2 Colorado, 614.

678. Promissory Notes.—The stamp of a bank on a promissory note is not an infallible indication of the legal holder and owner. *Barthe* v. *Armstrong*, 5 R. L. 213, C. C. 1869.

The holder and owner of a note may cancel any of the endorsations and reserve his recourse only against the maker, and may bring his action as if he had received it from the payee or any subsequent endorser, whose name is not cancelled. *Id.*, and 2289, C. C. Ca.

679. Given by an Insolvent.—A note to a creditor for the balance of his claim in consideration of his having signed a deed of composition is void. *Blackwood* v. *Chinic*, 2 Rev. de Leg. 27, Ca. K. B. 1809.

680. In an action to recover the amount of an I. O. U., *Held*, that such an instrument was negotiable like other mercantile paper. *Beaudry* v. *Laflamme & Davis*, 6 L. C. J. 307 ; S. C. 1862, Ca.

681. Payments by Endorsers.—Where a claimant in insolvency had received, as holder of a promissory note, a composition on the amount of his claim from an endorser, in consideration of which he had released the endorser, reserving his recourse against the other parties to the note, *Held*, that whatever the claimant had received from the endorser must be deducted from his claim against the maker's estate. *Bessette, et al.* v. *La Banque du People & Quevillon*, 15 L. C. J. 126 S. C. R. 1871, Ca.

682. Plaintiff sued upon the following instrument: "12 months from the 26th June, 1873, I (defendant) will pay J. C. (plaintiff) $90, for D. P., or otherwise settle the sum of $90 for him, on a note that he says he gave J. C., for $100." *Held*, 1. That this was not a promissory note, and required a consideration to support it. 2. That it was a promise made to D. P. and not to plaintiff. *Cochran* v. *Caie*, 3 New Brunswick Reports, 224.

683. A promise in writing to pay on a day certain £250 to A. B. or order, with an engagement to pay in cash or in goods, if the holder should choose to demand the latter, is a promissory note, for this engagement is no more than a power given to the holder to convert a promissory note into an order for merchandise if he see fit to do so. *McDonald* v. *Holgate*, 2 Rev. de Leg. 29, K. B. 1818; 2344, C. C., and art. 229, *infra*. Ca.

684. Promissory Notes.—A promise to pay a note to the holder which is not endorsed is sufficient to enable the holder to recover if the drawer knew that it was not endorsed. *Aylwin* v. *Cruttenden*, 2 Rev. de Leg. 30, K. B. 1820; 2285 C. C.

685. In an action for goods sold, in which the defendant pleaded payment and novation by a promissory note which he had given to the plaintiff, *Held*, that a writing merely certifying that a person is indebted to another in a certain sum of money, is not negotiable as a promissory note, and if it were it would have been no novation of the debt. *Dasylva, et al.* v. *Dufour*, 16 L. C. R. 294; C. C. 1866, Ca.

686. Issued under Fraud.—A son, having acknowledged to have stolen $25, the mother was induced to sign a promissory note under threats of having her son arrested. *Held*, that she was not liable on the note in question. *Macfarlane* v. *Devy*, 15 L. C. J. 85, Q. B. 1871; 994, C. C., Ca.

687. In Cases of Insolvency.—Action was brought on a promissory note having two years or thereabouts to run, on the ground that the maker had become insolvent and had left his domicile in Lower Canada, and the defendant demurred on the ground that the plaintiff had not alleged either fraud or secretion of his estate. *Held*, dismissing the demurrer, that the note was exigible on proof of insolvency. *Lowell* v. *Meikle*, 2 L. C. J. 69, S. C. 1853; Ins. Act, 1875, sec. 80, Ca.

688.—A note executed in 1863 for the balance due upon a note executed in 1853 (such new note being given because of a lack of space on the old note for entry of a credit), is not subject to the legislative scale of Confederate money. *Cobb* v. *Gray*, 78 N. C. 94.

689. **Payable on Demand.**—Action was brought on a promissory note payable on demand thirteen years after its date, and prescription being pleaded, *Held*, that it was due from the day of its date, and if action were brought on it, and no demand of payment proved, that the omission could not affect the action, and merely the costs, and therefore the prescription ran from the day of its date. *La Rocque, et al.* v. *André, et al.*, 2 L. C. R. 335, S. C. 1851; 2260, sec. 4 C. C. C.

690. **Municipality.**—On action to recover the amount of a promissory note signed by the secretary-treasurer of a municipality,—*Held*, that where the power of signing such promissory notes was not expressly given to the corporation by its charter or otherwise, that it could not be implied as necessary to accomplish any of the purposes for which the corporation was created. And *held*, also, that a promissory note signed by such corporation in settlement of a judgment against the municipality, was null, the legislature having empowered municipalities to raise money in a different way. *Pacand* v. *The Corporation of Halifax South*, 17 L. C. R. 56, S. C. R. 1866, Ca.

691. **Variance.**—In an action on a promissory note against an endorser, it is not necessary for the plaintiff to allege in his declaration endorsement subsequent to the defendant's, where the plaintiff does not sue upon any title derived through such subsequent endorsements. *Bank of America* v. *Senior*, 11 R. I. 376.

692. In an action on a note made in the United States, and payable there, defendant, after action

brought, tendered the amount in Canadian currency, equal at the then current rate of exchange to the amount of the note in American currency, with costs. *Held*, that judgment must be given for the amount of the note in Canadian currency with costs. *Daly* v. *Graham*, 15 L. C. R. 137, and 8 L. C. J. 340, C. C. 1864. And in another case of the same kind,—*Held*, that the note being payable to bearer, the maker must be held to have agreed to pay in the currency of the place where the bearer resided, and, consequently, that a tender of payment in greenbacks was insufficient. *McCoy* v. *Dineen*, 8 L. C. J. 339, S. C. 1864, Ca.

693. No set form of words is requisite to constitute a promissory note, and an instrument called a writing obligatory as a bond payable to order for value received, may be considered as a note in writing within the intent of the Provincial Statute 34 Geo. 3, Cap. 2, though it do not follow the very words of the act, and though it be merely described and designated in the plaintiff's declaration as writing obligatory or bond. *Hall* v. *Bradbury, et al.*, 1 Rev. de Leg. 180, Q. B. 1845.

694. An obligation before a notary to pay a certain sum of money without condition and at all events is a promissory note. *Auréle* v. *Durocher*, 5 R. L. 165, S. C. R. 1873 ; 2244, C. C.

695. **Illegal Consideration.**—A statute of the State provides that "all payments or compensations for liquors sold in violation of law, whether in money, labor or personal property, shall be held and considered, as between the parties to such sale, to have been received in violation of law, without consideration, and against equity and good conscience." With this law in force A. agreed to purchase of B. a half interest in a business and stock in trade, a portion of which consisted of liquor illegally kept for sale, and transferred a promissory note for $450 in part payment. A. afterwards repudiated the arrangement and sued for the value of the note. *Held*, that A. could recover so

much of the value of the note as might have been paid for liquor illegally kept for sale, the proportion to be recovered as paid for liquor to be determined by finding the proportional value of the liquor as compared with the rest of the purchase. *McGuinness* v. *Blegh*, 11 R. I. 94.

696. One H. made his promissory note to the order of Senior. It was endorsed by Senior, and subsequently by Stone, and by the A. Co. by Stone, treasurer. It passed into the possession of the Bank of America and was taken up by Stone, who brought suit on it against Senior in the name of the bank. At the trial, evidence was admitted by the presiding judge, notwithstanding Senior's objection, to show that Stone had paid the note to the Bank of America in full, and had left it for collection with the bank, and that the bank authorized Stone to bring suit in its name. Senior also requested the judge to instruct the jury that, as the note had been paid to the bank in full, it could neither bring suit on the note nor authorize Stone to do so in its name. This instruction was refused, and the jury was told that if the facts, as claimed by the plaintiff, were satisfactorily proved, the plaintiff could recover. *Held*, no error. *Bank of America* v. *Senior*, 11 R. I. 376.

697. In an action on a promissory note against an endorser, it is not necessary for the plaintiff to allege in his declaration endorsements subsequent to the defendant's, where the plaintiff does not sue upon any title derived through such subsequent endorsement. *Id.* 376.

698. A note payable to the order of W. was before issue endorsed by F. It was signed by G., and his signature was, at the request of W., changed to G., agent. The note was given for G.'s private debt. F. did not assent to the change, and there was no evidence to show that G's principals were accustomed to pay notes drawn in this form. In an action against F. *Held*, that the change was immaterial. *Held*, further,

affirming *Mathewson* v. *Sprague*, 1 R. I. 8; and *Perkins* v. *Barstow*, 6 R. I. 505, that F. was not entitled to notice of non-payment. *Manuf. & Merchants' Bank* v. *Follett*, 11 R. I. 92.

699. Due presentment of a note, when denied, is sufficiently shown by evidence that the note was in the bank where it was made payable, and in the possession of its officers, on the day of its maturity, and that the makers had no funds there for its payment. When this proof is made, it is not necessary, on this issue, to show that formal presentment and demand were made. When a note is in the bank, in the custody of the proper officer, on the day of its maturity, such possession is treated as due presentment. *Huffaker & Shy* v. *National Bank of Monticello*, 13 Bush, Ky. 644; also, 1 Daniels on Negotiable Instruments, p. 486, sec. 656.

700. **Property in.**—*Right to sue.*—E. & M., having been in co-partnership in the firm of Wm. M. & Co., and E. having subsequently entered into partnership with other parties under the firm name of J. E. & Co., by an agreement passed in July, 1855, M. agreed with J. E. & Co. to assume all the liabilities of Wm. M. & Co., to pay the sum due E. & Co. in four installments, and to give security on condition that he should be allowed to cut timber on certain timber limits of E. & Co. He subsequently cut timber without giving security, and the timber was transferred to the firm of Symes & Co., which had made advances to him. M. paid E. & Co. the first installment of the above mentioned debt by his notes, and for £1,500, which E. & Co. paid away to a third party, and one for £800, which E. & Co. placed to the credit of M. & Co. E. & Co., having by *raisie arret* before judgment seized the timber cut as in the possession of M., and having sued for the whole debt. *Held*, that E. & Co., having paid away the note for £1,500 to a third party, could not sue for the debt for which it was given without producing the note, and also that E. & Co., having carried the note for £800 to the credit of

Wm. M. & Co., could not withdraw it from that account without the consent of M. *Gibson, et al.* v. *Moffat & Young,* 2 L. C. L. J. 60, Q. B. 1866. *Held,* also, that the plaintiffs not having alleged the insolvency of M., in their declaration, could not base their right to sue for the whole of the debt on such insolvency, and the allegation of his insolvency in their special answer could not avail to supply the deficiency in their declaration.

701. Date of Issue.—The date of a promissory note is proof that the note was made on such date, and in the case in question. *Held,* that the party could not prove that the note had been made on a day posterior to its date, and that in consequence it fell within the operations of a subsequent deed of compromise between the respondents and their creditors, among them was the appellant. *Evans & Cross, et al.,* 15 L. C. R. 86, S. C. R. & 16 L. C. R. 469, & 2 L. C. L. J. 79 Q. B. 1866.

701a. Holder's Rights.—The holder of a promissory note does not require to prove that it was actually made on the date it bears, as the date makes proof of itself. *Hutchins, et al.* v. *Cohen & Cohen,* 14 L. C. J. 85, S. C. 1869.

702. When Payable.—On an appeal from a judgment condemning the defendants jointly and severally to pay the amount of the promissory note sued upon, *Held,* reversing the judgment of the court below, that a promise to pay at a specified place is not a promise to pay generally, and there is no liability on the part of the maker of a promissory note payable at a specified place, unless proof be made of a presentment and of demand of payment at such specified place, and of neglect or refusal there to pay the amount of such note. *O'Brien & Stevenson, et al.,* 15 L. C. R. 265, Q. B. 1865, 2307 C. C.

703. Given in Discharge of an Antecedent Debt in Rhode Island does not discharge the debt unless the note is given and received as absolute payment, and the burden of proof is on the debtor to show that it was so given and received. Nor does it make any difference that the makers of the note so given are fewer in number than the original debtors. *Nightingale* v. *Chafee,* 11 R. I. 609.

704. Promissory note given for a precedent debt in Rhode Island does not, *prima facie,* operate as absolute payment of the debt, but rather as an extension of credit or as only conditional payment; and if the note at maturity is not paid, the right to sue the original debt and enforce its securities revives. But though, *prima facie,* the note has only this effect, yet if it was given and received by the parties as absolute payment or satisfaction, the debt will, upon proof that the note was so given and received, be regarded as paid or satisfied. *Wilbur* v. *Jernegan,* 11 R. I. 113 ; also, *Nightingale* v. *Chafee,* 11 R. I. 609.

705. The holder of a negotiable note, who has bought it in good faith, and before its maturity, acquires a valid title to it, though it be shown that the vendor of the note was not its owner, and fraudulently disposed of it. *R. N. Ogden* v. *A. Marchand,* 29 La. 61.

706. The maker and the endorser of a promissory note, although not technically debtors in *soledo,* are yet liable, *each,* for the whole debt. *Paul Mack* v. *C. E. Fortier, et al.,* 29 La. 63.

707. The pledge or sale of a negotiable instrument before its maturity carries with it all the liens by which the instrument is secured, and by such sale, or pledge, the transferee divests of all power to affect the liens which secure the instrument. *Mechanics' Building Ass.* v. *C. L. Ferguson,* 29 La. 548.

708. In an action at law on a promissory note, facts which constitute mere matter of defence, and are available as such in the pending action, will not, in general, entitle the defendant to equitable relief. Such affirmative relief will be granted only when necessary

to prevent wrong or injustice. *Bank* v. *Weyland*, 30 Ohio, 126.

709. Assignor.—Burden of Proof.—In a suit by the assignee against the assignor of a note, where diligence by suit against the maker is not shown, the burden of proof is upon the plaintiff to establish the insolvency of the maker. *Clayes* v. *White*, 83 Ill. 540.

710. Payment.—Instruction.—In an action upon a promissory note, alleged to have been purchased by the defendant for the plaintiff's intestate, with money furnished by the latter, wherein defendant pleaded payment, it is proper to submit to the jury the question whether the transaction constituted a payment or a purchase of the note. While the mere delivery of money by the payer to the holder of a note is presumptive evidence of payment, yet this presumption may be rebutted by circumstances. *Dougherty* v. *Deeney, et al.*, 45 Iowa, 443.

711.—When Held as Collateral Security.—Where a promissory note had been transferred by endorsement as collateral security, and then, before maturity, with the knowledge of the endorsee, the payee had sold it to a third party, into whose possession it did not come until after maturity: *Held*, that the latter acquired it free from equities, and occupied the position of a good faith endorsee before maturity. *Grimm* v. *Warner, et al.*, 45 Iowa, 106.

712.—Where, at the request of the party with whom he deals, one makes his promissory note (which is to be partial payment for a piece of work to be done for him) payable to a third party, who is a creditor of the party with whom he contracts for the work, and it is credited by the payee to such party in good faith, the maker cannot set up a failure of consideration, as between himself and the party with whom he deals, in defence of a suit upon such note, in the name of the payee. *So. Boston Iron Co.* v. *Brown*, 63 Me. 139.

713.—In an action upon an unendorsed promissory note, by a plaintiff alleging himself to be the owner thereof by devise from the payee, the representative of the latter should be made a party defendant, or the complaint should allege that there is no such representative; but a failure to object to such defect is a waiver thereof. *St. John* v. *Hardwick*, 11 Ind. 251; also *Strong* v. *Downing*, 34 Ind. 300; *Shane* v. *Lowry*, 48 Ind. 205; *Shirts* v. *Isom*, 54 Ind. 13; *Bray* v. *Black*, 57 Ind. 417.

714.—Where a woman assigns by delivery a note payable to her order, and afterward marries the maker, her endorsement after such marriage transfers the legal title. The statutes of Maine give no mutual right of action to the husband and wife, and none such exists by common law. Such has been the uniform construction of this and similar statutes in Maine and Massachusetts. *Crowther* v. *Crowther*, 55 Maine, 358; also *Guptill* v. *Horne*, 63 Me. 405.

715. Evidence to impeach a promissory note in the hands of a *bona fide* purchaser for value, before maturity and without notice is inadmissible. *Waite* v. *Chandler*, 63 Me. 257.

716. **Promissory Note and Mortgage.**—*Married Woman.*—A married woman with the consent of her husband may make an equitable assignment of a note and mortgage executed to her, by the sale and mere delivery of the same to another. *Baker* v. *Armstrong*, 57 Ind. 189.

717. The holder of a solidary note cannot have its solidarity impaired, by the unauthorized action of his collection agent, who receipts in favor of one of the solidary debtors on the note for "his share" of the debt. *Cooley* v. *Broad*, 29 La. 345.

718. The holder of a negotiable note of a married woman, who has taken it for value, and before maturity, is yet liable to have pleaded against him every defence arising out of the wife's incapacity. *Conrad, et al.* v. *Lee Blanc, Sheriff*, 29 La. 123.

719. **Demand.**—In respect to the time within which it is necessary to present for payment a note, payable on

demand, in order to charge an endorser, that "it depends upon so many circumstances to determine wh·t is a reasonable time in a particular case, that one decision goes but little way in establishing a precedent for another." *Seaver* v. *Lincoln*, 21 Pick. 267.

720. Where in renewal of a matured promissory note executed by his decedent, the administrator or executor of an estate, as such, executes to the payee a new promissory note, he thereby becomes personally liable, but the estate is not bound. *Cornthwaite* v. *The First Nat. Bank, &c.*, 57 Ind. 268 ; also *Mills* v. *Kuykendall*, 2 Blackf. 47, and *Carter* v. *Thomas*, 3 Ind. 213.

721. Protest.—Where a bill is accepted by a firm, a notarial certificate of protest must state who compose the firm, and upon which of them the demand was made. *Oswego County Bank* v. *Warren*, 18 Barb. N. Y. 290.

722–723. Notice of Protest.— *When may be served by mail.— What is good service by mail.— Who deemed holder for purpose of receiving and giving notice of protest.— What is not unnecessary and unreasonable delay.*—When the endorser of a note lives in a different place from that in which presentment or demand is to be made, personal service of notice of protest is not required, but the notice may be served on him by mail, although he lives in the same place with the holder who serves the notice. Delivery to a city letter-carrier of a notice of protest enclosed in an envelope, properly addressed and with postage paid, is good service by mail.

724. Where a note held in New York was payable in Kutztown, Pennsylvania, and the holder placed it in a New York city bank for collection, which sent it to its Pennsylvania correspondent, a bank at Allentown, within eighteen miles of Kutztown, whence it was sent to a bank at Philadelphia, and thence to a bank in Reading, and thence to Kutztown for presentment, where it was dishonored :

Held, that each agent for transmission of the note for collection, having endorsed it, was the holder for the purpose of receiving and giving notice of protest; and that the return of such notice by the same channel, each bank forwarding them by the next mail, was not an unnecessary and unreasonable delay which discharged the first endorser. *Wynen* v. *Schappert*, 55 Howard, N. Y. 156.

725. In an action by an assignee, on a promissory note payable in a bank of this State, where the defences pleaded by the defendant maker were want of consideration, and that, after the execution of the note and before its assignment, the payee thereof, with the knowledge of the plaintiff, but without the knowledge or consent of the defendant, had procured the execution of such note by a third person, the plaintiff replied, that before procuring such assignment to himself, he had taken such note to the defendant, who, in answer to his inquiries concerning it, informed him that he had no defence thereto, and would pay it, and that, relying upon such statements, the plaintiff had procured an assignment of the note, for value. *Held*, on demurrer, that the reply is sufficient. *Vaughn* v. *Ferrall*, 57 Ind. 182.

726. Protest.—The defendant pleaded a general denial, there having been no notice of protest given him. The plaintiff answered that a verbal notice had been given to the defendant, and examined a notary to prove the giving of such verbal notice. The action was nevertheless dismissed. *Cowan* v. *Turgeon*, 1 Rev. de Leg. 231, Q. B. 1832; 2303 and 2327 *et seq.* C. C.

727. An endorsed note was discounted by a bank for the drawer, at maturity he took it up by a similar note on which the endorsements were forged, and destroyed the original note; he took up the second note by another note with forged endorsements. *Held*, that taking the last two notes in renewal did not extinguish the original note. The record of the protesting no-

tary being proved to contain a true copy of the first note, was admissible in evidence. The bank who discounted the first note was entitled to recover, on proof of its destruction and the genuineness of the signatures. *Ritter* v. *Singmaster*, 73 Penn. 400.

728. Purchaser *of a mortgage* from the assignee of a mortgage is put on inquiry as to his vendor's title, by the latter's failure to transfer all the securities. An assignment of a mortgage does not transfer undelivered collateral securities unless the parties so intend and a consideration is paid. *Fletcher* v. *Carpenter*, 37 Mich. 412.

729. Stock.—A note was given for additional stock in a manufacturing company; *Held*, that evidence of a parol agreement when the note was executed that it was not to be paid except on a contingency, was inadmissible.

Stock.—*Note.*—Hacker subscribed for additional stock in a corporation and she gave her note for the amount; a certificate was tendered her and refused, and no credit was given her in the stock ledger. *Held*, the note was not without consideration; she had the right to demand and receive the stock. *Hacker* v. *National Oil Co.*, 73 Penn. St. 93.

730. Protest Irregular.—If the protest for the non-payment of a promissory note be premature, or if time be given by the holder to the maker, the endorser is discharged, but if, with a knowledge of the protest having been made or of the giving of time, he, the endorser, subsequently promises to pay, his liability is revived. *The City Bank* v. *Hunter & Maitland*, 2 Rev. de Leg. 171, Q. B. 1847.

731. Practice.—*Garnishee order note not yet due.*—A promissory note not yet due does not constitute a debt within the meaning of sec. 63 of the common Law Procedure Act, 1856, which can be attached to answer a judgment debt. Motion to attach the amount of a promissory note. Plaintiff had, in October, 1876, obtained a judgment against the defendant for £73. 19s.

11d., which was still unsatisfied. The promissory note, the amount of which was sought to be attached, had been passed by one John Griffin to the defendant for the sum of £100, payable on the 28th of February, 1877, and consequently not due at the time of the present motion. The note was in the hands of the defendant, and it was deposed that Griffin was liable to the payee in the amount thereof. Morris, C. J.—You have no case of such an order made in this country to attach the amount of a promissory note. Keogh, J.—I have refused similar applications on several occasions. Lawson, J.—This being a negotiable instrument, no order can prevent its being endorsed over. Morris, C. J. said further—What evidence of a debt is there in a promissory note? There may have been no consideration. We will not make a precedent. Motion refused. *Pyne* v. *Kinna*, Irish Reports, Common Law Series, Vol. 11, p. 40.

732. A note was, "twelve months after date (or before, if made out of the sale of"—a machine), "I promise to pay to J. F. Huston or bearer" &c. *Held*, to be negotiable. A note to be negotiable must be for the payment of money at a fixed period on an event which must inevitably happen. *Id.*

A note is not negotiable if its payment depends upon a contingency, although that may in fact happen. *Id.*

A note may be negotiable if payable *certainly* at a fixed time, although subject to a contingency under which it may become due earlier. *Id. Ernst* v. *Steckman*, 74 Penn. St. Repts. 13.

733. The sale and delivery of a negotiable promissory note with endorsement thereon are a warranty of the genuineness of the endorsements. *Allen* v. *Clark*, 49 Rowell, Vt. 390.

PROTEST.

734. **Waiver.**—The husband being universal legatee of his wife endorsed for her a promissory note. *Held*,

that he was bound to pay the amount of the note, notwithstanding there was no protest, it being sufficiently established that he had consented in the name of his wife to waive protest in order to avoid costs, and that in fact the wife was only a *pret nom* to cover the trading of the husband. *Berian & McCorkill*, 14 L. C. R. 400, Q. B. 1864.

735. Endorser Discharged.—In an action against the maker and endorser: *Held*, that the omission to state in a notarial protest that it was made in the forenoon of the day of protest was fatal, and the endorser was discharged. *Joseph* v. *Delisle, et al.*, 1 L. C. R. 244, S. C. 1851; 2319 C. C.

736. *Held*, that the non-exhibition of the note to the maker at the time of protest, the maker being notoriously insolvent, will not invalidate the protest, and notice of protest to the endorser will hold them liable, notwithstanding such non-exhibition. *Venner* v. *Futvoye, et al.*, 13 L. C. R., 307; S. C. 1863.

737. The maker of a note was described in the protest, and also in the writ and declaration, as E. B. P., instead of Joseph B. P. *Held*, that a plea by the endorser to the effect that he never endorsed the note described by plaintiff, and that a protest of E. B. P.'s note was not a legal *protest* of J. B. P.'s note was bad, and would be dismissed. *Scullion* v. *Perry, et al.*, 9 L. C. J. 175, 1 L. C. L. J. 64, S. C. 1865.

738. Waiver of Notice.—A promise to pay a protested bill of exchange, of which no notice of protest has been given, if made with a knowledge of that fact, is a waiver of want of notice. *Ross* v. *Wilson*, 2 Rev. de. Leg. 28 K. B., 1812.

739.—In the case of a protest of a note dated at Montreal and payable at a bank in Albany, in the State of New York, a notice of protest mailed at Albany, addressed to an endorser at Montreal, protest being made, and notice mailed according to the laws of the State. *Held*, confirming court below, that it was not sufficient, inasmuch as the postal arrangements between the two countries required prepayment of the postage, at least from Albany to the line; but, had the postage been paid, the notice would have been sufficient, as notice of protest must be given, according to the *lex loci* contractus, but the protest itself made according to the law of the place where the note was payable. *Howard* v. *Sabourin*, 2 L. C. R. 121, and 5 L. C. R. 45, Q. B. 1854.

740. **Protested Draft** is not an obligation within the meaning of the proviso of the act of 16th of April, 1850, which declares that the assignees of an insolvent bank "shall receive in payment of debts due to said bank its own notes and obligations and the checks of its depositors at par." *Basehou* v. *Rhodes*, 85 Penn. 44.

741. In an action against an accommodation endorser of a negotiable note, the fact that the endorser resided at the time in Alexandria, where the note was discounted, and before the note became due he went into the Confederate lines, and was there when the note was protested, and at the time of such protest he had no known agent in Alexandria to receive notice of the dishonor of the note, is not of itself sufficient to render the endorser liable.

And in such a case, the fact that the endorser had a residence in Alexandria at the time the note was protested, and that a written notice of said protest was left at his residence, is not sufficient to render the endorser liable.

742. In such a case the plaintiff having purchased the note after maturity and dishonor, by purchase at a sale of the effects of a bank which had discounted it, he is not thereby prevented from recovering from the endorser the whole amount of the note, though he paid for it much less than the nominal amount. *McVeigh, et al.* v. *Allen*, 29 Grattan (Va.) 588.

743. **Notice of Protest** addressed to a female endorser and beginning "Sir" is bad, and an action against such endorser was dismissed. *Seymour, et al.* v. *Wright, et al.*, 3 L. C. R. 454, S. C. 1852. But,

held, in a later case, to be sufficient if duly served upon her. *Mitchell* v. *Browne,* 9 L. C. J. 168, and 15 L. C. R. 425, C. C. 1865.

744. There must be evidence of diligence of a protest for non-payment of a bill of exchange to charge the drawer. *Brent* v. *Lees,* 2 Rev. de Leg. 335, K. B. 1820.

745. Notice of dishonor need not be given by a notary, it may be given by any holder for himself and in his own language ; but it is not binding, whatever its form, unless the paper has been legally dishonored ; and every endorser is presumed to know what action will bind him and what will not. A letter addressed by the holders of a note to the endorser, describing the note and stating that it was unpaid and that the holders looked to him for payment is a sufficient notice of dishonor. *Cromer* v. *Platt, et al.,* 37 Mich. 132.

746. It is incumbent upon a party seeking to charge an endorser, to prove a legal notice, but this, like any other question of fact, is to be settled upon the testimony as it is given, and need not be proved beyond the possibility of mistake. *Seaton* v. *Scovill,* 18 Kansas, 433.

747. Where the holder, and party to whom notice is to be given, reside at different places, it is generally sufficient if notice is sent by the mail of the day next succeeding the day of dishonor. *Id.*

748. The holder of dishonored paper may give notice directly to all prior parties, or only to his immediate predecessor on the paper. In the latter case, such predecessor has the same time to give notice to his endorser as though he himself had been the holder and had the paper protested. *Id.*

749. A banker or agent to whom paper has been transmitted for the purpose of obtaining acceptance, or payment, is, so far as the question of notice is concerned, to be considered as though he were the real holder, and his principal a prior endorser. *I d.*

750. Where a promissory note provides that the en-

dorsers "waive presentment for payment, protest, and notice of protest and non-payment," the complaint in an action thereon need not allege "presentment," or "notice." *Henderson* v. *Ackelmire,* 59 Ind. 540.

751. Waiver of.—Where such note waives notice of non-payment, protest, etc., the complaint thereon need not aver such notice to an endorser. *Burroughs* v. *Wilson,* 85 Ill. 536.

752. Notice of.—The defendant was sued as endorser on a note. Seasonable notice of its non-payment was sent to his address at Baldwin, where he had formerly long resided ; but at, and for several years preceding the maturity of this note, he lived at Denmark. There were three post-offices in Baldwin, neither of which was designated simply by the name of the town ; but notice of the dishonor of a note maturing earlier at the same bank, addressed to him at Baldwin (as this was) was received and responded to, without any intimation that it was not properly directed ; and upon inquiry of those likely to know, the notary was told he still lived at Baldwin ; *Held,* that the plaintiff's allegation of notice was sufficiently proved, since legal notice is not, necessarily, actual notice. Reasonable diligence to communicate information of the non-payment of the note is all that is required, and that was issued in this case. *Saco Nat. Bank* v. *Sanborn,* 63 Me. 340.

753. Waiver of.—The accommodation endorser of a promissory note wrote the cashier of the bank where the note was made payable, on the day the note fell due, the note then being in the hands of an endorsee for value, and the bank being ignorant of its existence, that he would "waive protest" thereon. Afterwards, the endorsee endorsed the note to the bank for collection, and the bank brought suit thereon against the accommodation endorser. *Held,* that as at the time the letter was written and received the bank had no interest in or possession of the note, the letter was not, in legal effect, a waiver of notice of protest. *Nat. Bank of Poultney* v. *Lewis,* 50 Vt. 622.

PURCHASER.

754. Purchasers at public judicial sales or under a quit-claim deed usually buy at their own risk of the regularity of title. *McGoren* v. *Avery*, 37 Mich. 120.

755. With Notice.—A purchaser of land with notice of outstanding equities may protect himself by purchasing the title of another who was a *bona fide* purchaser, and this will not make him hold the property as a trustee. *St. Joseph Mfg. Co.* v. *Daggett*, 84 Ill. 556.

756. Who is a Bona Fide.—A creditor who makes advances under the security of a deed of trust, in good faith, and without notice of a vendor's equitable lien for the purchase-money, will be protected as an innocent purchaser. He should show that the vendor was seized in fee and in possession of the land. *Gerron* v. *Pool*, 31 Ark. 85.

757. Purchase, Option of.—W. conveyed to E. an undivided half part of two lots of land, and subsequently received from E. a bond in a penal sum of $4,000, giving W. the privilege at any time at his option within seven years from the date of the bond, to purchase the whole of said two estates for $8,000, provided that on such purchase E. should be by W. exonerated from all liabilities and losses, past and future, of a firm whereof E. was a member. W. died without having availed himself of the option, and more than three years before the expiration of the time prescribed. E. became his administrator. The widow and children of W. filed a bill against E., charging fraudulent concealment of the bond. E. produced the bond, denying in his answer the charges of the bill, whereupon the complainants asked leave to amend the bill by a prayer that E.'s title to the estate in question might be declared that of a mortgage for $8,000; that the estate might be sold to satisfy E.'s claim, and that an account might be ordered. *Held*, that the option of purchase given to W. by the bond was neither a chose in action, nor a transmissible right of property, but a personal privilege in W., and that on his death E. was freed from the bond. *Held*, further, that a purchase under the option by the administrator of W. must, if made, be for and in the name of W.'s heirs; but as this might change the succession to W.'s property, W.'s administrator could not be allowed the option given W. *Held*, further, that in no case could the exoneration required by the bond be given by the admistrator. *Newton* v. *Newton*, 11 R. I. 390.

758. **Bona Fide.**—A person to be a *bona fide* purchaser without notice, must be without notice of the rights and equities sought to be enforced at the time of the payment of the consideration. *Marsh* v. *Armstrong*, 20 Minn. 81.

759. **Insolvency of Purchaser.**—Unless actual possession of goods sold has been delivered to the purchaser, the vendor is not deprived of his right of lien as against the assignees of the purchaser, in the event of his insolvency. Where the vendors were also warehousemen of the goods sold under an arrangement with the purchasers to pay warehouse rent: *Held*, that as the goods remained in the possession of the vendors and no actual delivery had been made to the purchaser, the vendor's lien revived upon the insolvency of the vendees. *Grice* v. *Richardson*, 3 App. Cas. (Vic. 41–42, Eng. Law Reports), P. C. 319.

760. **Purchaser for Value.**—A creditor taking a chose in action as collateral security for a pre-existing indebtedness is not a purchaser for value. *Ashton's Appeal*, 73 Penn. 153.

Although a rule to open a judgment and let the defendant in to a defence has been discharged in a court of law, the defendant is not precluded from resorting to a court of equity for relief. *Id.*

PURCHASE-MONEY.

761. Purchase-Money.—Where the plaintiff purchased and paid for the land in question, and the deed made to the defendant J., under a verbal agreement that the plaintiff was to hold the deed, and that, concurrently with taking the deed to J., he and his wife were to execute a mortgage to the plaintiff to secure the purchase-money; J. did execute the mortgage, but his wife refused to join. *Held*, that the plaintiff was entitled to judgment for the amount due and that the land be sold to satisfy it. *Held, further*, that in such case no title vested in J., and his wife acquired no dower or homestead rights. *Held, further*, that plaintiff's demand is for the purchase-money, as against which homestead rights do not prevail. *Bunting* v. *Jones*, 78 N. C. 242; also *Suit* v. *Suit*, 78 N. C. 272.

QUANTUM MERUIT.

762. Quantum Meruit.—Although an action cannot be maintained upon a verbal contract not to be performed within one year, yet when such contract has been fully performed by one party, the other having obtained its benefits, he cannot refuse to pay the reasonable value thereof. T. agreed to work until coming of age, a period of six years or more, for M. Having performed the contract, T. may maintain an action quantum meruit for his services. *Towsley* v. *M.*, New Series, 30 Ohio, 184.

RECEIPTS.

763. Lost Note.—An instrument given by the payee of a lost note, upon the execution of another note in its stead by the maker, stipulating that if the lost note comes to hand it shall be null and void, is a receipt, and may be contradicted or explained by parol evidence. *Williamson* v. *Reddish*, 45 Iowa, 550; also *Price* v. *Mahoney*, 24 Iowa, 582.

764. *Receipts* may be explained or contradicted by

parol evidence. *Dunlap's Ex'r* v. *Shanklin*, 10 West Virginia, 662.

765. Receipt of Bank Check is not payment of antecedent debt until it is itself paid. *Phillips* v. *Bullard*, 58 Ga. 256.

RECEIVER.

766. Right to Bid in Property.—A receiver of an insurance company, holding notes given to the company and secured by deed of trust, has the rightful power to bid off the property to save a sacrifice. He succeeds to the rights of the company in this respect. *Jacobs* v. *Turpin*, 83 Ill. 424.

767. Where a creditor's bill charges that the debtor has choses in action, etc., in his possession, and asks for a discovery, and the debtor suffers the bill to be taken as confessed, it is not error to enjoin the debtor from disposing of his property, and to appoint a receiver to take charge of the same. *Runals* v. *Harding, et al.*, 83 Ill. 75.

768. Receiver of a Bank, appointed under Gen. Stat. R. I. cap. 140, may bring suit in his own name for a debt due to the bank. *De Wolf* v. *Sprague Manuf. Co.*, 11 R. I. 380.

REDEMPTION.

769. Redemption of Real Estate.—Real estate sold at sheriff's sale by virtue of a decree of foreclosure of a mortgage thereon, accompanied by a personal judgment against the debtor, may be redeemed by the judgment creditor, from the purchaser, where the amount realized by such sale is insufficient to satisfy such judgment. 2 R. S. 1876, p. 220, sec. 1; also, 2 R. S. 1876, p. 228, and notes on pp. 228 to 233. *The State, ex rel. &c.* v. *Sherill*, 34 Ind. 57; also, *Davis* v. *Longsdale*, 41 Ind. 399; also, *Greene* v. *Doane, et al.*, 57 Ind. 186.

REPLEVIN.

770. Replevin.—No previous demand upon a *bona fide* purchaser of a chattel from one who had no authority to sell it is necessary to enable the owner to maintain replevin. Such a person is not lawfully in possession as against the owner. *Prime* v. *Cobb*, 63 Maine, 200.

771. A sheriff who attempts to sell goods covered by a writ of replevin previously served upon himself or his receiptor, becomes a wrong-doer. *Mayhue* v. *Snell*, 37 Mich. 305.

772. Dillinger consigned goods to Moorehead for sale ; he pledged them for a loan to Macky, who knew they were owned by Dillinger : *Held*, that under the Factor Act of April 14, 1834, Dillinger could recover in replevin without tendering repayment of the loan. *Macky* v. *Dillinger*, 73 Penn. p. 85.

Moorehead had advanced to Dillinger on the goods before pledging them ; Dillinger demanded them from Macky, who declined to deliver without payment of his loan, saying nothing as to Moorehead's advance. Dillinger might recover the goods without payment of the advance. *Id.*

773. Macky gave a property bond and retained the goods : *Held*, that the amount due to the advance be recouped from Dillinger's damages. *Id.*

774. When a party declines to accept payment or performance, except in a way to which he is not entitled, he cannot insist that the action is prematurely brought. *Id.*

775. There is no set-off in replevin, but if the goods are subject to a charge, it can be enforced by way of recoupment. *Id.*

REPRESENTATIONS.

776. Representations.—Damages not recoverable for loss of speculative profits where money has been paid on the strength of mistaken representations. *Fitzsimmons* v. *Chapman*, 37 Mich. 139.

RESCISSION.

777. Rescission of Contract.—A contract can only be rescinded by the acts or assent of all the parties. A party, claiming to have rescinded a contract, cannot excuse himself for not returning a promissory note, by showing that it is worthless by reason of its maker's insolvency. Where a party had produced and surrendered to a referee at the trial certain notes, but had neglected seasonably to return other notes, and the object was insisted upon, it was held that by leave of court he might resume the notes so surrendered. *Spencer* v. *St. Clair*, 57 Hall, N. H. p. 9; *Cook* v. *Gilman*, 34 N. H. 556; *Evans* v. *Gale*, 21 N. H. 240; *Winkley* v. *Foye*, 28 N.H. 513.

778. I. sold stock to T., and agreed that when T. should desire it, he would take it back and repay the price. *Held*, that upon tender of the stock T. might recover the price with interest. *Laubach* v. *Laubach*, 73 Penn. 389.

779. On a refusal by a vendee to accept goods sold him, the measure of damages is the difference between the contract and the market price at the time of refusal.

Where the contract is that the vendee may rescind the contract, the vendor to pay back the price, or the contract is rescinded by the vendee by reason of inherent vice; the measure of damages is the price paid and interest. *Laubach* v. *Laubach*, 73 Penn. 389.

RETROSPECTIVE.

780. Retrospective Operation *of Statutes of Limitation.*—Act 145 of 1871 amended the statute of limitations so as to run against Canadian as well as domestic creditors, but allowed one year from time when the act would take effect for bringing suit on all claims ; that it would otherwise bar action, because it clearly fixed the date of limitation. *Krone* v. *Krone*, 37 Mich. 308.

REVIVOR.

781. Revivor of Debt.—Where a note and mortgage are once barred, a subsequent revivor of the note by a part payment, promise, or acknowledgment of the payer, will revive the mortgage so far as it affects the interests of the payor in the mortgaged premises. But such revivor of the note will not revive the mortgage as against a grantee in the mortgaged premises prior to the revivor of the note. In case of a note and mortgage, the latter being merely an incident to and security for the former, the mortgage is not barred until the note is. *Schmucker, et al.* v. *Sibert, Assignee*, 18 Kansas, 104.

SALE.

782. Sales.—A "dealer" is one who makes successive sales as a business. A single sale in gross of a stock of liquors, without license as a wholesale liquor dealer, is not an illegal sale avoiding a note given therefor. *Overall* v. *Bezeau*, 37 Mich. 506.

782½. Sale of Goods.—*Contract.*—*Fraud.*—*False Pretences.*—*Pawning of Property.*—The purchaser of a chattel takes it, as a general rule, subject to what may turn out to be informalities in the title. By a purchase in market overt the title obtained is good against all the world. If not so purchased, though purchased *bona fide*, the title obtained may not be good against the real owner. Where the original owner has parted with the chattel to A. upon a de facto contract, though there may be circumstances which enable that owner to set aside that contract, the *bona fide* purchaser from A. will obtain an indefeasible title. The question, therefore, in many cases will be, was there a contract between the original owner and the intermediate person. *Cundy* v. *Lindsay*, Eng. Law Reports, 41–42, Vic. 3 App. Cases, 459.

783. Sale under the guise of a renting of personal property passes the title to the property to the vendee. When the transaction shows a sale it does not matter whether the parties intended the title to pass or not. The sale being completed by an agreement as to price and terms of payment, and delivery of possession to the vendee, the law, in furtherance of public policy and to prevent frauds, will treat the title as being where the nature of the transaction requires it should be. *Greer* v. *Church & Co.*, 13 Bush, Ky. 430.

784. Parties considering sale complete as to price and delivery, title passes; otherwise not. *Flanders & Huguenin* v. *Maynard*, 58 Ga. 56.

785. While it is true that it is essential to a sale that both parties should consent to it, yet the consent of the former owner need not be expressly given, but may be inferred from the circumstances of the transaction. *Ketchum* v. *Duncan*, 96 U. S. S. Ct. 659.

786. **Sale of Chattels.**—A vendor of goods and chattels who is induced by fraudulent means to part with his property under color of a contract of purchase may disaffirm the sale and reclaim the property. In such case no title passes to the fraudulent vendee, even though delivery be made; nor will execution creditors, or purchasers, or mortgagees from the fraudulent vendee, acquire a title superior to that of the original vendor, unless they be purchasers or mortgagees *bona fide* and for a valuable consideration. *Williamson* v. *N. J. Southern R. R. Co.*, 29 N. J. Eq. 311.

786½.—In replevin of whiskey, brought by A. against C., there was evidence that A. sold the goods in Cincinnati to B., who did business in Boston; that, by the terms of the agreement, the whiskey was to be delivered and re-gauged on the cars at Cincinnati, and, on receipt of an invoice of the whiskey, B. was to send to A. at New York his promissory note for the price, on three months' time, dated at Cincinnati as of the date of the delivery on the cars, and an invoice and a form of a note dated at Cincinnati, on ninety days, were sent to B. ; that B. did not sign this note, but pledged the goods to C. for a valuable consideration, failed in business, and two days afterwards sent a note to A. in New York, dated at Boston, and payable three months after date; that A. replevined the whiskey in Boston on the day the note arrived in New York, and two days afterwards tendered the note to B. in Boston, who refused to receive it. *Held*, that the evidence would warrant the jury in finding that the sale was upon a condition which was broken, and that there had been no waiver of the condition; and that, if so, B. acquired no title to the goods which he could transfer to C. *Armour* v. *Pecker*, 123 Mass. 143.

787. **Personal Property.**—*Purchase of one in Possession.*—Possession of personal property is not title. It is *prima facie* evidence of title, but nothing more, and will not protect one who buys on the faith of it against the holder of the title. *Ketchum* v. *Cummings*, 53 Miss. 596.

787½. A sale of goods in the hands of a bailee is good against an execution-creditor, if the vendor do not retake possession. *Worman* v. *Kramer*, 73 Penn. 378.

788. Faust's property was about to be sold by the sheriff; an attorney by arrangement with Faust and a judgment-creditor agreed to buy it for Faust; under this it was struck down to the attorney; it was afterwards agreed that Haas, another judgment-creditor, whom the proceeds would reach, should pay the purchase-money to the sheriff, take the deed and give Faust a time named to repay him. Under this arrangement the deed was made to Haas under the direction of the purchaser; Haas claimed to hold the property: *Held*, that he was trustee *ex maleficio* for Faust. Where artifice or trick are resorted to to procure property at sheriff's sale at an under value, the purchaser

takes as trustee for person misled. *Faust* v. *Haas*, 73 Penn. St. 295.

789. A sale of goods which is not accompanied by immediate delivery, and followed by actual and continued change of possession, as required by section 14 of Statute of Frauds, R. S. 339, is void as against the creditors of the vendor. *McCraw* v. *Welch*, 2 Colorado, 284.

790. Where a creditor, who has bought certain movables from his debtor, by crediting the latter on his account with the price of the movables, instantly resells the property to the debtor, the sale will be valid, as between them, whether any delivery was made to the creditor or not. *Edward J. Gay & Co.* v. *Crichlow & Donelson, et al.*, 29 La. 122.

791. **Implied Warranty.**—*Latent defect.*—The vendor of an article sold for a particular purpose does not impliedly warrant it against latent defects to him unknown, and caused by the unskillfulness or negligence of the manufacturer or previous owner, except where the sale is in itself equivalent to an affirmation that the article has certain inherent qualities inconsistent with the alleged defects. *Bragg* v. *Morrill*, 49 Rowell, Vt. p. 45.

792. On a sale of personal property by a debtor, there must be a real, permanent delivery and change of possession, to enable the purchaser to hold the same against an officer levying an execution upon it for the debt of the vendor. *Allen* v. *Carr*, 85 Ill. 388.

793. **Conditional.**—A sale and delivery of goods, on condition that the property is not to vest until the purchase-money is paid or secured, does not pass the title to the vendee until the condition is performed. *Aultman* v. *Mallory*, 5 Neb. 178.

794. **Warranty.**—*Implied Acceptance.*—Representations by the vendor, of the quality of the thing sold or of its fitness for a particular purpose, intended as a part of the contract of sale and relied upon by the vendee, constitute a contract of warranty. And when

there is such contract, the vendee has a right of action, by proving the contract and its breaches, and is under no obligation to return the property or to give notice of its defects; his retention and use of it, and neglect to give notice of its defects, being material only upon the question of damages. The court charged that if plaintiff kept it longer than was reasonably necessary to inspect and vest it in the respect counted upon, without giving notice of any defect, he had impliedly accepted it. *Richardson* v. *Grandy, et al.*, 49 Rowell, Vt. 22.

SATISFACTION.

795. Satisfaction.—Payment of part of a debt without release under seal, although received in full satisfaction, will not discharge the debt. *Hartman* v. *Danner*, 74 Penn. St. 36.

SAVINGS BANK.

796. Savings Bank.—*Loss of Deposit Book.*—A depositor in a savings bank, one of whose by-laws, contained in his deposit book, provides that, "as the officers of the institution may be unable to identify every depositor, the institution will not be responsible for any loss sustained, when a depositor has not given notice of his book being stolen or lost, if such book be paid in whole or part, on presentation," cannot maintain an action against the bank for an amount which, in good faith and without notice that the book had been stolen, it paid to a person who, fraudulently personating the depositor, presented the book and obtained the amount. *Goldrick* v. *Bristol County Savings Bank*, 123 Mass. 320.

SECURITIES.

797. Securities.—*Stolen.*—The owner of negotiable securities which have been stolen may follow them and reclaim them, in whose hands soever they may be found: and when shown that the securities had been stolen from the owner, the burden is upon the holder to show that he took them in the usual course of business and for value. *Robinson* v. *Hodgson*, 73 Penn. St. 202.

In trover for such securities, merely showing that they were in possession of another from whom defendant or his immediate bailor received them is not a defence. *Id.*

A holder's possession is *prima facie* evidence of ownership, because the presumption is that it was honestly acquired. *Id.*

SECURITY.

798. Security.—*Confession of Judgment by Principal.*—A confession of judgment by a principal, has on the surety only the force of a private agreement between the principal and his creditor. Even after a judgment against the principal, any agreement made with him by the creditor, without the assent of the surety, which defers payment, or in any wise impairs the recourse of the surety against the principal, will discharge the surety. *Allison* v. *Thomas & Rosenfeld*, 29 La. 732.

799. Security.—When the owner of a note holds collateral security for the same, the release of such security does not discharge a surety upon the note, if such release was given at the surety's instance and with his consent. *Pence* v. *Gale*, 20 Minn. 257.

SET-OFF.

800. Set-off.—H., being indebted to W. on a note under seal for $109, took from a third party an assignment of a note of W. for $58.83, with the knowledge of W., and with the understanding between the parties that it would be credited against the note for $109. *Held*, that the equity to such credit attached to the note for $109, and followed it into the hands of an assignee, though without notice. *Hall* v. *Hickman*, 2 Del. 318; also *Oliver*, use of *Griffith* v. *Lowry*, 2 Harring. 467.

801. Under the Gen. Statute, c. 130, sec. 3, a demand for money paid cannot be set off unless it is a sum that is liquidated, or one that may be ascertained by calculation. *Taft* v. *Larkin*, 123 Mass. 598.

802. Debts are not mutual when one is by the defendants as principal and surety, to the plaintiff as trustee for a minor, and the other is by plaintiff as an individual to the defendants as partners. *Vason, et al.* v. *Reall, Trustee*, 58 Ga. 500.

803. The assignee of a mortgage, unless the mortgagor has estopped himself, holds it subject to all the equities to which it was liable in the hands of the assignor.

The mortgagor having given a certificate that he has no defence, is estopped from setting up a defence against an assignee.

804. Any subsequent assignee may avail himself of a certificate of "no defence," given to the first, if he shows that he or a prior one under whom he claims, was an assignee for value without notice.

805. Burns, through an agent of a trust company, borrowed from them on a note and assigned stocks, &c., as collateral; the agent borrowed from Ashton, and afterwards took an assignment of Burns's note and collaterals. *Held*, that Ashton took the collaterals subject to the equities between Burns and the company. *Ashton's Appeal*, 73 Penn. 153.

806. Set-off.—Whenever a demand is for damages, which the law is capable of measuring accurately by a pecuniary standard, it is a proper subject of set-off under our statutes. *Sledge* v. *Swift, Murphy & Co.*, 53 Ala. 110.

807. The right of set-off in an action is governed by the law of the place where the action is brought. In an action brought in Ohio by the endorser against the maker of a promissory note, paya-

ble to order, executed in Kentucky, and endorsed before due, the maker cannot set-off a debt due to him from the payee, notwithstanding the Kentucky statute, which declares such notes, "assignable so as to vest the right of action in the assignee," but provides that such assignment shall not "impair the right to any . . . off-set the defendant has or might have used" against the payee. *Second Nat. Bank of Cincinnati v. Hemingray*, 31 Ohio, 168.

808. A set-off may be pleaded in an action brought by a receiver of an insolvent national bank. Where usurious interest is reserved or charged on a note or bill discounted by a national bank, the entire interest reserved or charged will, in an action on the note or bill, be adjudged forfeited. *Hade v. McVay, Allison & Co.*, 31 Ohio, 231.

809. **Deposits in Bank.**—A voluntary assignee allowed certain bank deposits to remain in the name of the assignor, and without bringing suit for them, after the maturity of notes held by the bank on which the assignor was liable as endorser: *Held*, that the bank could retain the deposits in set-off against the notes, as by Gen. Stat. R. I. cap. 202, sec. 14, the right of set-off is determined by the state of the claims at "the time of the commencement of the action." *Nightingale v. Chafee*, 11 R. I. 609.

810. **Legacy and Legatee.**—A legacy, presently payable, cannot be set-off in equity against a debt of the legatee to the estate, not yet due. *Hayes, Adm'r v. Hayes*, 2 Del. 191.

811. **Of Debt due the Former.**—In a suit against a party and his sureties, a debt or demand due from the plaintiff to the principal defendant may be set-off. *Himrod, et al. v. Baugh*, 85 Ill. 435.

812. **Nominal Partners.**—*Demand against one.* — A demand against one person cannot be set-off against him and his nominal partner in a suit by them on a note made to the firm. A set-off must be against all the partners. *Jones v. Howard*, 53 Miss. 707.

813. **Partnership.**—Where a surviving partner purchases from the administrator of his deceased partner the interest of the latter in the partnership property, as assets of the estate, he cannot, in a suit to collect the purchase-money, set off a debt due him from such decedent in his lifetime, even if such set-off grew out of a settlement of partnership matters. *Welborn* v. *Coon*, 57 Ind. 270.

SHAREHOLDERS.

814. **Liabilities.**—Certain shares in a company incorporated by letters patent, issued under 27 and 28 Vict. ch. 23, were allotted, by a resolution passed at a special general meeting of the shareholders, to themselves, in proportion to the number of shares held by them at that time, at 40 per cent. discount, deducted from their nominal value, and scrip issued for them as fully paid up. G., under this arrangement, was allotted nine shares, which were subsequently assigned to the appellant for value as fully paid up shares, and he accepted them in good faith as such, and a year afterwards became a director in the company. The shares appeared as fully paid up on the certificates of transfer, whilst on each counterfoil in the sharebook the amount mentioned was "Shares, two, at $300=$600." *Held*, reversing the judgment of the Court of Appeal for Ontario, that a person purchasing in good faith, without notice, from an original shareholder, under 22 and 28 Vict., ch. 23, as shares fully paid up, is not liable to an execution-creditor of the company whose execution has been returned *nulla bona*, for the amount unpaid upon the shares. (The Chief Justice and Ritchie, J., dissenting.) *McCraken* v. *McIntyre*, 1 Canada S. C. 479.

SIGNATURE.

815. **Signature.**—*Held*, that the genuineness of the signature to or endorsement of a note ceases to be pre-

sumed the moment the defendant denies it in his pleas supported by affidavit, and the plaintiff must make proof of the same; and that in the present case the plaintiffs were guilty of neglect in accepting the note without sufficient caution. *Dorwin, et al.* v. *Thompson*, 3 C. L. J. 130, S. C. 1867, Ca.

816. **Proof of.**—If a defendant by exception admits his signature to a note of hand, and plead a term for payment, it is not necessary for the plaintiff to prove the signature, even though the exception be dismissed and there is a *defense en fait*. *Vallieres* v. *Roy*, 2 Rev. de Leg. 335, K. B. 1820; 1223 C. C. & 145 C. C. P. Ca.

817. **Signature on Check Forged.**—A dealer with a bank trusting to his clerk's report that his bank book was correct, omitted to examine it, and did not discover that checks, forged in his name by the clerk, had been paid by the bank, charged in the book, and cancelled, and returned with it, until some months after their payment: *Held*, that he was not estopped from denying the genuineness of the checks. *Weisser* v. *Denison*, 10 N. Y. Ct. of App., 1854 (6 Seld.), 68.

818. **Signature; Genuineness of.**—*How proven.* — Standards of comparison, to be used by experts upon the trial of an issue as to the genuineness of a signature when not a paper already in the case or admitted to be genuine, are not admissible for that purpose, unless they are clearly proved by witnesses who testify directly to their having been written by the party whose signature is in question.

819. Where a receipt was offered as such standard of comparison, and a witness testified that the defendant gave him a receipt that looked very similar to the one offered, but that he could not positively say it was the identical one offered in evidence: *Held*, that the evidence was too uncertain to warrant the admission of the paper as a standard of comparison. *Pavey* v. *Pavey*, 30 Ohio, 600.

820. In an action by the endorsees of a promissory note against the alleged makers, in which the defendants by their plea denied their signature, *Held*, confirming courts below, on evidence that one of the firm by whom the note purported to be signed had therein admitted that the signature was that of the firm, and had been written by himself, that as there was no clear and legal proof of want of genuineness in the signature the admission could not be set aside on mere presumption arising from knowledge of the maker's handwriting, and also that another promissory note signed by the firm could not be sued for the purpose of creating a standard of comparison of handwriting, such signature not having been itself established to be genuine. *Reid, et al.* v. *Warner*, 17 L. C. R., 485, Q. B. 1867, Ca.

821. Verification of.—Where the signature to a bill or note is denied, experts may be appointed on motion of one of the parties, and their report promulgated as conclusive. *Lord* v. *Laurin, et al.*, 9 L. C. J. 171, and 15 L. C. R. 452, C. C. 1865, 322 *et seq.* C. C. P. Ca.

STATED ACCOUNT.

822. Stated Accounts were given in an answer in equity, and the benefit thereof claimed as if pleaded. They were supported by sufficient evidence. *Held*, the burden of proof was on the party impugning the accuracy of the accounts. *Seamans* v. *Burt*, 11 R. I. 320.

823. What constitutes, is a matter of evidence. Setting down a plea of, for argument, is equivalent to a demurrer. *Allen* v. *Woonsocket Co.*, 11 R. I. 288.

824. The fact that a balance is shown in an account and claimed in a suit, does not make it less an open account. The term "open account" is used in contradistinction to a stated account, wherein the account is closed by an assent to its correctness by the party charged. *Whittlesey* v. *Spofford*, 47 Texas, 13.

STATUTE OF LIMITATIONS.

825. Statute of Limitations.—A promise by M. that "he would see his brother and would pay the debt," sufficient to remove the bar of the statute of limitations. A promise relied on to avoid the statute of limitations, made to an attorney, is in law a promise made to the principal, and can be declared on as such. *Kirby* v. *Mills*, 78 N. C. 124.

826. Residence and not citizenship is contemplated in the statute prescribing limitations upon the time of bringing actions, and the statute runs in favor of a debtor who has his domicile in the State. The statute ceases to run when the debtor becomes a non-resident, but revives upon his demise. *Savage* v. *Scott, et al.*, 45 Iowa, 130.

827. Part payment of the consideration of a parol promise not to be performed within the year, does not withdraw the agreement from the operation of the statute. *Reinheimer* v. *Carter*, 31 Ohio, 579.

828. The statute of limitations in force where the remedy is sought, and not that existing where the contract was made, must govern the remedy. *Sampson* v. *Sampson*, 63 Me. 329.

829. Statute of limitations runs against an infant having only color of title to the land. *Soule* v. *Barlow*, 49 Rowell, Vt. 329.

830. Statute of limitations can apply to future transactions only, unless they are expressly given effect on previous transactions, or unless some of their terms cannot be met otherwise. *Perrin* v. *Kellogg*, 36 Mich. 316.

830½. A credit upon an account after the cause of action on the same is barred by the statute of limitations, will not be treated as part payment thereof, unless shown to have been so intended by the parties. *Kaufman* v. *Broughton*, 31 Ohio, 424.

831. Accrual of, After statute begins to run.—Where the statute of limitations has begun to run during the life of the devisor, no disability in the devisee will arrest it. *Bozeman, et al.* v. *Browning, et al.*, 31 Ark. 364.

832. Under the Gen. Sts. c. 155, sec. 14, a payment of interest on a promissory note by the principal does not take the debt out of the statute of limitations as against a surety. *Faulkner* v. *Bailey*, 123 Mass. 588.

833. Part payment upon a bond made by the administrator of one of the joint makers within the statutory period will prevent the running of the statute of limitations in favor of the remainder. *The County of Vernon to use of School Fund* v. *Stewart*, 64 Mo. 408.

834. **Statute of Limitations** begins to run on an administrator's bond from the expiration of four and a half years after issuing letters of administration. *Biddle* v. *Wendell*, 37 Mich. 452.

835. Plaintiff, in order to remove the bar of the statute of limitations, having shown that defendants were non-residents of the State wherein the cause of action accrued, it was *held*, that the burden was on defendants to show that they had owned attachable property within the State. *Rixford* v. *Miller, et al.*, 49 Rowell, Vt. 319.

836. If money is loaned, to be repaid on demand, and no note or obligation is given in writing to repay it, the statute of limitations commences running from the time of the loan. When the statute of limitations holds, the debt cannot be revived, except by a promise in writing signed by the debtor. *Estate of Galvin*, 51 Cal. 215.

837. A payment by one of several makers of a joint and several promissory note, were in fact partners when they signed the note, will take it out of the statute of limitations as to the others, if the note be a partnership debt, and the payment made out of partnership funds. *Mix* v. *Shattuck, et al.*, 50 Vt. 421.

838. Payments made by the treasurer of a partnership from partnership funds, and by him endorsed on

a partnership note, take the note out of the statute of limitations, in the absence of any showing that he acted without authority and without duty. *Walker v. Wait, et al.*, 50 Vt. 668.

839. A partial payment of a debt, replied to the statute of limitations, raises only a *prima facie* presumption that such payment is an admission of continued indebtedness. *Strong v. The State, ex rel. &c.*, 57 Ind. 428.

840. In an action on account for money loaned, where the six years' statute of limitation is pleaded, a reply that such money is part of a mutual running account, remaining unsettled, and extending up to the time of bringing the action, is sufficient on demurrer. *Harper v. Harper*, 57 Ind. 547.

841. **As to Married Women.**—Since the passage of the Married Woman's Act of 1861, the statute of limitations runs against a married woman the same a against a *feme sole*. The expression in *Morrison v. Norman*, 47 Ill. 477, and *Noble v. McFarland*, 51 Ill. 226, to the effect that the Married Woman's Act of 1861 has no effect upon the saving clause in the limitation laws, is overruled. *Cortner, et al. v. Walrod*, 83 Ill. 171.

842. The payment by the principal, year by year, of the interest on a joint and several promissory note, will prevent the statute of limitations from attaching to the note in favor of the surety. The rule on this subject, laid down in *Ellicott v. Nicols*, 7 Gill, 86, has been the accepted law of his State for nearly thirty years, and in the absence of legislation to the contrary, it is not to be questioned. *Schindel v. Gates*, 46 Md. 604.

843. An acknowledgment of a debt, made not to the creditor, but to a stranger, does not avoid the running of the statute of limitations. *Schmucker v. Sibert*, 18 Kansas, 104.

844. The presumption that a bond has been paid which arises after a lapse of twenty years, has not been changed or abolished by the passage of the act of limitation to suits on bonds. Such presumption is not

a legal bar; it is a presumption of fact which must be held to be conclusive, unless rebutted by evidence showing satisfactorily that the bond has not been paid, or furnish good and sufficient reasons why longer forbearance has been given. *Hale, et al. v. Park's ex'r.*, 10 West Va. 145.

845. A promise by a member of a late partnership, made after dissolution and before a suit is barred by the statute of limitations, to pay a partnership debt, will not prevent the running of the statute so as to estop the other partner from availing himself of the defence of the statute as against the original cause of action; and this whether the creditor was aware of the dissolution or not. *Tate v. Clements*, 16 Florida, 339.

846. In order to obtain the benefit of the statute of limitations, a defendant must insist on it as a bar to his answer. If, instead of so doing, he simply denies the allegations of the petition, he cannot, upon the trial, also insist upon the bar of the statute. *Townsley v. Moore*, 30 Ohio, 184.

847. A debt was due October 6th, 1862; suit was brought October 6th, 1868. *Held*, not barred by the statute. When suit is brought within six years after the day on which the cause of action arose, that day is to be excluded from the computation. *Menges v. Foick*, 73 Penn. St.137.

848. The receipt for nine hundred dollars, borrowed, to be returned "when called for," created a cause of action from its date, and against it the statute ran from the time of its execution. The mere removal of a debtor, without communicating to his creditor the place of his new domicile, does not constitute such a fraud as will stop the running of the statute. *Eborn v. Zimpelman* 47 Texas, 503.

849. The act of 1868, ch. 357, provides, that "In actions hereafter brought, where a party has a cause of action of which he has been kept in ignorance by the fraud of the adverse party, the right to bring the suit shall be deemed to have first accrued at the time at

which such fraud shall, or with usual and ordinary diligence might have been known and discovered." *Held*, 1st. That it was not thereby meant that in all cases a party must commit a fraud *distinct* from, and *independent* of the original fraud, for the purpose of keeping the injured party in ignorance of his cause of action, nor that the mere concealment of the fraud is insufficient. 2d. That where one practices fraud to the injury of another, the *subsequent concealment* of it from the injured party is *in itself a fraud*, and if he is thereby kept in ignorance of his cause of action, he is kept in ignorance by "the fraud of the adverse party." *Wear* v. *Skinner*, 46 Md. 257.

850. To remove the bar of the statute of limitation, plaintiff introduced a letter from defendant, in which defendant "in regard to settlement, that he was ready any day after that week, and willing to leave it out to be settled, but that he thought it would be better to settle it themselves, if they could," and that he did not see where plaintiff got his statement of what had been put upon the farm; and asked when plaintiff would "look the business over." *Held*, that the letter was an admission of the existence of an unsettled account, and an expression of willingness to settle it, unaccompanied by an expression of unwillingness to pay the balance that might be found due, and that it took plaintiff's claim out of the statute. *Bliss* v. *Allard*, 49 Rowell, Vt. 350.

STOCK AND STOCKHOLDERS.

851. **Stock.**—As between a corporation and corporator, the stock-book is evidence of their relation; the certificate is secondary evidence. Assignment of a certificate is only an equitable transfer, and must be produced to the corporation and a transfer made. *Bank of Commerce's Appeal*, 73 Penn. St. 59.

852. **Stock Pledge.**—Stock was pledged as collateral for a note; the pledgee took a mortgage as further security; the stock at the time was of greater value than

the amount of the mortgage; the pledgee had not the stock during the pledge, so as to re-deliver on redemption. The mortgage was to be credited with the value of stock when executed. *Ashton's Appeal*, 73 Penn. 143.

853. **Stock.**—An agreement for a valuable consideration by A. to purchase from or sell to B., at the option of the latter, a certain number of shares of stock within a limited time at a specified price, is not *per se* a gaming contract. An illegal intent will not be presumed; and in the absence of proof that the parties were merely speculating upon the fluctuations in the price of the stock, without any intent that A. should deliver or accept, but simply should pay differences, the contract is valid and may be enforced. *Story v. Soloman*, 71 N. Y. 420.

854. **Stock Brokers.**—*Agreement to carry Stock on Margin.—Right to Sell when Margin not kept good.—Evidence as to Circumstances under which written Instrument was executed.—Nonsuit.*—It is competent for a party to show any facts and circumstances surrounding the making of a contract, which would enable the jury to determine the subject-matter to which the contract was in fact applicable. It is an elementary rule of construction that every written instrument should be interpreted in the light of the circumstances surrounding its execution, and it is error for the court to exclude evidence of the circumstances under which the instrument was executed. It is only where there is no evidence in law, which, if believed, will sustain a verdict, that the court is called upon to nonsuit. *Bickett v. Taylor*, 55 Howard, N. Y. 126.

855. **Stockholder.**—If any one stockholder is required to pay debt due by the corporation, he is entitled to contribution from all the other stockholders whose subscriptions are unpaid. If any stockholder who has not paid up his subscription claims to be a creditor of the corporation, his unpaid stock is liable for the debt, and he cannot recover from another stock-

holder the full extent of his claim. By the act of 1872, ch. 325, sec. 59, all the stockholders of a corporation are severally and individually liable to the creditors of the corporation of which they are stockholders, to an amount equal to any unpaid subscription held by them respectively. *Weber* v. *Fickey*, 47 Md. 196.

856. A person is presumed to be the owner of stock when his name appears on the books of a company as a stockholder; and, when he is sued as such, the burden of disproving that presumption is cast upon him. *Turnbull* v. *Payson*, 95 U. S. 418.

857. A party who made a contract with an organization which had attempted irregularly to create itself into a corporation, and which acted as such, or who subscribed to its capital stock, cannot, in a suit by the corporation, defend himself against a claim growing out of such contract or subscription, by alleging the irregularity of such organization. *Chubb* v. *Upton*, 95 U. S. 665.

858. A subscriber to the capital stock of a railroad corporation, who has failed to pay for the shares subscribed for, as required by the terms of his subscription, is properly chargeable with interest from the time of the default, and cannot compel the company to issue the stock until not only the principal but the interest is paid. *Gould* v. *Town of Oneonta*, 26 Sickels (71 N. Y.) 298.

859. **Stockholder.**—*As a debtor restrained from transferring his stock.*—Under articles of association which had been adopted as part of the charter of the bank it was provided that so long as a stockholder might remain indebted to the bank, his stock should not be transferable. *Held*, that the defendant was not liable in damages for refusing to permit the endorser, while still remaining liable on his endorsement, to transfer his stock on the books of the bank. *McDowell* v. *Bank of N. & B.*, 2 Del. 1.

860. **Stockholders.**—*Liability of, for Corporation Debts.*—The Michigan Statute (Comp. L. sec. 2852)

does not make individual stockholders primarily liable for corporation debts. The liability of a stockholder for a corporation is discharged by the creditors' extending the time and accepting the note of the corporation. *Hanson* v. *Donkersley*, 37 Mich. 184.

SUBROGATION.

861. Subrogation.—*How and to what extent allowed.—Principal and security.—Complaint.—Demurrer.—* It seems to be a settled rule of equity that if A. owes B. and he and C. are bound for it, and A. gives C. a mortgage or bond to indemnify him, B. shall have the benefit of it to recover his debt. But a private arrangement as to liability of securities, as between themselves, comes neither within the rule nor the principle upon which it rests.

862. The complaint alleged that the plaintiffs, who are bankers, issued letters of credit to the Atlantic De Laine Co. Hoyt, Sprague & Co. guaranteed to plaintiffs that the De Laine Co. would keep its contract, and in default thereof H., S. & Co. would hold plaintiffs harmless of loss. E. H., who was a partner of the firm of H., S. & Co., guaranteed to his said firm the payment of any and all sums of money which should remain due and owing to said H., S. & Co. after all the property of the Atlantic De Laine Co. should have been applied to the payment of the debts of said Co., the intention of said guaranty being to secure to H., S. & Co. the payment in full of any ascertained balance of account due them by said Atlantic De Laine Co., and in case of his death his personal representatives were to pay such ascertained balance, for which he would be liable under the above guaranty, without delay, out of his assets in their hands applicable to the payment of his debts. The plaintiffs ask as relief that the balance of account due to H., S. & Co. from the Atlantic De Laine Co. may be ascertained and determined, and that the plaintiffs may be adjudged to be

subrogated to all rights of said H., S. & Co. to collect the said balance so to be ascertained from the executors of E. H., and that said executors be directed to pay the assets in their hands applicable to the payment of the debts of said E. H. to the plaintiffs, to the extent necessary to satisfy their claims and demands. On demurrer to the complaint by the executors of E. H. *Held*, that the action would not lie. E. H. was, in no just sense, a principal. The only principal was the Atlantic De Laine Co. H., S. & Co. were sureties. *Held*, further, that H.'s guaranty was to secure an ascertained balance, and it is only when all the property of the De Laine Co. shall have been applied in payment of its debts that, within the terms of the guaranty, the balance becomes ascertained. *Morgan, et al. v. Francklyn*, 55 Howard, N. Y. 244.

863. **Subrogation of surety by payment.**—A surity who pays the debt of his principal is subrogated to all the remedies of the creditors as against the principal, or others who become liable for the debt. *Talbot, et al. v. Wilkins, et al.*, 31 Ark. 411.

SUNDAY CONTRACTS AND SALES.

864. **Sunday Contracts.**—A written contract made on Sunday, but bearing the date of another day of the week, may be transferred, and will be enforced in the hands of a transferee in good faith and without notice. *Johns v. Bailey, et al.*, 45 Iowa, 241.

865. A contract by a livery stable keeper to hire a horse on Sunday, for purposes of business or pleasure, is void; otherwise, if it is for purposes of charity or necessity, etc. *Stewart v. Davis*, 31 Ark. 518.

866. A promissory note or agreement in writing, dated on Sunday, in payment of a horse purchased on the same day, is null and void, under 45 Geo. 3. L. C. R., 221, S. C. 1859. A promissory note, payable to order, may be validly made on the Lord's day, com-

monly called Sunday. *Kearney* v. *Kinch, et al.*, 7 L. C. J., 31 S. C. 1862.

868. The defendant sold a horse to the plaintiff on Sunday; the plaintiff gave his bank check for the price of the horse on the same day; the defendant at the same time deposited a bill of sale of the horse with a third person, to be delivered to the plaintiff when the check was paid; the check was paid, and the horse and bill of sale were delivered, all on a secular day afterwards. *Held*, that an action of assumpsit to recover back the price paid for the horse on account of a deceit practiced in the sale would not lie, because based upon a transaction tainted with illegality. *Plaisted* v. *Palmer*, 63 Me. 576.

SURETIES AND SURETY.

868. **Sureties,** not having paid the debt for which they are bound, are not creditors of their principal. The surety's liability for his principal is not a valuable consideration, as against creditors of the principal, for a bond conditioned for the payment of a sum of money as a debt. *Jefferson* v. *Tunnell, et al.*, 2 Del. 135.

869. **Contribution from Estate of Co-surety.**—A., B. and C. were co-sureties; C. died, and A. and B. were forced to pay the debt after the administration on the estate of C. had been settled, and more than two years after the grant of letters. *Held*, that they could subject assets descended to the heir to contribution. *Williams, et al.* v. *Ewing & Fanning*, 31 Ark. 229.

870. **Sureties.**—The sureties on a joint and several bond, given by them with A. and B. as principals, to dissolve the plaintiff's attachment of "the goods and estate of the said A. and B.," the condition of which is that A. and B. shall pay to the plaintiff "the amount, if any, which he shall recover in such action." are not discharged by the discontinuance of the action as to A. *Poole* v. *Dyer*, 123 Mass. 363.

871. 1st. To entitle a surety to an assignment and

execution against his co-sureties under sec. 7 of art. 9 of the Code, vol. 1, it is incumbent upon him not only to satisfy the judgment, but to pay the *whole* amount of it. *Wilson, et al., Adm'rs* v. *Ridgely, et al.,* 46 Md. 235.

2d. Whilst it is an undoubted proposition that the liability of the surety is not to be extended by implication beyond the terms of his written contract, by which his responsibility is to be measured, the bond constituting such contract must have such construction given to it as to carry out the intention of the parties thereto, and in this respect there is no difference between such contract and any other. *Engler* v. *People's Fire Ins. Co.,* 46 Md. 322.

872. Where all the stockholders of a corporation give their joint and several note, for money loaned to it, they are co-sureties as between themselves, in proportion to the relative amounts of stock owned by them respectively. *Coburn* v. *Wheelock,* 34 N. Y. 440; S. C., 42 Barb. 267.

873. A surety paying a judgment against his principal and himself will be substituted to the lien of the judgment upon land in the hands of a *bona fide* purchaser. See Judgments, No. 3, and *Edison* v. *Huff, et al.,* 29 Va. 338.

874. A bond on which the principal and surety are both bound, one paid by the surety in the lifetime of the principal, without assignment by the creditor, or agreement to assign, is forever dead as a security, as well in equity as at law. There can be no subrogation in such a case. *Cromer* v. *Cromer's Adm'rs,* 29 Va. 280.

875. **Surety.**—Where one person becomes surety for the payment of money by another, who is himself a surety for a third person, they are not co-sureties; and on payment of the principal obligation by the first surety, the secondary one is discharged. *Remington* v. *Staats,* 1 S. C. 394.

876. Where a party, when asked to sign a note,

as surety, refuses unless another person will first execute the same, and the principal maker forges the name of such other person, and thereby induces the party to sign, and procures money of an innocent party who has no notice of the fraud, the fact of the forgery and the fraud will not release the surety so executing the same. The case of *Seely* v. *The People, &c.*, 27 Ill. 173, is departed from so far as it conflicts with the rule as above laid down. *Stoner* v. *Millikin, et al.*, 85 Ill. 218.

877. **Surety on a Promissory Note.**—A verbal notice by a surety on a promissory note to the holder thereof, to proceed at once to collect the note of the principal, and a verbal agreement by said holder so to do, do not waive the notice in writing required by the statute, and a failure to proceed according to the verbal agreement will not operate to release the surety. *Chrisman* v. *Tuttle*, 59 Ind. 155.

878. An extension of the time of payment of a promissory note, upon the consideration that the maker will annually pay interest on the note at the rate stipulated therein, will not release the surety. *Id.*

879. **Surety.**—A surety cannot be held under a judgment void as to his principal. *McCloskey, Bigley & Co.* v. *Wingfield & Bridges*, 29 La. 141.

879½. **Surety—*Released.*—The surety of an administratrix who fails to perform her duties as prescribed by law, has a right to be released from his bond. *Sanders* v. *Adeline Edwards*, 29 La. 696.

880. A mortgage was given to secure the payment of notes; their time of payment was extended by the holders, there being no evidence of a consideration for such extension. *Held*, that this did not discharge the surety. *Zane* v. *Kennedy*, 73 Penn. St. 182.

880½. An agreement without consideration to give time to a debtor is not binding on the creditor, and would not prevent the surety from paying the debt and seeking reimbursement from the principal. *Id.*

881. A surety, who holds several securities by way

of indemnity, may resort to either of them for payment. *Muller* v. *Dows*, 94 U. S. 444-

882. Married Woman. can contract no liability as surety for her husband, nor make a mere personal obligation not connected with, nor charging property, nor bind herself by mere personal promise jointly with her husband, or as his surety. A husband cannot sue his wife at law or in equity to enforce a purely executory contract. *Jenne* v. *Marble*, 37 Mich. 319; *Kitchell* v. *Mudgett, et al.*, 37 Mich. 81.

883. Surety.—Part payment of a debt already due is not a sufficient consideration for an agreement to extend the time for the payment of the residue. *Turnbull* v. *Brock*, 31 Ohio, 649.

884. A surety who takes of the debtor a mortgage for his indemnity as such surety, is to be regarded in equity as a *bona fide* purchaser within this rule, and will be protected to the extent of his liability as surety. Such mortgage executed to one or more of several sureties on the official bond of an officer, inures to the benefit of all the sureties, as well to those who subsequently become such under an order of court requiring "additional sureties" in pursuance of law, as to those who were sureties at the date of the mortgage. *Bank* v. *Teeters*, 31 Ohio, 36.

885. A *bona fide* purchaser of a debtor's land from a fraudulent vendee, without notice of fraud, or of the rights of the creditor, acquires an equity superior to that of a creditor, who obtained a judgment against the debtor, and levied his execution on the land, after the date of the fraudulent sale, and prior to that of the *bona fide* purchaser. *Second National Bank* v. *Teeters*, 31 (De Witt) Ohio, 36.

886 An undertaking by an infant as surety for the stay of execution is not void, but only voidable, and when ratified by him after arriving at majority, becomes a valid and enforceable contract. *Harner* v. *Dipple*, 31 Ohio, 72.

887. Surety or Endorser of a Bankrupt is released from

liability by the bankrupt's payment of the debt to the creditor who accepts payment in fraud of bankruptcy law, without the consent of the surety or endorser, although the assignee of the bankrupt may recover the amount so paid of the creditor. The judgment in favor of the assignee against the creditor establishes conclusively that the payment was accepted, with implied notice of the bankrupt's insolvency and of his intention to defraud the bankrupt. act. *Northern Bank of Ky.* v. *Cooke,* 13 Bush, Ky. 340.

888. **Surety.**—A security taken by one of several co-sureties, to indemnify him against the joint liability, inures to the benefit of all. *Elwood* v. *Deifendorf,* 5 Barb. 398.

889. Where one of two co-sureties pays the debt of their principal, and obtains an assignment of a mortgage held by the creditor as collateral security, which he subsequently forecloses, and himself becomes the purchaser of the mortgaged premises for a nominal sum, his co-surety is only entitled to have the fair cash value of the premises, on the day of sale, credited on the original debt; he has no interest in the lands. A commission of five per cent. and the expenses of foreclosure, are proper items of deduction from the value of the mortgaged premises. *Livingston* v. *Van Rensselaer,* 6 Wend. 63.

890. If the surety does not assent to an alteration of the terms of his undertaking, it ceases, when materially altered, to be his contract, and has thenceforward no more force as to him than if the whole writing had been a forgery, unless it has previously become effectual by delivery, and the alterations be made by a stranger. *Blakey* v. *Johron,* 13 Bush, Ky. 197.

891. A surety after judgment continues for most, if not for all purposes, a mere surety, and is entitled to demand the same good faith on the part of the plaintiff as before judgment. *Kouns* v. *Bank of Ky.,* 2 B. Mon. Ky. 303. Also *Hughes's adm'r* v. *Hardesty,* 13 Bush, Ky. 364.

892. A surety, against whom judgment has been rendered, may offset, against an assignee of the judgment, whatever claims he may have purchased against the plaintiff in the judgment, in good faith, without notice of the assignment. *Townsend* v. *Quinan*, 47 Texas, 1.

893. A surety cannot benefit by an exception personal to the principal. *Jordan & Co.* v. *Anderson*, 29 La. 749.

894. The mere neglect of a privileged creditor to sue will not release the surety of the debtor, even to the extent of the value of the privilege held by the creditor, unless it be proved that in consequence of such neglect, the privilege was lost. *J. D. Hill & Co.* v. *Mrs. Bourcier, et al.*, 29 La. 841.

895. In an action on a bond against a surety, judgment having been obtained against the principal, he is a competent witness for the surety. Although there was an expectation by a surety, by the statements of the principal when a bond was signed, that there was to be another surety, the bond was binding on the one signing although not executed by the other. The principal owed a note, which, being due, he procured a surety on another in payment of the first. The surety signed it in blank, gave it to the principal to fill up. and use it in payment of the first note. *Held*, that thereby the surety made the principal his agent to complete the note. The surety could not relieve himself from liability to the obligee who took the note *bona fide* for a valuable consideration, by showing that his instructions as to filling up the note were not followed, The surety having created confidence by putting the note in blank into the principal's hands, must suffer the loss as between himself and another innocent party. *Simpson* v. *Bovard*, 74 Penn. St. Repts. 351.

896. **Promissory Notes.**—*Signature of, on faith of that of co-surety, which proves to be forged.*—A surety upon a bond will not be discharged from liability by the fact that the name of a co-surety, on the faith of

which his signature has been procured, was a forgery, nor by the fact that the surety whose name was forged gave him no information of the fact, where the condition upon which the surety signed is unknown to the officer to whom the bond is given, at the time he accepts the same. *State, et al. Brown* v. *Baker, et al.*, 64 Mo. 167 ; *State, et al.* v. *Potter*, 63 Mo. 212.

897. Judgment was rendered against one of the makers of a promissory note, who appealed to the court of common pleas, where the plaintiff again recovered. The undertaking of the surety was to pay any judgment rendered against appellant. *Held*, that the surety is liable, notwithstanding another maker of the note was made a party in the appellate court, and judgment was rendered against both makers. *Helt* v. *Whittier*, 31 Ohio, 475.

898. **Release.**—An agreement between the payee and principal of a note, for the extension of the time of its payment for a fixed and definite period, in consideration of the same rate of interest as that named in the note, is valid, without the payment of the interest in advance, and, if made without the knowledge of the sureties, will discharge them. *Fawcett* v. *Freshwater*, 31 Ohio, 637.

899. **Surety.**—*Release of by Failure to present Debt against Estate of deceased Principal.*—The statute providing that, where the principal maker of a joint note dies, the payee or assignee shall present the same against the estate of the decedent for allowance, and that, upon a failure to do so, the sureties shall be released, is not a mere statute of limitations. On the contrary, the statute forms a part of the contract, upon which the sureties have a right to rely, even in case of a note payable to the trustees of schools ; and if the note is not presented within the time limited by the statute, the sureties will be released. *House* v. *Trustees of Schools*, 83 Ill. 368.

900. **Proceedings.**—Where, in an action on a promissory note against several apparently joint makers, one

of the defendants appear, and, upon default of his co-defendants, and without any notice to them other than the original summons in the cause, alleges and obtains a judgment against them, that they are principals and he a surety only, and asks and obtains a decree that execution be first levied on their property, such judgment and order, as between the defendants, are utterly void for want of proper notice, and will not support a plea of a former adjudication of such matter. *Fletcher* v. *Holmes*, 25 Ind. 458. In *Pattison* v. *Vaughan*, 40 Ind. 253, and *Feutriss* v. *The State, ex rel. etc.*, 44 Ind. 271, appear in conflict, but those decisions were announced overruled by the court in *Joyce, et al.* v. *Whitney, et al.*, 57 Ind. 550. *Held*, further, the complaint of one defendant against another, to establish the alleged suretyship of the former, is not a mere cross-complaint, but is a new and original proceeding which cannot be tried upon the summons issued by the plaintiff. *Id.*

TAXATION.

901. On Corporations.—A profit upon the capital or investment of a corporation, either made or passed to the stockholders without declaration of a dividend, or a dividend declared, becomes the measure of a State tax on dividends. If a dividend be declared, the stock is taxable on the basis of the declaration, and the company is estopped by the declaration whether the dividend be earned or not. *Commonwealth* v. *Pittsburg, Fort Wayne & Chicago Railway Co.*, 74 Penn. St. 83.

902. What Exempt.—Solvent debts, promissory notes and mortgages are not liable to taxation. *People* v. *Hibernia Savings and Loan Society*, 51 Cal. 243; also, *Bank of Mendocino* v. *Chalfant*, 51 Cal. 369.

903. Tax Exemptions.—*Corporations.*—The return of the city tax assessor, setting forth the amount of the taxable capital of a banking corporation, will be held as true, until the contrary has been shown by the bank.

904. When a bank claims that a portion of its capital is invested in United States bonds, stocks, or currency, it must show affirmatively the exact amount of its capital so invested. Otherwise, its capital thus invested will not be exempt from taxation. The mere fact that at various periods during the year the tax is assessed, the bank "held" large amounts in United States currency, will not exempt its capital from taxation to the extent of those amounts, unless the bank proves that the currency so "held" was a part of its capital.

905. **Deposits.**—While the ordinary deposits of United States currency (or national bank notes), in a bank by its customers, enter into, and form a part of its assets, they at the same time create liabilities of the bank, and thus offset themselves as assets. Such deposits, therefore, do not constitute a portion of the capital of a bank, and hence the bank cannot claim that its capital shall be exempt from taxation to the amount of such deposits. The capital of a bank which is subject to taxation, as capital, is made up of the balance of its assets remaining after deducting the debts, that portion of its assets exempt from taxation, and that portion which is taxed under another name as capital.

906. United States currency and national bank notes belonging to a bank, although non-taxable, are a part of its assets, and in ascertaining the real amount of its taxable capital, such currency, and notes, must be held as compensating the debt due depositors, and thus *pro tanto*, extinguishing the liability of the bank. *City of New Orleans* v. *New Orleans Canal & Banking Company*, 29 La. 851.

907. **Tax Sale.**—A tax sale made on a day other than that provided by law confers no title. *McGehee* v. *Martin*, 53 Miss. 519.

908. **Deed on Tax Sale.**—A tax collector's deed, which describes the land conveyed as "200 acres in sec. 2, t. 12, range 1 east," is void, for uncertainty in the description. *Yandell* v. *Pugh*, 53 Miss. 295.

909. **Taxing Stock of Corporation.**—The revenue act does not make a corporation liable for taxes assessed on its

capital stock, when such capital is represented by shares of stock which are not the property of the corporation. *People* v. *National Gold Bank*, 51 Cal. 508.

910. Tax Titles.—The purchaser of property, sold for taxes, in accordance with the provisions of law, holds, *prima facie*, after the delay for redeeming has expired, a valid title, and such title cannot be disregarded, or assailed collaterally, like a simulated title, but must be attacked in a direct action to annul. *Lannes* v. *Workingmen's Bank, et al.*, 29 La. 112.

911. The deed of a State tax collector is not conclusive of the legality of the title conveyed by it. If such a title is properly put at issue, its validity must be proved by the party claiming under it. *State, ex rel. Louis Fix* v. *F. J. Herron, Recorder of Mortgages, et al.*, 29 La. 848.

912. The power to sell land for the non-payment of taxes is a naked power, not coupled with an interest, and in all such cases every pre-requisite to the exercise of the power must precede its exercise. In interpreting statutes authorizing the sale of land for non-payment of taxes, the title to be acquired must be regarded as *stricti juris*. Whoever sets up a tax title must show that all the requirements of the law have been complied with, unless the former owner is the purchaser. *Cahoon* v. *Coe*, 57 Hall, N. H. 556.

TENDER.

913. *Tender* of payment to one of several creditors and a demand from him of an assignment of the security, although the security may not be in his possession, bind, all the obligees, and his refusal is equivolent to the refusal of all. *Merriken* v. *Goodwin, et al.*, 2 Del. 236.

914. Where a debt is unliquidated, the acceptance by the creditor of money tendered by the debtor as "in full of all account," precludes the creditor from recovering more. And this, although the creditor de-

clares at the time that he receives it only to apply on the debt, so long as the debtor does not assent to his so receiving it. *Potter* v. *Douglass*, 44 Conn. 541 ; *Clark* v. *Dinsmore*, 5 N. H. 136. *Miller* v. *Holden*, 18 Vt. 340.

915. Where a purchaser of stock makes a demand for the same, and is ready to pay the price, but the seller refuses to comply, on the ground of his inability to deliver it, no further tender is requisite. *Wheeler* v. *Garcia*, 40 N. Y. 584 ; *Currie* v. *White*, 45 N. Y. 822, reversing *S. C.*, 1 Sw. 166. S. P., *Bellinger* v. *Kitts*, 6 Barb. 273.

916. The endorser of a note, on a tender of payment, may insist on its delivery to him, as a condition of such payment. *Wilder* v. *Seelye*, 8 Barb. 408.

917. **What constitutes.**—To constitute a tender, there must be a production and manual offer of the money, unless dispensed with by some positive act or declaration on the part of the creditor. *Bakeman* v. *Pooler*, 15 Wend. 637 ; *Strong* v. *Blake*, 46 Barb. 227. See *Holmes* v. *Holmes*, 12 Barb. 137 ; *Bellinger* v. *Kitts*, 6 Barb. 273 ; *Meserole* v. *Archer*, 3 Bos. 376 ; *Vaupell* v. *Woodward*, 2 Sand. Ch. 143.

918. A tender, by the president of a bank, in money belonging to the bank, to his private creditor, is not sufficient ; inasmuch as the act would be a fraud both on the part of the debtor and creditor, who had notice of the ownership of the funds. *Reed* v. *Bank of Newburgh*, 6 Paige, 337.

919. **Offer in Writing.**—*Effect of, when not accepted.*— An offer in writing to pay a debt when not accepted is a sufficient tender of money under the code, and such tender will discharge a lien for such defendant, on personal property, created by a chattel mortgage. *Bartel* v. *Lope*, 6 Oregon, 321.

920. **When Necessary.**—Tender of advances and charges on goods to a warehouseman is unnecessary if upon an offer to pay the same he declines to state the amount. So, also, if he declines to deliver the goods upon an-

other ground, as that his receipt for the goods is outstanding. *Hanauer* v. *Bartels*, 2 Colorado, 514.

921. Effect of.—A tender does not extinguish the right of action, but only precludes a claim for interest. *Raymond* v. *Bearnard*, 12 Johnston, 274; *Kelly* v. *West*, 4 J. & Sp. 304. The only effect of a tender after judgment is to bar a claim for damages or interest. *Lansing* v. *Low*, 5 Cow. 248.

922. Tender of Interest.—*How and to whom made.*—A mortgage debtor must seek his creditor to pay the interest on his mortgage, if he is within the State, and for this purpose must go to the residence or place of business of the mortgagee. A tender of interest, if not made to the creditor, must be to one authorized by him to receive it. 50 Howard, N. Y. Practice Reports; also, 55 Howard, N. Y. Practice Reports, 188.

TRADE-MARK.

923. Trade Mark.—A. C. & Co., being the successors by purchase of Stillman & Co., woollen manufacturers, continued to use "Stillman & Co." as trade-mark on their ticket for goods. Latimer, Stillman & Co., the lessees of a mill formerly used by Stillman & Co., known both as the "Stillman Mill" and as the "Seventh Day Mill," used "Stillman's Mills" as a trade-mark. On a petition for injunction, brought by A. C. & Co. against Latimer, Stillman & Co., to prevent their so using the word "Stillman," it appearing that no deception could be charged on either complainants or respondents, and that no person of the old firm of Stillman & Co. was a member of the firm of A. C. & Co.: *Held*, that the injunction could not be granted. *Held*, further, that a manufacturer has the right to label his goods with his own name or that of his mill, if no fraudulent purpose is intended. *Query:* If a trade-mark whose reputation depends on the excellence of the manufacture, or the skill and honesty of the manufacturer, can be legally assigned?

924. *Query.*—If the English practice of retaining a firm name, when no original partner remains, is generally recognized in American law? *Carmichel* v. *Latimer*, 11 R. I. 395. See *Motley* v. *Downman*, 3 M. & C. 1; also, *Crawshay* v. *Thompson, et al.*, 4 M. & C. 357.

925. Where a manufacturer has habitually stamped his goods with a particular mark or brand, a court of equity will restrain another party from adopting it for the same kind of goods. *McLeon* v. *Fleming*, 96 U. S. S. C. 245.

TRANSITU.

926. Stoppage of goods in.—A. sold goods to B., to be paid for upon their delivery, either in cash or in the notes of B. The goods were shipped on a vessel under a bill of lading, by which they were to be delivered to B. on his paying the freight. Before the vessel arrived, B.'s notes were protested because of his inability to pay them in the usual course of business, and an agent of A., having heard that B. had failed, sent a person to stop the goods *in transitu*. This person, whose acts were subsequently ratified by A., before B. paid or tendered the freight, or came into possession of the goods, but after they had been attached by a creditor of B., demanded the goods of the master of the vessel, and forbade his delivering them to B. *Held*, that A. had seasonably exercised the right of stopping the goods *in transitu*. *Durgy Cement & Umber Co.* v. *O'Brien*, 123 Mass. 12.

TRUSTEE.

927. Promise to allow personal debt as credit.—Promise by a trustee to allow his personal debt as a credit upon a note held by him as trustee, is not binding on the trust. Breach thereof is no defence to the note, even though the personal debt may have become debarred by the statute from delay to sue induced by the promise. *Vason, et al.* v. *Beall, trustee*, 58 Ga. 500.

928. Of deposit in bank.—A father made a deposit in his own name as trustee for his daughter, and died. The daughter, while a minor, married, and the husband and minor wife preferred a petition for the appointment of a new trustee. *Held*, that the decree appointing a new trustee shall direct him to pay the interest of the deposit to the wife, but not to pay over any part of the principal without an order of the court. *O'Brien, petitioner*, 11 R. I. 419.

TRUST.

929. Trust.—No presumption of a resulting trust arises from a wife's possession of premises under a voluntary conveyance by her husband. *Osborn v. Osborn*, 29 N. J. Eq. 385.

930. A person who acquires a legal title, with notice that the equitable title is in some other person than his grantor, will be decreed to hold the legal title for the benefit of the equitable owner. *Gale v. Morris*, 29 N. J. Eq. 222.

931. A., an habitual drunkard, conveyed lands to B. without consideration, and B. immediately reconveyed to A., for life, with remainder to his heirs, reserving a nominal rent, which was never in fact paid or claimed. *Held*, that the two instruments must be construed together and that B. had no beneficial interest in the lands, but merely took the title in trust. *Moore v. Carling*, 29 N. J. Eq. 432.

932. Trust Fund.—Where a trust fund has been perverted, the *cestui que trust* can follow it at law as far as it can be traced. *United States v. State Bank*, 96 U. S. S. C. (Otto) 30.

933. Trust Assignment.—*Mutual rights of Beneficiaries.*—Where the holder of one of several notes secured by a trust assignment without preference has, under a bill filed by him against the grantor and trustee alone, had the property sold and the proceeds applied to the satisfaction of his note, the holders of the other notes may, by suit in this court, hold him liable for their proportion of the proceeds. *Smith* v. *Cunningham*, 2 Tenn. Chancery, 565.

934. Trust ex Maleficio.—If one, having an interest in land, is induced to confide in the verbal promise of another that he will purchase at sheriff's sale for the benefit of the former, and in consequence is allowed to obtain legal title, his denial of the confidence is such fraud as will make him a *trustee ex maleficio*. *Wolford* v. *Harrington*, 74 Penn. St. 311.

935. Trusts and Trustees.—*Deposits in Bank.*—B. deposited in a savings bank certain moneys in his own name as trustee for R. B. gave the bank book to R., who returned it to B., in whose control it remained. B. was childless, R. was his step-daughter. It was in evidence that B. was a man of few words and that he treated R. as his daughter. In an equity suit by R. against the administrator of B., claiming the deposit as trust funds held by B. for R., *Held*, that the trust was completely constituted. *Held*, further, that the trust being constituted, the fact that it was voluntary was no reason for refusing relief.

To constitute a trust, it is enough if the owner of property conveys it to another in trust, or if the owner of personalty unequivocally conveys it to another in trust, or if the owner of personalty unequivocally declares, either orally or in writing, that he holds it *in præsenti*, in trust for another.

A bill in equity to enforce a trust, brought against an administrator, alleged that the respondent as administrator withdrew a bank deposit, being the trust funds in question. The answer alleged the respondent's appointment as administrator in Massachusetts, and that as such he withdrew the deposit and held the same as part of his decedent's estate:

Held, in the absence of denial by the administrator that he held the deposit as administrator in Rhode Island, that the court would presume he held it as administrator in Rhode Island, and would order him to account directly with the complainant, the trust having been proven. *Ray* v. *Simmons*, 11 R. I. 266 also *Stone, et al.* v. *King, et al.*, 7 R. I. 358. It is enough if, having the property, he conveys it to another in trust, or, the property being personal, if he unequivocally declares, either orally or in writing, that he hold it *in præsenti* in trust or as a trustee for another. *Ex parte Pye*, 18 Ves. Jun. 140; *Milroy* v. *Lord*, 4 De G. F. & J. 264; *Richardson* v. *Richardson*, L. R. 3 Eq. 686; *Kekewick* v. *Manning*, 1 De G. M. & G., 176; *Morgan* v. *Malleson*, L. R. 10 Eq. 475; *Penfold* v. *Mould*, L. R. 4 Eq. 562; *Wheatley* v. *Parr*, 1 Keen, 551 and note; *McFadden* v. *Jenkyns*, 1 Hare, 458.

USAGES OF TRADE.

936. Usages of Trade.—Where a party conversant with the rules and usages of the Chicago board of trade employed a commission merchant to make purchases of grain for future delivery for him, and afterwards sued the merchant for a loss incurred by the sale, which was made for want of necessary advances to meet a decline in prices, it was *held*, that proof of the usages of the board of trade was properly admitted to justify the act of the defendant. *Corbett* v. *Underwood*, 83 Ill. 324.

USURY.

937. Usury.—A note and mortgage executed to secure a loan of gold at a higher rate of premium than the market value of the gold are usurious. Defendant was desirous of negotiating a loan from plaintiff, and on that day he procured from plaintiff $1,700 in gold coin, and executed his note therefor for $2,000, payable in one year, with interest at ten per cent. At the time the premium upon gold was from 3¾ to 10 per cent. The defendant testified that he was to allow 10 per cent. premium upon the gold, and was to pay 15 per cent interest for the use of the money; that the 10 per cent. premium and 5 per cent. interest were taken out of the sum called for upon the face of the note, and that the arrangement was made as a cover for usury. *Austin v. Walker*, 45 Iowa, 527. It was said "The form of the transaction is nothing, the cardinal inquiry being, when the contract specifying the amount reserved is express, did the parties resort to it as the means of disguising the usury, in violation of the laws of the State where the contract was made or to be executed?" And, in arriving at this intention, all the facts are to be taken in consideration. *Arnold v. Potter*, 22 Iowa, 194.

988. A surety cannot avail himself of usury paid by his principal. *Lamoille County National Bank v. Bingham*, 50 Vt. 105.

939. Although the code provides the mode and manner in which a defendant may plead usury, its provisions do not in any manner deprive a party of existing remedies for relief against the payment of illegal interest, even though he may have failed to avail himself of the plea. Such being the law, there is no reason why a party may not except to the confirmation of an award on the ground of usury, even though no such defence was made before the arbitration. *Woods v. Matchett*, 47 Md. 390.

940. Appeal from the Circuit Court for Carroll county, in equity. On a bill filed to restrain the execution of a judgment of fraud, it was *held:* 1st. That the complainant had not made out a case entitling him to have the judgment set aside. 2d. That inasmuch as there appeared to have been usurious charges against him in the transaction between him and the defendants, he was entitled to have the judgment reduced to the sum found to be due by charging him with the net amount loaned him, and the average interest thereon, and allowing him for the amount of credits to which he was entitled, including bonus and interest on bonus. 3d. That although it was quite probable that this method did not ascertain the precise amount of usury paid by the complainant, yet no more could be allowed him, as there was no proof in the record to justify the

court in allowing any more, owing to the defective manner in which the complainant had kept his accounts, and his own forgetfulness of matters material to their elucidation. *Hill* v. *Reifsnider, et al.*, 46 Md. 555.

941. An allegation in answer that the complainants, as executors, received a certain amount usuriously, is not sustained by proof that one of them individually received a part of such sum from defendant's agent. *Cleveland* v. *O'Neil*, 29 N. J. 457.

942. Suit by a national bank upon a bill of exchange; defence, usury. The bank, in discounting the bill, reserved a greater amount than was allowed for interest by the law of the State where it was situated. There was no proof of the current rate of exchange. *Held*, that the bank was entitled to recover. *Wheeler* v. *National Bank*, 96 U. S. 268.

943. As a general rule, in setting up the defence of usury, the usurious contract must be described with precision and accuracy, and proved as laid. *Cox* v. *Westcoat*, 29 N. J. 551.

944. But when the complainant voluntarily confesses the taking of usury, and there is a variance between the contract alleged and that proved, the court, in order to give the defendant the benefit of facts admitted, will direct an amendment of the answer. *Cox* v. *Westcoat*, 29 N. J. 551.

945. **Consideration of Contract to forbear.**—Under our former statute, usury was a cause of forfeiture of all interest, and a promise to pay usury was not a sufficient consideration for a promise to forbear. *Roberts* v. *Stewart*, 31 Miss. 664. But under our present statute, usury forfeits only the illegal excess, and the right to get interest for a given time is a valuable consideration to uphold a promise to forbear, and the illegal excess is appropriable in legal contemplation to the discharge *pro tanto* of principal. *Brown* v. *Prophit*, 53 Miss. 649.

946. Usurious Contracts.—Where a sale is made under a mortgage, whether the contract was usurious or not is immaterial as an inquiry as to the validity of the sale; usury affects only the distribution of the proceeds, not the sale itself. If more than legal interest has been extorted by the mortgagee, the court, in distributing the proceeds, may direct it to be withheld or refused. *Carroll* v. *Kershner*, 47 Md. 262.

947. Usury.—Defendant endorsed certain notes for the accommodation of D., which were discounted by plaintiff. In an action upon the endorsements defendant offered to show that plaintiff in its dealings with D. took upon discounts made for him more than lawful interest. *Held*, that as the offer embraced transactions with which defendant was not connected, it was too broad, and so was properly rejected. *First Nat. Bank* v. *Wood*, 71 N. Y. 405.

948. Factor and Broker.—When an agreement is entered into between a factor and a holder of produce for an advance of money on the produce as part of an entire contract, embracing the storage, safe keeping and sale of the produce, and the compensation stipulated is greater than the legal rate of interest on the advance, it is a question of fact whether usury was intended, and if relief is sought on the ground of usury the fact must be averred in the bill and established by proof. Thus, where the complainants, as manufacturers of whisky, made a contract with the defendants, factors and commission merchants, for the storage of their whisky and an advance of money thereon, upon certain terms and conditions, the commission and charges agreed to be paid being more than the legal rate of interest on the advances, it was *held*, upon a bill filed stating a contract which was not usurious and not established by proof, that the complainants were not entitled to relief, although the agreement proved was for a rate of compensation greater than legal interest on the money advanced. *Stark* v. *Sperry*, 2 Tenn. Eq. 304.

949. *Usury.*—Hartman lent money to Duphorn for a year at 8 per cent., on a note, stated to be at 6 per cent., with Danner as surety; about maturity Hartman agreed to an extension for a year, upon Duphorn paying 2 per cent. usury, and in the same way for a third year. The usury was paid after the maturity of the note. Danner had no knowledge of the usury or the extensions. *Held*, that the contract for usury being illegal, it was without consideration, and therefore not binding on Hartman, and he could recover from Danner notwithstanding the giving of time. The payment of the usury after maturity of the note was a payment on account, which the debtor was under obligation to make, and therefore no advantage to one, or disadvantage to the other, so as to create consideration. *Hartman* v. *Danner*, 74 Penn. St. 36.

950. If an usurious contract is made, whether expressed or implied, at the time of, or subsequent to the entering into of the agreement, to take or reserve more than lawful interest, it is such an agreement as falls within the prohibition of the statute. *Peddicord et al.* v. *Connard*, 85 Ill. 102.

951. If, where a party overdraws his account with a bank, the bank, at the end of each sixty days, compounds the interest on the sums overdrawn, so as to make it the same as in discounting a loan, and the same is included in a note, the transaction will be tainted with usury, which may be set up in defence to a suit on the note, and no interest will be allowed on the sums overdrawn, either on the amount or the note. *Id.*

952. Where a party having an account in bank, which he overdraws from time to time, makes a settlement with the bank by having his bank book written up and his checks surrendered, and he paying the charges made against him, he cannot, after a considerable lapse of time, open such settlement to recover unlawful interest charged to him on the sums overdrawn. *Id.* 102.

953. In a suit upon a note the defendant, in her affidavit of defence, averred that the loan for which the note was given had been carried by her father for two years, at ten per cent. interest, and that the note signed by her was the renewal of one which was the last of a series given by him. The court below entered judgment for the amount of the note, and only abated the excess of interest for the four months which defendant's note had run: *Held* (reversing the court below), that she had the right to set up also the excess of interest paid by her father against the plaintiff's claim. *Miller* v. *Irwin*, 85 Penn. 376.

954. In April, 1870, the plaintiff executed four promissory notes, payable in one year, with interest at ten per cent., which were secured by mortgage on real estate. After the maturity of the notes the plaintiff endorsed thereon the following promise: "For value received I promise to pay twelve per cent. per annum from maturity until paid. Signed. T. W. T. R., Nov. 29, 1871." *Held*, that the notes were not affected with usury. The promise endorsed on the notes by the plaintiff is utterly void, and cannot modify or impair the original contract. If the original contract is *bona fide*, and wholly free from the taint of usury, then no subsequent agreement to pay usury, or an usurious premium upon the debt, will invalidate the original contract with the vice of usury, or prevent a collection of the debt with legal interest. *Richards* v. *Hountze*, 4 Neb. 206.

955. **Usury** is the charging of unlawful interest, and unless there is a law which limits the rate of interest to be charged for the use of money, there can be no usury. *Newton* v. *Wilson, et al.*, 31 Ark. 484.

956. It is sufficient to sustain the defence of usury if the weight of evidence be in its favor. *Chew* v. *Ferrari*, 29 N. J. Eq. 380.

957. **Liquidated Damages.**—Where a party executes his note for money loaned him, bearing ten per cent interest, with a provision that if the same is not paid within ten days after maturity, interest shall after-

wards be paid at the rate of twenty per cent., as liquidated damages, there will be no error in allowing such rate in accordance with the contract, especially where usury is not pleaded. *Walker, et al.* v. *Abt, et al.*, 83 Ill. 226.

958. On petition for foreclosure, brought by the purchaser of the mortgage notes against the purchaser of the equity of redemption, the defendant sought to abate the claim by showing that the notes were given in part for usurious interest. *Held*, that the right so to do was personal to the maker of the notes, the same as the right to recover money paid for usury is personal to the payer. *Reed* v. *Eastman*, 50 Vt. 67.

959. On Sale of Property.—If a party loans money, and at the same time sells lots to the borrower at a fictitious value, taking a note for the whole, merely to secure an unlawful rate of interest on the loan, the transaction will be usurious. But the fact that a party sells property and loans the consideration to the purchaser, with other funds, affords no presumption the transaction is usurious. *Mosier* v. *Norton, et al.*, 83 Ill. 519.

The defence of usury is regarded as in the nature of a penal action, and not only is great strictness required in the pleadings, but the contract must be proved as alleged by a clear preponderance of the evidence. *Id.*

960. No one but the person paying usury can recover it back. Thus, an accommodation maker of a promissory note cannot avail himself in a suit upon the note he has so given, of a payment of usury thereon by the party accommodated. *Aliter* of interest paid by such party. *Cady* v. *Goodnow*, 49 Rowell, Vt. 400.

961. Purchaser of mortgaged property, who paid full price for same, may set up usury in mortgage, though it had been foreclosed, and the usurious interest paid, before his purchase. *Lilienthal* v. *Champion, et al.*, 58 Ga. 158.

962. Recoupment.—Interest in excess of six, but not exceeding ten, per cent. per annum, voluntarily paid for the use of money, cannot be recouped, though no agreement in writing was made for its payment. *Reynolds* v. *Rondabush*, 59 Ind. 483.

963. **Recoupment.**—*Repeal of Statute.*—By the act of March 9, 1867 (1 R. S. 1876 599), concerning interest on money and the recoupment of usury, so much of section 5 of the act of March 7, 1861 (1 R. S. 1876, 599), on the same subject, as amended by the act of December 19, 1865 (3 Ind. Stat. 316), as prohibited the recoupment of usury, was repealed, but that part of such section prohibiting a direct action therefor is still in force. *Holcraft* v. *Mellott*, 57 Ind. 539. Where, in an action on a promissory note wherein the defendant answers, seeking to recoup usurious interest, alleged to have been paid, the plaintiff dismisses his complaint, such dismissal carries all the pleadings out of court, and the defendant cannot prove or recover such usury. *Id.*

Recoupment of usurious interest, alleged to have been paid on a promissory note in suit, can be had only to the extent of any balance due on such note, and judgment for any excess of such usury can be rendered. *Id.*

In recoupment the defendant can only use his claim in diminution or abatement of the plaintiff's cause of action, and cannot, as in set-off, recover for the excess of his claim over that of the plaintiff. *Id.*

964. The taint of usury cannot be eradicated by the substitution of one security, or one set of securities, for another, so long as the original debt survives. *Miller* v. *Irwin*, 85 Penn. 376.

965. **Usurious Brokage** taken by a third person, whether an agent of the mortgagee or not, if taken without his knowledge or consent, will not taint the mortgage. The rule that such brokage, to be valid, must be taken by virtue of an independent agreement between the borrower and the broker, not approved. *Gray* v. *Blarcom*, 29 N. J. 454.

966. Where usurious interest is reserved or charged on a note or bill discounted by a national bank, the

entire interest reserved or charged will, in an action on the note or bill, be adjudged forfeited. The action authorized by section 30 of the national banking act of 1864, to recover from the bank twice the amount of usurious interest paid, was within the jurisdiction of the State courts. *Hade* v. *Mc Vay, Allison & Co.*, 31 Ohio (DeWitt), 231.

967. To render a transaction usurious, there must be an unlawful or corrupt intent, confessed or proved. *Nourse* v. *Prime*, 7 Johns. Ch. 69 ; *Woodruff* v. *Hurson*, 32 Barb. 557.

968. Taking more than legal interest by mistake is not usury. *Marvin* v. *Hymers*, 12 N. Y. 223 ; *Mosher* v. *Randall*, 52 N. Y. 649 ; *Bailey* v. *Lane*, 21 How. Pr. 475.

969. If the plaintiff's principal and interest are both put at hazard, the contract is not usurious, however hard and unconscionable the bargain. *Cummings* v. *Williams*, 4 Wend. 679 ; *Spencer* v. *Tilden*, 5 Cow. 144 ; *Holmes* v. *Wetmore*, 5 Cow. 149 ; *Pomeroy* v. *Ainsworth*, 22 Barb. 118.

970. A contract is not usurious, if it depend on *contingencies*, whether, on return of the property, the lender will have received more than its value at the time of making the contract, and legal interest thereon. *Hall* v. *Haggart*, 17 Wend. 280.

971. Where one man advances money to purchase lands for the benefit of himself and others, to be refunded with interest, out of the proceeds only, a stipulation that he shall receive more than an equal proportion of the lands, in consideration of such advance, is not usurious. *Queckenbush* v. *Leonard*, 9 Paige, 334.

972. A loan of money upon condition that the borrower would sell to the lender real estate of a speculative character, to the amount of the loan, at its then market value, is not usurious, though both parties expected it would greatly increase in price. *Fellows* v. *American Life Ins. & Trust Co.*, 1 Sand. Ch. 203.

973. There can be no usury on a loan of chattels, whatever the percentage upon their value agreed to be paid for their use, unless intended as an indirect loan of money. *Bull* v. *Rice*, 5 N. Y. 315.

974. A loan, secured by a pledge of stock, under an agreement that the lender shall have the benefit of their rise in value, is usurious. *Cleveland* v. *Loder*, 7 Paige, 557.

975. If the purchaser of land, who has paid a considerable portion of the purchase-money, be unable to pay the balance on the day fixed, and the fiction of a re-sale be resorted to, as a cover for usury, the second contract is void, but the balance of the original purchase-money is recoverable. *Crippen* v. *Heermance*, 9 Paige, 211.

976. If the vendor of land agree to sell for $10,000 in cash, but the vendee being unable to pay cash, it is agreed that a deed and bond and mortgage for $12,000, payable at a future time, with interest, shall be executed, to remain in the vendor's hands, until he can dispose of the bond and mortgage for $10,000, which is done; the transaction is not usurious. *Brooks* v. *Avery*, 4 N. Y. 225.

977. A usurious loan on a contract to procure the assignment of choses in action, at a future day, which have then no existence, and the loan being ultimately secured by the notes of the borrower, is void. *Seymour* v. *Strong*, 4 Hill, 255; *Rapelye* v. *Anderson*, 4 Hill, 472.

978. A loan made by an insurance company, on condition that the borrower will effect an insurance with them, on the ordinary terms, is not usurious. *Utica In. Co.* v. *Cadwell*, 3 Wend. 296; *New York Fire In. Co.* v. *Donaldson*, 3 Edw. Ch. 199.

979. A loan-company, authorized to loan money on pledge, and to charge interest for a full month, where the loan is for a period of over fifteen days and less than one month, is not entitled, where a loan made for twenty days remains unpaid, to demand interest at the

same rate for any subsequent time. *Macomber* v. *Dunham*, 8 Wend. 550.

980. Giving a note for a larger sum than the party discounting it expected to advance, with an agreement that it shall be negotiated only for the amount advanced, is not usurious. *Schoop* v. *Clarke*, 1 Keyes, 181; S. C., 4 Abb. Dec. 235.

981. The reservation of interest, payable quarterly, upon a sum payable at a future day, is not usurious. *Mowry* v. *Bishop*, 5 Paige, 98.

982. On Bill of Exchange. — Suit by a national bank upon a bill of exchange; defence, usury. The bank, in discounting the bill, reserved a greater amount than was allowed for interest by the law of the State where it was situated. There was no proof of the current rate of exchange. *Held*, that the bank was entitled to recover. *Wheeler* v. *National Bank*, 96 U. S. S. C. 268.

983. A *bona fide* contract for the delivery of personal chattels cannot be usurious. *Stockwell* v. *Holmes*, 33 N. Y. 53.

948. A note with interest from a day past, is not usurious on its face. *Marvin* v. *Feeter*, 8 Wend. 533; *Lynde* v. *Staats*, 1 N. Y. Leg. Obs. 89.

985. The original taint of usury attaches to all consecutive obligations and securities growing out of the original vicious transaction. *Vickery* v. *Dickson*, 35 Barb. 96; S. C., 62 Barb. 272; *Stanley* v. *Whitney*, 47 Barb. 586.

986. What is Usury.—Discounting a note on the theory that 360 days make a year, though the practice be universal, is usurious. Payment and receipt of usurious interest is *prima facie* evidence of a corrupt agreement. *New York Farmers' In. Co.* v. *Ely*, 2 Cow. 678; *Bank of Utica* v. *Wager*, 2 Cow. 712; S. C., 8 Cow. 398; *Utica In. Co.* v. *Tilman*, 1 Wend. 555.

987. If a person discounting a note, give a check payable in uncurrent funds, the transaction is not usurious, in the absence of an agreement that the amount should be so paid. *Codd* v. *Rathbone*, 19 N. Y. 37. S. P., *Slosson* v. *Duff*, 1 Barb. 432; *Robbins* v. *Dellaye*, 33 Barb. 77.

988. Taking a security, bearing interest, and giving checks for the amount, payable in six months, without interest, is usury. *Lane* v. *Losee*, 2 Barb. 56.

989. To constitute usury, there must be a loan, a taking of more than lawful interest, and a corrupt agreement. *Bank of Utica* v. *Wager*, 2 Cow. 712; *Talmage* v. *Pell*, 4 N. Y. 463; *Mumford* v. *American Life In. Co. and Trust Co.*, 4 N. Y. 463; *Crocker* v. *Colwell*, 46 N. Y. 212.

990. An agreement to pay more than legal interest, made at the time of the loan, will avoid a note taken therefor, though on its face it be only for the amount loaned with legal interest; otherwise, of a subsequent agreement to pay usurious interest. *Merrills* v. *Law*, 9 Cow. 65; S. C., 6 Wend. 268; *Austin* v. *Fuller*, 12 Barb. 360.

991. An agreement that the borrower shall receive uncurrent notes at a higher rate than their market value, renders the loan usurious. *Cleveland* v. *Loder*, 7 Paige, 557; *Pratt* v. *Adams*, 7 Paige, 615. Otherwise, if the discount be very trifling, and the notes pass current in the market in the way of trade. *Slosson* v. *Duff*, 1 Barb. 432.

992. Accommodation Paper.—The purchase of accommodation proper for gross sum, which, on calculation, give more than seven per cent. discount is usurious. *Bossange* v. *Ross*, 29 Barb. 576.

993. Accommodation note negotiated upon a usurious consideration is void. *Blodgett* v. *Wadhams*, Lalor, 65; *Callin* v. *Gunter*, 11 N. Y. 368. *Newell* v. *Doty*, 33 N. Y. 83.

994. If a party accept stock at par, which is depreciated in the market, and give his bond and mortgage for the par value thereof, the transaction is not usurious. *Willoughby* v. *Comstock*, 3 Edw. Ch. 424.

995. The loan of certain notes, at their nominal

value, which are actually worth less than that amount, is not necessarily usurious as a matter of law, there being no intent to evade the statute. *Sizer* v. *Miller*, 1 Hill, 227; *Dry Dock Bank* v. *American Life In. and Trust Co*, 3 N. Y. 344.

996. A credit given on a payment in advance, for a larger sum than the actual payment, does not amount to usury; it is but a discount of a portion of the debt. *Righter* v. *Stall*, 3 Sand. Ch. 608.

997. Nor is it usurious, on selling a note payable at a future day, with interest, to take a note for the principal and interest, computed to the day of sale, without making a rebate of interest. *Lynde* v. *Staats*, 1 N. Y. Leg. Obs. 89.

998. If two persons exchange notes for the purpose of raising money, and one procure the other's note to be discounted at a premium exceeding the lawful rate of interest, the transaction is not usurious. *Rice* v. *Mather*, 3 Wend. 62; *Odell* v. *Greenly*, 4 Duer, 358.

999. If notes be exchanged for the purpose of enabling one of the parties to sell the other's note at a usurious rate of discount, with the knowledge of the lender, the transaction is void for usury. *National Fire Ins. Co.* v. *Sackett*, 11 Paige, 660.

1000. Usury.—If an accommodation note be sold at a usurious rate of discount, the maker is not estopped from setting up the defence of usury, though the payee represented it as business paper. *Hall* v. *Earnest*, 36 Barb. 585. S. P., *Parshall* v. *Lamoreaux*, 37 Barb. 189.

1001. Usury.—The fact that the maker of an accommodation note takes security for his indemnity, does not render the note a security for value, so as to shut out the defence of usury. *Parshall* v. *Lamoreaux*, 37 Barb. 189.

1002. Usury.—An exchange of notes with commission of two and a half per cent., if intended as a loan of money, is usurious. *Dunham* v. *Dey*, 13 Johns. 40; *Dunham* v. *Gould*, 16 Johns. 367; *New York Dry*

Dock Co. v. *American Life Ins. & Trust Co.*, 3 Sand. ch. 215, *S. C.*, 3 N. Y. 344.

1003. Where, in an action on a promissory note, the defendant answers that such instrument is the last of a series of usurious renewals of a usurious promissory note, and that the real principal, and lawful interest thereon, have been overpaid, and asking to recoup the excess, an objection that the date of such renewals, and payments thereon, are not alleged, should be made not by demurrer, but by motion to make specific. *Holcraft* v. *Mellott*, 57 Ind. 539.

1004. Where usury was set up in the ordinary form appropriate to pleading usury taken in this State, and it appeared that the agreement was not made in this State, and it also appeared that a premium had been taken for loan of the money and a further premium for further forbearance : *Held*, that unless the complainant would deduct the preminms and all interest received thereon, the defendant should have leave to amend his answer so as to set up the taking of the premiums. *Glading* v. *Cuberly*, 29 N. J. 104.

VENDOR.

1005. **Guaranty of Title.**—Vendor who has guaranteed a good title to the property he has sold cannot collect the price of the sale from the vendee until he has made the title good. *Wamsley* v. *Hunter*, 29 La. 628.

1006. **Vendor's Lien.**—The vendor of real estate has a lien upon the property sold for the unpaid purchase-money, independent of the existence of a lien evidenced by a title bond or mortgage. *Rosler* v. *Hale*, 10 Iowa, 470: *Malony* v. *Fortune*, 14 Iowa 417 ; *Harlan* v. *Sigler*, Morris, 39 ; *Griffey* v. *Payne*, Morris, 68 ; *Jordan* v. *Wimer*, 45 Iowa, 65, Seevers, Ch. J., dissenting.

1007. **Promissory Notes.**—If the vendor of land retains the legal title until payment is made, or if he creates an express lien in his deed to secure the purchase-money, an assignment of the notes given therefor carries with it the security to the same extent as it existed for the benefit of the vendor. *Moore* v. *Lackey*, 53 Miss. 85.

1008. A note for the purchase-money of land, payable in Mississippi certificates of indebtedness, is secured by the vendor's equitable lien the same as if payable in money. *Deason* v. *Taylor*, 53 Miss. 697.

1009. Vendor and Vendee.—A person who, having discovered a flaw in a title to land, purchases the title for speculation, with a view to ousting the possessor, who claims to be the real owner, is not a *bona fide* purchaser. *Wanner* v. *Sisson*, 29 N. J. 141.

1010. Vendor of Lands, who had taken a note therefor, which he had endorsed and negotiated, was held liable without notice on the ground that he had retained the title of the land as security. *Develing* v. *Ferris*, 18 Ohio, 170.

1011. Vendor and Purchaser.—Title does not vest till the delivery of the deed. *Heffron* v. *Flanigan*, 37 Mich. 274.

1012. Vendor's Lien.—Giving a receipt or taking a note, with security, from the purchaser, or taking a note of a third party, specifying in either case it is for the purchase-money, will not, while the title remains in the vendor, be an extinguishment of the vendor's lien unless the purchase-money has been actually paid. *Dunlap, ex'r. v. Shanklin*, 10 West Virginia Reports, 662.

1013. Vendor and Vendee.—*Delivery of goods.*—As soon as an order for goods is accepted by the vendor, the contract is complete without further notice to the vendee; and such contract is fully performed on the part of the vendor by the delivery of the goods in good condition to the proper carrier. A delivery to a carrier designated by the vendee is of the same legal effect as a delivery to the vendee himself; if no particular route or carrier is indicated by the vendee, it is the duty of the vendor to ship the goods ordered in a reasonable course of transit. *Ober* v. *Smith*, 78 N. C. 313.

WAREHOUSE RECEIPT.

1014. Warehouse Receipts.—A warehouseman's receipt for goods not in his warehouse at the time of the execution and delivery of the receipt, although he was the owner, *did not pass any right or title* to the holder of such receipt so as to affect innocent third parties. *But after removing the goods* to his *warehouse*, the warehouseman might, by a subsequent stipulation or ratification of his original contract, before the rights of others intervened, again pledge the property to secure the liability, for the security of which the original receipts were given. *The new* receipts took effect at the time of their execution and delivery, although they were dated back to correspond with the dates of the original receipts. *Cochran & Fulton* v. *Ripy, Hardie & Co. et al.*, 13 Bush, Ky. 495.

1015. A party having property stored in a warehouse may sell or dispose of the same in the absence of a warehouse receipt, and this right is not taken from him by the statute. The character of symbol that would in construction of law pass the possession to one making an absolute purchase would pass the possession to a party holding the property in pledge to secure the payment of a debt. *Id.*

Warehousemen's receipts are negotiable and transferable by endorsement in blank, or by special endorsement, the endorsers being liable as are endorsers of bills of exchange. *Id.*

1016. No one can obtain the property but the holder of the receipt, unless he produces the written consent of the holder as well as the receipt itself; and as to property owned by the warehouseman, for which he gives a receipt, he can assert no claim or set-off as against the holder, unless the receipt on its face shows such right to exist. *Id.*

1016½. The right to pledge or pawn goods as a security for the payment of a debt existed independently of the statute, and was made to rest upon the doctrine of the common law. It is a bailment of personal property only, and the right in the bailee or pledgee is never consummated until the latter has possession of the property. *Id.*

WARRANTY.

1017. **Warranty.**—A., by a contract in writing, pledged to B. certain tobacco, reciting that it was A.'s "own property, and free from all incumbrances and all of the crop" of a certain year. B. borrowed money of C., and delivered the tobacco to him and gave him an assignment of all his "right, title and interest in and under the contract, together with all the property therein mentioned." *Held*, that there was no implied warranty of title to the tobacco or of its quality, between B. and C. *National Bank of Northampton* v. *Mass. Loan and Trust Co.*, 123 Mass. 330.

1018. **Breach of warranty** may be set up as a defence without returning the goods, unless the contract of sale expressly requires their return. The omission to return them only affects the amount of damages recoverable. Where goods were sold with warranty, and the defence to an action for part of their price was grounded on a breach thereof, an inquiry as to whether part of the goods were sound that had been returned as unsound, was relevant on the cross-examination of the plaintiff, who had testified as to the contract and its performance. *Hull* v. *Belknap, et al.*, 37 Mich. 179.

1019. **Warranty Implied** *on the part of the Vendor of a Bond or other Security*, that it is a valid and subsisting security for the amount expressed. Defendant sold and assigned to plaintiff a bond and mortgage which were usurious and void. Defendant was personally concerned in the making of them and in the unlawful acts which vitiated them. *Held*, that there was an implied warranty on the part of defendant of the validity of the bond and mortgage, for the breach of which he was liable. Defendant executed a warranty of the validity of the mortgage. *Held*, that as the bond was the principal debt upon which the mortgage was dependent, if the bond was invalid the mortgage also; and therefore that the warranty was, in effect, that the bond as well as the mortgage was valid. *Ross, Respt.* v. *Terry, Applt.*, N. Y. Reports, 18 Sickels, 613.

1020. Where L. purchased of R. a certain number of barrels of rosin, under the following contract, viz.: "Received of L. $700 in part payment of 500 barrels of strained rosin, to be delivered, &c.," and thereupon. at the place of delivery, L. examined and selected the number of barrels purchased from a lot of barrels largely in excess of the amount purchased; and the barrels so selected afterwards proved in a great measure not to be "strained rosin:" it *was held*, that the agreement of R. to deliver, &c., amounted to a warranty on his part, that the rosin received by L. should be strained rosin. In such case, the fact that L. had an opportunity to inspect the rosin before or when it was delivered, and did in fact select the particular barrels purchased, did not amount to a waiver of the warranty that they should be of the specific description. Where goods are warranted to come within a specific description, the vendee is entitled, although he does not return them to the vendor or give notice of their failure to come within the description warranted, to bring an action for breach of warranty. *Lewis* v. *Rountree*, 78 N. C. 323.

WRITTEN INSTRUMENTS.

1021. **Writing.**—Courts must interpret written instruments, but they follow the meaning attributed to the terms by those whose custom it is to use them. Where a contract may have two interpretations, courts will follow that which the parties have put upon it and cited upon. *Gass' et al. appeal*, 73 Penn. St. 39.

1022. Written Agreement.—An agreement for the sale of personal property at a price not less than fifty dollars, is void under our statute of frauds, unless the same, or some note or memorandum thereof expressing a consideration, be in writing, and subscribed by the party to be charged. A promise made by one party without a corresponding obligation or promise by the other party is void. *Corbitt* v. *Salem Gaslight Co.*, 6 Oregon, 407.

INDEX.

[The references are to the paragraphs.]

Acceptance—Verbal acceptance of an order,...............(Ill.)	1
Accommodation—Evidenced by the acceptance of drawees' names on it before delivery...............(Miss.)	2
Account Stated—Circumstances attending its delivery must at least justify an inference of assent...............(N. Y.)	3
Administrators—Written acknowledgment alone by an administrator will not bind the succession...............(La.)	4
Advice of Counsel—As a defence, is good if obtained in a proper manner...............(Ill.)	5
Agent—Taking insufficient security when loaning the money of his principal...............(N. Y.)	6
Goods bought by the agent...............(Mass,)	7
Dealing with an agent before notice of his recall...............(U. S.)	8
Advice of, to sell certain bonds and reinvest proceeds in others...............(Mass.)	9
Cannot act for both seller and buyer...............(Wis.)	10
Principal not liable for illegal acts of...............(La.)	10½
His acts are those of the principal, not his own...............(Ill.)	11
Claiming to be authorized to act for another...............(La.)	12
Principal bound for agent's necessary acts...............(La.)	13
Where agent has fraudulently sold principal's property...............(La.)	14
Personal liability of...............(Ill.)	15
Dealing under a power of attorney...............(La.)	16
Good faith alone does not exonerate agent from responsibility to his principal...............(Ky.)	17
Partner, after dissolution of firm, has no agency growing out of his former partnership...............(Fla.)	18
Unauthorized sale by...............(Kan.)	19
Undisclosed principal...............(Mass.)	20
Authority to invest money...............(Iowa.)	21
When notice to agent is notice to principal...............(Penn.)	22
President of railway acting as agent thereof...............(Oregon.)	23
Agreement—Forbidden by law expressly or by implication...............(Ky.)	24
To furnish certain articles without stipulating terms of payment...............(Me.)	25
To pay interest upon interest...............(N. Y.)	26
Assignee—Of mortgage—in possession...............(Ill.)	27
Time of filing claims before...............(Iowa.)	28

Assignment—Blank assignment construed most to advantage of
    defendant..(Ark.)   29
    Tender of debt requires return of collaterals, and refusal discharges
      surety...(Del.)   30
    Of wages under seal duly recorded......................(Mass.)   31
    Giving preference......................................(N. Y.)   32
    Of stock as against attaching creditor..................(Tenn.)   33

Assumpsit—Lies on a claim of ownership..................(Mich.)   34

Attachment—Of property assigned........................(N. Y.)   35

Attorney—General powers, directing the levy...............(N. Y.)   36
    Purchasing of his client a claim..........................(Me.)   37
    Must prove capacity to recover his fees...................(Me.)   38
    Contingent fee..(Ill.)   39

Bailee—Voluntary relinquishment of possession..............(Me.)   40
    Forfeiture of his rights..................................(Me.)   41

Banks—Depositor must first demand his deposit..............(N. Y.)   42
    Uniform custom of dealing with depositor.................(N. Y.)   43
    Taking negotiable instrument for collection................(Neb.)   44
    Overdraft by an agent, of his principal's account..........(Colo.)   45

Bills of Exchange—Disposal of proceeds of............(R. I., U. S.)   46
    " Accepted payable after my advances are paid "..........(Miss.)   47
    Drawn and accepted by same parties—Custom—Re-exchange.(Eng.)   49
    Assigns a fund in the hands of another...................(N. C.)   48
    Accommodation—Drawer and endorser—Remittitur of judgment
      against acceptee....................................(Miss.)   50
    Time of protest to hold endorser........................(Canada.)   51
    Rights of holder.......................................(Canada)   52
    How payable when drawn in N. Y. and accepted in Montreal,
      Canada...(Canada.)   53
    Damages notwithstanding want of protest.................(N. Y.)   54
    Where the instrument is doubtful........................(N. B.)   55
    Notice of drawer's effects..............................(Canada.)   56

Bills of Foreclosure—May be in name of owner of note........(Ill.)   57

Bill of Lading—May disprove by parol proof..................(La.)   58
    Must deliver with usual despatch.........................(Vt.)   59
    Imparted on its face as an absolute undertaking, on the back of
      which were printed rules and regulations..................(Vt.)   60

Bills and Notes—Possession *prima facie* evidence of ownership.(Ky.)   61
    Alteration of a writing by a third person without consent or
      knowledge of obligee..................................(Ky.)   62
    Material alteration of completed note....................(Ky.)   63
    If on the transfer an endorsement is omitted................(N. J.)   64
    Negotiability, Endorsement, Assignor, Liability..............(Mo.)   65
    Bearing the stamp of a bank.............................(Eng.)   66

Bill of Sale—Absolute bill of sale, executed to secure a debt, operates
    as a..(Ark.)   67

Bonds—Negotiable city bond be stolen......................(N. J.)   68
    Jointly and severally. In debt on writing obligatory.........(R. I.)   69
    Official responsibility of secretary and president..............(Md.)   70
    Municipal corporation cannot issue bonds, except under authority
      from the legislator..................................(U. S.)   71
    Form, irregularity, fraud, or misconduct, no defence........(U. S.)   72
    Where there is a total want of authority to issue.............(U. S.)   73

Buyers must consider the statutes under which bonds have been issued..(U. S.) 74
And mortgage to bank. Deposit set off....................(N. Y.) 75
Of the State to certain railways.............................(Fla.) 76
Under seal, though voluntary................................(Del.) 77
Stolen and altered before they are sold...................(Mass.) 78
As surety for faithfulness of a third person..................(Md.) 79
Where guaranty is subsequent to contract....................(Md.) 80
Signed by guarantor and delivered to the agent of the guarantee. (Md.) 81

Brokers—Commission for furnishing a purchaser...............(Ky.) 82

Certificates—Of deposit to order after fifteen days.........(Canada.) 83
Of deposit, very high and satisfactory as to the sum deposited.(Ill.) 84
Of deposit, interest on after due..............................(Mo.) 85
Of incorporation, defective in form...........................(Md.) 86

Charges on Book—Sales to the agent of a corporation.......(Conn.) 87

Chattel Mortgage—On growing crop............................(Fla.) 88
Where mortgagee remains in possession......................(Wis.) 89
A continuing security..(N. Y.) 90
Fraudulent although on valuable consideration..............(Minn.) 91
To secure debts maturing at a future time..................(Tenn.) 92
Subject to prior mortgage as expressed therein.............(Mass.) 93
Not necessary to be in writing...............................(Ala.) 94
On conditions uncertain.....................................(Mass.) 95
Valid only by retention of possession.......................(R. I.) 96
Title after due delivery by and return to mortgagor.........(R. I.) 97
Neglect to make and sign affidavit..........................(N. H.) 98
To secure several notes held by different parties...........(N. H.) 99
Description necessary in a chattel mortgage.................(Iowa.) 100
Use by mortgagee temporarily with assent of mortgagor......(Md.) 101
Absence of specific appropriation of payments...............(Md.) 102
Does not protect materials from execution..................(Mich.) 103
Valid as between the parties..................................(Ill.) 104
Mortgage property sold without notice.......................(N. H.) 105
Fair efforts by mortgagee at public sale to realize a good price.(N. Y.) 106
Usury, sale under the mortgage, purchase by mortgagee. Action to redeem..(N. Y.) 107
Upon after-acquired goods..................................(Mich.) 108

Checks—Of firm, to pay individual partner's debts by consent—may be rescinded...(Ill.) 110
"To hold as collateral for 1,000 P. T. oil, pipage paid" &c..(Penn.) 111
Garnishee order on check in debtor's hands..................(Eng.) 109
Check given to another by one who died before payment thereof.
(Ohio.) 112
Appropriation as a payment...................................(Eng.) 113
On another bank handed to teller by a depositor and credited on his pass-book, but which was returned dishonored............(Cal.) 114
Is an appropriation of so much of the maker's funds in the bank. Maker cannot object to delay in its presentation...........(Me.) 115
Rightful possession when made payable to a particular person confers no authority..(Ohio.) 116
Payment of a forged check...................................(Mass.) 117
Apparent on its face that it was not drawn in the usual course of business..(Penn.) 118
Teller receives from depositor a check on his bank drawn by another of his depositors which was dishonored..........(Cal.) 119
Payment of check endorsed by wrong person in name of payee.
(Penn.) 123

Copy of, in protest, not enough for suit....................(Ind.) 124
Notice of non-payment required........................(Ind.) 125
Diligence required in presentment for payment..............(Ind.) 126
Given in contravention of Bankrupt Act..................(N. Y.) 127
Not describing any particular fund........................(N. Y.) 130
Holder on whom it has been fraudulently passed............ 131
Bank enjoined from making any payment................(S. C.) 129
Drawn on one bank and required to be presented for payment to another..... 128
Is a payment until presented and refused................(Irish.) 132
Agreement between the payee and drawer of a check contemporaneous with its execution............................(Ind.) 133
Protest not required to make drawer liable to the payee......(Ind.) 134
Date of, is *prima facie* evidence of the time it was made....(N. Y.) 135
Has no conception until delivered........................(N. Y.) 136
Dated on day of its execution, and deposited for 14 months with third party to be delivered to payee on certain contingency.(N.Y.) 137
Must be drawn on a particular and specific fund...........(N. Y.) 138
Deposits withdrawn by maker prior to presentation of check(N. Y.) 139
Payee of, before acceptance, has no action against the drawee.(U. S.) 120
Rights of parties not changed by fact of a settlement of accounts. (U. S.) 121
Payment to a stranger on unauthorized endorsement.......(U. S.) 122

Collections—Collector is not a *bona fide* holder of draft left with him for collection..(N. Y.) 141
Liability of agent for money collected....................(N. Y.) 142

Collateral Security—Railway bonds as collateral still held although suit and arrest has been made............................(Me.) 140
Attorney can receive nothing but money except by express authority. (W. Va.) 143
Order to "return at once without protest if not paid." Collecting bank reported paid, but it was not......................(Conn.) 144

Compromise—Of a criminal action....................(Oregon.) 145

Comity—Courts guided by the law merchant...... ....(La.) 152

Common Carriers—Agent—Bill of Lading—Evidence—Damages. (Vt.) 153

Community of Property—Purchased, whether in the name of husband or wife..(La.) 154
After dissolution of community............. ....(La.) 155

Composition—Obtained by fraud.........................(Ill.) 156

Confederate Currency—Value of such money at time of payment of security debt may be recovered.........................(Texas.) 146
Payment in such currency is valid......................(Texas.) 147
Sale of property on value of Confederate currency in gold.(W. Va.) 148
Decree on contract payable in Confederate currency should be for an equal value thereof in legal tender notes of the United States. (U. S.) 149

Conflict of Laws—Of the right and the remedy..............(Ill.) 150
Resident of one State doing business as a firm in another State where the law prohibits such a course to its own citizens...(La.) 151

Consideration—Waiver of a legal or equitable right as a consideration...(Ark.) 157
Debt barred by statute sufficient consideration for new promise.(Ga.) 158
Agreement to forbear is a valid consideration..............(Ark.) 159
Failure of, on a note..(Ill.) 160
May be impeached by parol evidence although expressed on face of the note..(Ill.) 161

Contract—Of sale induced in part by desire on behalf of both vendor and purchaser to cause certain notes of the vendor's to be paid, on which he has forged the name of endorsers..............(Vt.) 162
May be avoided by one party thereto on account of his dissatisfaction...(Mass.) 163
In form of a license..(N. J.) 164
No protection in court for the rash against the consequences of their imprudent contracts.............................(N. J.) 165
Condition precedent.....................................(Oregon.) 166
Common carriers' express stipulation will exempt him from liability for negligence..(N. Y.) 167
Execution of, when not signed by all parties................(Cal.) 168
Meaning of the words "Value received"..................(Colo.) 169
May be rescinded.......................................(Oregon.) 170
As security...(N. C.) 171
Subsequent—Degree of proof to establish...............(Oregon.) 172
At public sale..(R. I.) 173
For purchase of grain for future delivery....................(Ill.) 174
To sell house and lot, a mere memorandum................(R. I.) 175
For sale of wheat in store to be delivered at a future time.....(Ill.) 176
Made on change must be construed as if the rules of the board were a part of it..(Ill.) 177
For an advance of money on goods to be shipped for sale on commission on which the claim of ownership is defined......(Ohio.) 178
Mistake in drafting contract.......................(Eng. & Me.) 179
Competent any time before a breach of contract to alter or make a new one.. 180
To recover property, made at the time of purchase...........(La.) 181
Made on Sunday..(Ind.) 182
Under seal between twelve persons, with an explanation of liability of each to the other and to other parties...................(Md.) 183
Empowering a person to act as agent in a special way........(Md.) 184
Will not be enforced, a void contract........................(Ky.) 185
Due notice of acceptance is required.......................(Penn.) 186
Between creditor and principal, or creditor and surety.......(Md.) 187
Verbal, for longer time than a year.........................(Ohio.) 188
Fraud, consideration, performed, rescission, *restitutio in integrum*.
 (Irish.) 189
When rescinding must put parties in their original state....(Irish.) 190
Forfeiture caused by act of party..........................(N. Y.) 191
Conveyance—Recorded after fifteen days is notice to purchasers, mortgagees and judgment creditors subsequent to such record.
 (N. J.) 192
Voluntary, is void as to creditors holding debts previously contracted..(Del.) 195
When second deed will not have priority over first although recorded before it..(N. J.) 193
Deed not recorded within fifteen days, is void as to subsequent deed for a valuable consideration, without notice........(N. J.) 192½
When grantee is a *bona fide* purchaser......................(Va.) 194
Withholding deed from the records for several years........(N. J.) 196
Made by a man before his marriage in fraud of the dower rights of his intended wife..(N. Y.) 197
Voluntary, is void if it tends to hinder and delay creditors...(Del.) 198
Purchaser of property sold him to defraud creditors must be innocent and pay for it......................................(N. J.) 199
In fraud of creditors will be reclaimed for benefit of creditors.(N. J.) 200
Fraudulent, grantee thereof responsible if he sells it before proceedings to set aside.....................................(N. J.) 201

By a solvent father to his two sons in consideration of services rendered..................(N. J.) 202

Corporations—Receiving money in excess of its powers. Such money must be returned..................(Mass.) 203
Officers of, not authorized to borrow money..............(Colo.) 204
Unauthorized agent must be repudiated and notice given....(Colo.) 205
Promise to pay, or see them paid, must be in writing to be binding.
..................(Tenn.) 206
Liability of officers who state to a creditor that the corporation is solvent although it is not..................(Tenn.) 208
Bonds payable to bearer or order with coupons annexed are negotiable..................(N. J., Mass.) 209
Where an instrument is incomplete..........(Vt., Mo. & N. Y.) 210
Status of a, doing business in a State other than that in which it was incorporated..................(U. S.) 211
Trustees, action against, for injuries caused by fraudulent acts, or misapplication of corporate funds..................(N.Y.) 212
Preemption under contract between stockholders not to sell stock without notice of ten days..................(R. I.) 213
Refusal or neglect by officers to bring suit against a defaulting officer. Cannot gratuitously condone or release the fraud of one of its officers..................(Mass., R. I., N. J.) 214
Subscriptions not always vitiated by non-payment..........(Miss.) 215
President of Bank—Authority to make contracts..........(Miss.) 216
Bank that issues bills for circulation is a public corporation.(N. C.) 217
Certificate of stock stolen and the owner's name forged to a power of attorney under which a new certificate is given to an auctioneer, who in turn sells it for value to an innocent buyer........(Mass.) 207

Coupons—Title to detached interest-coupons passes from hand to hand as a bank note passes..................(U. S.) 218

Damages—Measure of, under count for goods sold............(Ill.) 220
In suit on first of several notes where it does not appear the notes were received as payment, nor in whose hands the others are.
(Wis.) 219
Neglect or delay in the transportation of goods.............(Vt.) 221

Debtor and Creditor—Two notes given, but one of which is secured by mortgage. Application of a small payment thereon...(N. J.) 222
Priority of debts, one due to wife whose husband is embarrassed.
(N. J.) 223
Release—Concealment of means which is not an absolute discharge.
(N. Y.) 224

Deed—When distances and areas do not correspond........(Iowa.) 225
Description in, by words and figures, which shall govern.....(Mo.) 226
No title passed until deed is delivered......................(Ill.) 227
Of trust, legal effect of, merely a mortgage................(Ohio.) 228

Deed of Trust—Legal effect of..................(Ohio.) 228
Is not an absolute transfer..................(Texas.) 229
Delivery of, to a trustee who has no interest in the trust is not required..................(Ill.) 230
As security for future advances..................(Ill.) 231
Sale under, when no money need be paid..................(Ill.) 232

Defences—Executory contract entered into under false representations, the result of accepting conveyance..................(N. Y.) 233
It is no defence to an action that the contract was not within the powers granted in the corporate charter..................(N. Y.) 234

Demand—When a demand is not required..................(Iowa) 235

Deposits—Although a bank does not appropriate deposits of the maker of a note in its hands, does not discharge the surety..(Ill.) 236
Special deposits withdrawn by a person having authority, though the bank acted without knowledge of that fact............(Ga.) 237
Payment to dorsee after death of depositor................(Irish.) 238
Discount—Interest may be retained when taking the note....(N. Y.) 239
Giving certificate of deposit payable at a future day for a bill discounted at same time................................(N. Y.) 242
When discounted by creditor at more than legal rate of interest. (N. Y.) 243
Purchase of a note at a discount is not usurious...........(N. Y.) 244
Ante-dating a note, bearing interest, as of a date when the money was due on the contract...............................(N. Y.) 245
Taking out seven per cent. in advance is not usurious......(N. Y.) 240
May include three days' grace...........................(N. Y.) 241
Dividend—Pledged involuntarily to the bank for indebtedness of shareholder...(Me.) 246
Duties—Of an officer are implied by his acceptance..........(Penn.) 247
Endorsement—Of a negotiable note or bill before maturity by the payee creates an absolute warranty to the immediate and subsequent endorser.....................................(Minn.) 248
"Assigned to A" made in the name of payee, the latter is *prima facie* endorser..(Ind.) 249
Released from liability.... ....(Canada.) 250
Change of domicile of endorser..........................(Canada.) 251
To get benefit of security held by the creditor, the endorser must first pay the paper, and assert his rights to subrogation...(N. Y.) 252
Liability of endorser....................................(Canada.) 253
Last endorser has paid the amount......................(Canada.) 254
Accommodation endorser................................(N. Y.) 255
Endorsed with the understanding that plaintiff should place his name above his (the defendant).......................(Canada.) 257
Endorser discharged may assume his liability again as though due process had been had...............................(N. Y.) 256
No notice of dishonor by non-acceptance is required in Spain.(Eng.) 258
After the maturity of a note.............................(Del.) 259
Endorser says "Then I will waive protest" upon time being granted...(N. Y.) 260
Endorser—Rights of, when some money had been paid to holder on note..(Canada.) 261
Note carries mortgage with it.............................(Iowa.) 262
Waiver on demand and protest.........................(Oregon.) 263
Endorser cannot maintain suit against assignee of paper not commercial..(Ala.) 264
Promise by, after failure to protest with notice...........(Oregon.) 265
Delay of payment granted to maker without notice to endorser. (Canada.) 267
A promise to pay after maturity of note by endorser dispenses with necessity of demand and notice........................(Cal.) 268
Endorser in blank first by payee and then by a third person. (Kansas.) 269
Stranger endorses negotiable paper is *prima facie* liable to the payee as original promissor................................(W. Va.) 270
Note under seal, payee agreed to continue it if maker would give security, and he gave an endorsement in blank...........(Penn.) 271
When, is a competent witness to prove an agreement in writing made with holder of note at the time of his endorsement..(U. S.) 266

Exemptions—Partnership property..........................(Mass.) 272
Evidence—To vary written contract—Sale—Sale upon approval.
     (Vt.) 273
Fair Dealing—Presumption in...........................(Oregon.) 274
False Pretences—What pretences will not constitute a cause of
     action..(Me.) 275
False Representations—Will not avoid contract in all cases(Oregon.) 276
Fixtures—Mortgage on building covers certain property and does
     not other certain property.............................(Mass.) 277
Actual connections to the realty, or something appurtenant thereto.
     (N. J.) 280
Foreclosure—Of mortgage by payee of certain notes which he en-
     dorsed in blank, conditioned that payee shall pay, or cause to be
     paid, said notes...(Ind.) 279
Foreign Corporations—Taxation on here, is an indirect prohibition
     against foreign corporation...........................(Oregon.) 278
Frauds—Whatever creates justice will destroy fraud.........(N. J.) 281
     Is never presumed, must be proven to exist.............(Md.) 282
     Recommendation for credit..............................(Md.) 283
     Contract for the purchase of goods with intent not to pay for them.
     (Ohio.) 283½
     Vendor and vendee. Interest of vendor.................(Iowa.) 284
Fraudulent Representations—Basis upon which charge should be
     made..(N. Y.) 285
     Mere fraudulent representations not actionable.............(Ill.) 286
     Infancy is a bar to an action for.........................(Vt.) 287
     Material representations by a vendor.....................(N. Y.) 288
Guaranty—Construction of documents.....................(Irish.) 289
     What constitutes a....................................(Iowa.) 290
     Signature in blank of a third person on a note in the hands of the
     payee..(Ill.) 291
     Guarantor undertook to insure the payment of all indebtedness of
     his principal..(Iowa.) 290½
     Assignor agrees to pay on notice of non-payment...........(Geo.) 292
     Sufficiency of a complaint founded upon a special promise to an-
     swer for the debt or doings of another..................(Minn.) 293
Homestead—Incumbrance upon. Its validity.................(Iowa.) 294
     Although mortgaged, may be sold free of such lien and regardless
     of it... 295
     Deed of ordinary form by husband and wife is sufficient to pass the
     title of..(Colo.) 296
     Deed of homestead must be executed anterior to the creation of the
     debt to be collected, to secure exemption therefrom........(Mo.) 297
     Living temporarily elsewhere, will not necessarily create abandon-
     ment of homestead.....................................(Mich.) 298
Husband and Wife—When wife executes a mortgage at the instance
     of the husband, who deceived her........................(Kan.) 299
     Husband having reduced to his possession the funds of his wife.
     (Del.) 300
     Husband becomes absolute owner of wife's legacy...........(Ark.) 301
     Materials for improvements on wife's property.............(Md.) 302
     Husband cannot loan money to his wife, both being insolvent at
     the time..(N. C.) 301½
     Property conveyed to the wife for which payment was made out of
     husband's property.....................................(Me.) 302½
     May pay his wife's claim in preference to other creditors.....(Me.) 303

Action against husband and wife for necessaries...........(Penn.) 304
Wife may mortgage her estate to secure her husband's creditors.
....(Penn.) 304½
Contract between, void...................................(Ark.) 305
Conveyance of land by husband to wife through trustee, not void
as to future creditors....................................(Ohio.) 306
Indemnity—Subsequent circumstances. Mortgage on his land, to
secure interest of another................................(Ind.) 307
Innocent Purchasers—Should be protected by the early record of all
deeds for land..(Ky.) 308
Innocent Holders—Of negotiable paper....................(Iowa.) 309
Insurance—Policy of, should be construed most strongly against the
insurer...(Vt.) 310
Life, forfeiture of, on failure to pay premium..............(N. Y.) 311
Marine. Who may effect an insurance, &c..................(N. Y.) 312
Interest—Action for money loaned and for interest upon money
loaned, and upon an account stated ....(Colo.) 313
Sureties liable for interest as damages in an action on official bond.
....(Colo.) 315
Compound interest...(N. Y.) 323
Ten per cent. can be taken................................(Mich.) 316
Need not say in contract ten per cent., the sum to be paid will do.
....(Mich.) 317
Agreement to pay compound interest if claim is not paid when due.
....(N. Y.) 321
Rate agreed upon under previous laws which is in excess of present
rates...(Conn.) 318
An allowance for the the failure of payment at maturity....(Colo.) 320
Promise to pay in labor and materials in annual payments. Interest
does not begin to run until the year is completed.....(Mich.) 324
Where installment falls due within the year...............(Mich.) 324½
Interest specified in note may be recovered.......... .....(Colo.) 325
Note containing "with interest, at the rate of sixteen per cent."
bears the legal and not the conventional rate after maturity.(Ark.) 327
Promise to pay on demand, interest runs from date of note.(Canada.) 326
On account, runs from day of settlement....................(Cal.) 328
Runs on deposits from time the bank failed.................(U. S.) 329
A judgment to bear interest at ten per cent. until paid.......(Ky.) 330½
When at the place of contract the rate differs from that of payment.
....(U. S.) 331
Interest on interest.......................................(N. Y.) 332
Act of 1872 provides "that no greater rate of interest than six per
centum per annum."......................................(Conn.) 333
On coupons..(N.Y.) 334
When the contract does not fix rate.........................(Ky.) 335
Both parties living in the State, creditor is entitled to war interest.
....(Va.) 314
Act of April, 1873. Code of 1873, ch. 173, § 14, p. 1120, abates
war interest. Not constitutional ....(Va.) 319
Agreement to pay twelve per cent. interest embodied in note, dated
in 1871...(Va.) 322
Interlineations—Defining remarks of court in Stanbery v. Moore,
56 Ill. 472, on interlineations... ....(Ill.) 330
Irregularity—Consenting to proceeding he might prevent by resisting.
....(R. I.) 337
Lapse of Time—Does not bar a direct trust ....(Del.) 338
Lien—Is neither property nor a debt........................(Ark.) 339

Transfer cannot be made but may be released.............(Ark.) 340
Change of...(Iowa.) 341
Life Policy—Is a chose in action........................(Mass.) 342
Married Women—Husband's consent may be implied.........(Ill.) 343
  Endorsing for her husband..............................(Ohio.) 344
  Cannot bind herself under statutes.....................(N. H.) 345
  When her note with husband's is valid in law...........(Colo.) 346
  Mortgaging her property to secure husband's debts......(Oregon.) 347
  Note is void at common law, no change..................(Fla.) 348
  Money loaned to wife for use of husband................(Mass.) 349
Marshalling Securities—Required to realize on collaterals first.(Del.) 350
  Mortgage on two tracts of land, on one of which B. held a mortgage also...(Ark.) 351
Merger—Conveyance of fee to mortgagee...................(N. J.) 352
Mistakes—In payment of money may be recovered back.....(N. Y.) 353
  Sufficient to decree the reform of a deed..............(Md.) 354
  Party to a lease misnamed...............................(Ill.) 357
  Assertion of payment leads to refusal of payment from endorser.
    (N. Y.) 356
  Produced wrong contract when making settlement.........(N. Y.) 355
  To avoid agreement, must be not of law but of fact.....(Del.) 358
  Made by a bankrupt in his statement....................(N. Y.) 359
  Deed may be corrected..................................(Oregon.) 360
  Degree of proof required to reform instrument on the ground of mistake...(Oregon.) 361
Mortgage—Of land, as security for note, the latter being sold, an assignment of the former to the third party, may be enforced.
    (Mass.) 362
  Right of entry under it................................(Vt.) 363
  Manner of making an entry..............................(Vt.) 364
  Writ of entry against heirs of mortgagor...............(Mass.) 365
  Absolute assignment to an agent who sells it...........(N. J.) 366
  Mortgagee's power to sell the mortgage.................(Ill.) 367
  Where one of a series of notes secured by a mortgage is sold..(La.) 369
  On a vessel, like a deed absolute on its face..........(Ill.) 368
  Equitable mortgage arises from non-payment of purchase-money.
    (N. J.) 370
  Foreclosure of senior mortgagee........................(Ohio.) 371
  When one person advances money for another with which to purchase land, taking the conveyance in his own name......(Ill.) 372
  Given by the wife with her husband's authority on her separate property, without the authorization of the judge.......(La.) 373
  An instrument of conveyance that on its face purports to be given as security...(Mich.) 374
  Sale of, by a mortgagee, same effect as a sale by the mortgaging debtor...(N. Y.) 375
  Two mortgages on same land, date the same, to secure his bond and three sureties......................................(N. J.) 376
  Besides which a chattel mortgage on fixtures to secure same debt, consisting of several bonds held by different parties.....(N. J.) 377
  Securing a negotiable note.............................(Ky.) 378
  Assumption of, contained in a deed to a married woman without her knowledge or consent..............................(N. J.) 379
  Conditions in "that if on demand, there shall be paid".......(Ill.) 380
  Assignee of a, takes it subject to all.................(N. J.) 381
  Grantee of a mortgagor of land cannot because of fraud maintain bill against assignee of the mortgage.....................(Mass.) 382

Is security, although contains no covenant of warranty.....(Mass.) 383
When mortgage and a note are held as security for mortgagor's note also held by mortgagee, the latter of which he sells......(Mass.) 384
If third mortgagee of land which is subject also to a fourth mortgage, sells............(Mass.) 385
A. gives his note and executes a mortgage to B. to enable him to raise money for him. B. without A.'s knowledge or consent gave the note to C. to secure his own debt, and then getting another note from A. by artifice, assigned mortgage and second note to D............(Mass.) 386
Bona fide assignee from an agent of the mortgagor can hold it.(N. J.) 387
Unauthorized cancellation of.........(La.) 388
On an undivided portion of land on which mortgagee is joint owner and holds a lease on all of it............(Mass.) 389
Withholding from record does not necessarily invalidate the mortgage as against creditors............(Ohio) 390
Where one of seven notes secured by a mortgage, is forcibly retained by creditor as a credit on his claim against the mortgagee who afterwards sells mortgage to an innocent party.....(N. Y.) 391
Note secured by a mortgage will carry the mortgage therewith, provided the holder of the note has actually negotiated for the note or parted with the value, upon the strength of the security. (N. Y.) 392
Conveyance of real estate on parol promise of defendant to raise plaintiff some money............(Penn.) 393
Lien—Priority............(Kansas.) 394
Third party not affected by notice of a mortgage, except the notice conveyed to him by the inscription of the mortgage........(La.) 395

National Bank—Is liable to be sued in any court having jurisdiction. (N. Y.) 396
Stockholder's liability............(Conn.) 397
Prohibited from taking mortgage on real estate, by act, sec. 8-28. (N. Y.) 398
Bank may take a mortgage to secure anticipated liabilities, as well as those existing at the time, unless restricted by its charter.(N. Y.) 400
Special deposits—Gross negligence............(Penn.) 399
Habitually receiving special deposits............(Ga.) 401
Federal agencies are exempt from State legislation so far.....(Md.) 402
To protect a trustee who is a stockholder of a national bank.(Conn.) 403
Omission of officers to exact security for money lent........(Colo.) 404
Ordering payment of the debts of an insolvent bank, who are stockholders............(Conn.) 405
Suit against, in State courts............(Vt.) 406
When national banks are not responsible for special deposits...... 407
Stockholders assent as security for the bank.........(Conn.) 408
Executors, administrators and trustees, are exempt as stockholders. (Conn.) 416
State law requiring cashier of each bank to transmit to certain town clerks a list of its shareholders, is not void.........(U. S.) 409
Stock of, assessed for taxation at actual value............(U. S.) 410
Depositor's claim at the time of suspension of bank........(U. S.) 411
Comptroller's declaration as to individual liability of stockholders. (U. S.) 412
When loan exceeds one tenth actual paid-in capital.........(U. S.) 417

Negligence—Who must suffer if one of two innocent persons must suffer a loss, as in signing deed, &c............(Ill.) 418
Contributory and comparatively............(Ill.) 419
Burden of proof............(Ill.) 420

As between two innocent parties........................(Ill.) 421
Negotiable Instruments—Endorsement in blank on negotiable paper is a *prima facie* evidence of the holder's clear right thereiu.(U. S.) 423
Given in payment of a patent right which is denounced as a fraud. (Penn.) 422
Rights of a *bona fide* holder of paper received from one who had misappropriated it.................................(U. S.) 424
Consist in failing or omitting to do what prudence would dictate. (U. S.) 425
Taken before maturity by a *bona fide* holder frees it from all infirmities, unless it is absolutely void for want of power in the maker. (U. S.) 426
Original holders of which are infected with fraud, subsequent holders stand the same................................(U. S.) 427
Though subject to prior equities. The purchaser without notice. (U. S.) 428
Negotiable Note—Made by wife, endorsed and presented by her husband for discount, is *prima facie* a nullity, unless for by evidence *aliunde* the instrument that it was made in her separate business or for the benefit of her separate estate..........(N. Y.) 429
Is not changed to a non-negotiable note by being payable one or two years after date, or was given for or secured by a lien on real estate......................................(Ky.) 431
One day after date is due on day after it was made, cannot be sued until the day following..............................(Ga.) 432
Non-Negotiable Notes—Pleading—Complaint—Demurrer—Defence. (N. Y.) 430
Notary Public—No general power to administer oaths......(Texas.) 433
Sureties on his bond are liable for damage caused by his affixing his paraph to any mortgage note which he knew to be forged....(La.) 434
Note—Given for too much not void. May recover *pro tanto*....(Ill.) 435
Notes and Bills—Signed by one as principal—Proof that the contract was that of surety.............................(Mo.) 436
Payable a specified number of months after date without grace. falls due.....................................(N. Y.) 437
Parol evidence to change the mode of payment............(Tenn.) 438
When note payable on demand becomes overdue..........(Conn.) 439
Notice—An association (not incorporated) desired to raise money, individual members thereof made notes in large sums and placed them in the hands of one of their number for sale. He used his own notes instead, because those given him were too large.(Penn.) 440
To the cashier, is notice to the bank.....................(N. J.) 441
To sue. To release a surety under the statute................(Ill.) 442
Offer to Endorse—When defendant becomes liable.............(Ga.) 443
Officers—The illegal cancellation of an official bond will not release the sureties..(La.) 444
Cashier cannot bind the bank as an endorser on his individual note. (U. S.) 445
Over-due—Coupons detached from railroad bonds payable to bearer are negotiable instruments............................(N. Y.) 446
Bona fide pledgee may hold bonds he received from an agent after they were over-due.................................(N. Y.) 447
An honest purchaser from the agent of the company can give a good title to another, although the bonds become due before the last transfer...(N. Y.) 448
Owelty—Manner of paying proceeds of sale..................(R. I.) 449

Parol Evidence—to vary terms of written contract..........(Ohio.) 450
Patent Right Notes—Statutes requiring notes given for patent rights to bear the fact on their face is unconstitutional..........(Mich.) 451
Partner—Surviving partner of a firm may assign a note payable to the late firm, by endorsement so as to vest legal title in the assignee.
(Ill.) 452

Partnership—Note of the firm to one of its members for borrowed money may be enforced at law in name of an indorsee......(Vt.) 453
Partner's attempt to bind his co-partner after dissolution of firm.(Cal.) 454
Partnership not taken under misapprehension, how maintained.
(Mass.) 455
Claim against firm can be established against estate of deceased partner...(Texas.) 456
Obligations created after dissolution of firm..............(Texas.) 457
Death of any of its members dissolves a firm, unless otherwise arranged for in agreement.............................(Texas.) 458
New partner not liable for old debts of previous firm........(Ky.) 459
Two partners constituting old firm cannot bind third partner, who with them, constitutes new firm of same name without his consent, by borrowing money and using it to pay debts of old firm.
(Ky.) 460
Parties in an action—For breach of contract..................(Ill.) 461
Partnerships and Partners—Power of one partner to bind his co-partners, rests alone upon the usages of merchants, and does not amount to a rule of law in any other than commercial partnerships...(Ky., Wis., &c.) 462
Partner in non-commercial partnership........................... 463
Engaged in business of mining................................... 464
Action against B. as to whether one W. and B. were partners.(N. C.) 465
Liability of a firm of real estate brokers when one partner receives money to buy land for a third person....................(Ill.) 466
Agreement between A. and B. to build five houses, certain expenses and profits to be divided between them...........(R. I.) 467
One partner, at its dissolution, sold all his interest to his partner, who gave his note therefor. Set-off against such note......(Me.) 468
Individual debts. Levy made on partnership property......(Ind.) 469
By levy on partnership property by the creditor of an individual creditor, acquires no interest whatever in the property itself, but only a lien on said property............................(Ind.) 470
Action at law cannot be maintained by one partner against another involving the state of the partnership accounts, unless on a promise to pay a balance agreed upon........................(Md.) 471
Partnership—Incoming partner. Liability...............(Kansas.) 472
One partner, without the consent, expressed or implied, cannot apply a claim of the firm to the payment of his individual debt.
(Wis.) 473
Partners have no implied authority to confess judgment for each other...(Mich.) 474
Remaining partners, on buying out retiring partner, agree to pay firm debts. Retiring partner afterwards paid some of old firm debts, and shortly after the new firm failed..............(Penn.) 475
Contracts made by one partner on behalf of the firm.......(N. H.) 476
Violation of good faith, for any partner to stipulate clandestinely with third person for any private and selfish advantage.(W. Va.) 477
When general reputation insufficient to prove partnership—What is not reputation..(N. Y.) 478
Community of profit and loss is the test of a partnership, even when the dispute is between the partners......................(Ala.) 480

Partner of an insolvent firm, conveyed his separate estate in satisfaction of a debt due to a separate creditor..................(Del.) 481
Sale by a partner, in payment of his own debt, of goods belonging to the firm, so intrusted to him by the firm, as to induce the public to believe them to be his..............................(Mass.) 479

Partnership Property—Attachment of partnership property for a partnership debt will prevail over a prior attachment of the same property for a separate debt of one partner...............(Iowa.) 482

Payable in Bank—Note so payable in a bank named, but not located, it will be presumed, unless the contrary appear, that the bank is located in this State...............................(Ind.) 483
Acceptance of a check for a draft, and neglects to present the check in due time, is a payment of draft.......................(N. Y.) 484
Money voluntarily paid in discharge of a claim made, or to buy off from, and quit a criminal prosecution.....................(Vt.) 485
Payment to sheriff of redemption money under foreclosure in United States treasury notes and national bank notes............(Minn.) 486
Where there are several debts, when at the time of sending a draft, the sender was, as a member of the firm, indebted to the party to whom the draft was sent ....(Ill.) 487

Payment—Creditor holding notes or other obligations for the payment of money, assigned to him by his debtor as collateral security, and neglects to use diligence to collect them..........(Wis.) 489
Stipulation on note that no credit shall be allowed on it, unless endorsed upon it by the payers.............................(Wis.) 490
When draft of third party is received by a creditor from his debtor for a pre-existing debt, presumed to be a conditional payment, unless agreed otherwise..................................(Penn.) 491
Taking a note from the debtor, or a note make by a third party, is no discharge of the debt, unless agreed so to be.........(W. Va.) 492
Partial payments are applied when their sum equals or exceeds the interest..(Miss.) 494
Partial payments are made on debt past due, are applied to accrued interest, and residue to principal.........................(Ala.) 495
In an action upon a note, money paid by the maker after the date of the note, and not endorsed thereon.....................(Colo.) 496
Voluntary payment to a bank holding a mortgage on the land owned by wife, and for which money was paid, cannot be recovered by wife..(Penn.) 497
Option to pay in money or property.........................(Ark.) 498
Part payment before due is a consideration to support a contract to give time...(Penn.) 499
By mutual mistake for that which has no legal existence or validity. (Mich.) 500
Tender, any third person who demands no subrogation, may tender to a creditor either in his own name or in that of the debtor.(La.) 501
Giving a note of a third person is evidence of payment of a pre-existing debt, unless proved otherwise....................(Mass.) 502
Proof of, may be made by parol evidence...............(Canada.) 503
What amounts to a...(Ill.) 504
Made voluntarily—Recovery..............................(Iowa.) 505
Partner may invest upon a foreclosure of a mortgage given to secure a note of firm before a personal judgment can be rendered against him upon the note. " If he pays the note, he becomes subrogated to the rights of the mortgagee "................(Iowa.) 506
Indorsement of a partial payment on back of note when controverted by payer, is not evidence sufficient to suspend statutes of limitation...(Ky.) 507

Action lies on note payable by installments as soon as first day of payment is passed, but only for first installment.......(Canada.) 508
On conditional sale of goods, does not give the seller a lien upon goods sold on such terms.................................(Ohio.) 509
Disposition of—Payer has a right to direct the application of his payment where he owes the creditor several debts........(Ohio.) 510
Mortgagor of land is the executor of the will of the mortgagee, and charges himself with the amount of the mortgage debt as assets in his hands as executor...............................(Mass.) 488
Bank check, given and accepted by the parties to it as payment of the balance found due on accounting together...........(Mass.) 493

Personal Covenants—in the husband's mortgage do not bind the wife, although she joined in its execution....................(Mich.) 511

Personal Liability—Wife not liable for deficiencies on a foreclosure of a mortgage from her husband and herself............(Mich.) 512

Pledge—Collateral left with a national bank with written authority to sell them at its discretion............................(U. S.) 514
Subsequent bankruptcy of the pledgor of a negotiable instrument. (U. S.) 515
Lending money on pledge of stock held in trust............(N. J.) 516
To constitute a pledge there must be a delivery and retention by the pledgee of the thing pledged........................ ....(Me.) 517
Sale of the pledge...(Ill.) 518
When pledgor tenders the sum due, but takes no steps to recover possession..(Ill.) 519
Actual possession necessary when practical.................(Wis.) 520
What constitutes a...(Ill.) 521
Withdrawal of pledge from national bank by giving it his individual check on himself, and shortly thereafter failed........(Md.) 522
Taking a negotiable note before maturity for consideration and without *mala fides*, creates a good title...................(Md.) 523
Nothing less than proof of a knowledge of facts that show want of authority to transfer a note will be sufficient to defeat title to such note..................... ....(Md.) 524
Holder is not bound to make inquiry, and mere negligence, however gross, not amounting to willful and fraudulent blindness...(Md.) 525
If the bank knew the note pledged was not the property of the party offering it...(Md.) 526
Possession is necessary to perfect the title to a pledge, and voluntary delivery back terminates the title....................(Md.) 527
Possession is of the essence of a pledge, and without, no privilege can exist as against third persons..................(U. S.) 528
Thing pledged may be in the temporary possession of the pledgor, as special bailee, having previously been in the possession of pledgee..(U. S.) 529
Pledges made with one party for the benefit of another, and handed over to the pledgor for collection........................(U. S.) 530
Ruling in Casey *v.* Cavaroc (supra, ¶ 467), applies to cases of Casey *v.* National Bank (96 U. S. S. Ct. 492)....................(U. S.) 531
Evidence of pledge made to insure defendant who became bail for another at plaintiff's request............................(Vt.) 532
Accommodation bill has been pledged for less than its face, and the pledgee transfers it for full value......................(N. Y.) 533
Ceases to be operative when its object is effected..........(Mich.) 534
Where a certificate of stock pledged as collateral security, is transferred by the pledgee to a creditor of his own............(Mass.) 513

Possession—By a man or his tenant, is notice of the title.....(N. J.) 535

No length of constructive possession will ripen a defective title to
land..(N. C.)   536
Entering into possession of land owned by wife under a deed from
her husband, alone...(N. C.)   537
Of a note, bond or bill, unattended by circumstances which in a
reasonable mind ought to excite suspicion..........................(Ill.)   538

Power—Committed to two or more persons........................(Texas.)   539
Of attorney, gives power to sell, and a sale is made under it, title
passes whether reference is made to the power or not....(Texas.)   540

Preference—Sale of property by an insolvent debtor, made in good
faith, to pay a particular creditor of his, to the exclusion of
others, without any intention to defraud, but simply to prefer
one creditor to another...(Kansas.) 541
Bond given by a debtor in failing circumstances covering all his
property..(Del.)   542

Presumptions—In the absence of proof to the contrary it will be presumed that notaries of other States have no greater powers than
are possessed by those of this State................................(La.)   543

Principal and Agent—Fraudulent misrepresentations by an agent.
(Canada.) 544
Secret gratuity given to an agent to influence his mind in favor of
giver...(Eng.)   545
One purchasing goods for another makes himself personally liable
if he contracts in his own name without discovering his principal.
(N. Y.)   546
Also held that a subsequent disclosure of the principals by defend-
ant, and the commencement of an action against them by plain-
tiffs was not conclusive of an election to hold them only.(N. Y.)   547
Where agents, without express authority, assume to act for their
principals..(Miss.)   548
Ratification by a principal of his agent's acts is only binding when
made on full knowledge of the facts...............................(Ky.)   549

Principal and Surety—When real estate of the surety has been levied
upon and sold by sheriff under execution issued upon a judgment rendered against principal and surety.......................(Ind.)   550
Bond executed in blank by H. and sureties to enable him to raise
$300 by loan, from B., was filled up for $354.48...........(Del.)   551
Release of surety by cashier of a bank.............................(Neb.)   552
When holder holds other securities for the payment of the note, is
no ground for the release of surety...............................(Neb.)   553
Cashier states to a surety, who is not an officer of the bank, that the
note upon which he is surety has been paid by the principal,
bank is estopped from denying the truth of such statement, when
to do so would entail loss upon the surety.......................(Neb.)   554
When a firm is surety, and one of its members is also a member of
the board of directors of the bank, all the members of such firm
are affected with the notice which the one who is a director is
presumed to have..(Neb.)   555
Release of the principal, against whom, with the surety a joint judgment has been obtained, operates as a release of the surety.(Miss.) 556
Agreement between holder of note and the principal maker thereof,
that the latter may retain the sum due for a definite time upon
his promise to pay usurious interest.............................(Miss.)   557
Action upon an administration bond under R. S., c. 72, § 9, a judgment against the administrator in favor of the creditor of the
estate for whose benefit this suit is brought....................(Me.)   558

Surety cannot be held on a bond which he only signed upon a condition that was not performed..........................(Mich.) 559
Extension of note in consideration of the execution of a deed of trust by a principal debtor, whereby property not subject to execution was made liable for its payment, is good for a promise of extension of payment........................ ....(Mo.) 560

Privilege—If proceeds of the movable and unmortgaged property of a succession do not suffice to pay off its privileged debts, those debts must be first preferred for payment to the proceeds of its property incumbered by the youngest mortgage............(La.) 561
Seizure of property under execution of a valid judgment gives superior lien..... ....(La.) 562

Profits—Probable profits are not a proper basis upon which to estimate damages...(Me.) 563
Property purchased by a wife on the credit of her separate estate, or of her profits from it, or her earnings..................(Penn.) 564

Promise—On demand of payment, the endorser replied that he had "not expected to have it to pay, and that it was impossible to pay it at present"...(Mich.) 565
Original promise is the basis of action........................(Ky.) 566
Promise to a debtor, for valuable consideration, to pay his debt to a third person...(Kansas.) 567

Promissory Note—Illegality of note made in a foreign state, claimed because made upon a consideration void in that state......(Colo.) 568
Will not always discharge liability.........................(Conn.) 569
Note made in Georgia in 1863 is shown to be solvable in Confederate notes, the sum thereby payable in actual money is ascertained by the value of coin or legal currency of the United States at the time...(U. S.) 570
Indorsed payment in same terms used in the note, has same construction as to kind of money value..................(U. S.) 571-572
Written contract made at same time of executing and indorsing note and relating thereto, cannot be contradicted by parole testimony... ....(U. S.) 573
In absence of proof when notes were transferred, the law presumes that they were, when under-due.........................(U. S.) 574
Defendant's name on back of note in blank, written before delivery to payee, is presumed to be the surety of the maker for his accommodation..(U. S.) 575
Payable conditional that a case pending in the courts is decided in favor of the payee, and proceeding is decided against him..(Cal.) 579
Interest payable quarterly................... ....(Conn.) 580
If maker was required to act after maturity of his note, and before payment with reference to his equitable rights ....(Texas.) 581
Descriptio personæ—Executor when personally liable on, reimbursement out of estate.......... ....(Mo.) 585
"We, as trustees, but not individually, promise to pay," signed A., B. and C., trustees, purporting on its face to be secured by a mortgage...(Mass.) 586
Given at the request and for the benefit of his son..........(Mass.) 587
Payable to the order of the wardens and vestry of a church or order, but before it passed into plaintiff's possession the corporation became in fact extinct..(Vt.) 589
Alteration of by one of the makers, increasing the amount by inserting words and figures in blank spaces left in the printed form. (Mass.) 594
Under the Act of April, 1873, governed by the law merchant—Set-off...(Ark.) 595

Situation of a person, to whom money is paid by mistake on a forged note..(Mass.) 598
Obtained through fraud by A. from B., payable to C., whose endorsement was forged. B. at maturity, paid it to the bank.(Mass.) 599
Obtained from a person while under influence of liquor without sufficient consideration...(Ala.) 600
Signing a note after two others had signed, added to his signature the word "surety." At maturity the note was renewed at bank by giving another signed in the same manner by third party.(Vt.) 601
Signing name on back of note at the time it is made and before it comes into the hand of the payee........................(Colo.) 602
The fact that he did not participate in the consideration of the note does not tend to explain or rebut his liability as maker....(Colo.) 603
Entitled to the whole of the business hours of the last day of grace to pay a note secured by chattel mortgage, and is not in default until the expiration of that time.........................(Minn.) 604
Principal and surety—Liability of co-sureties—Want of consideration..(Vt.) 605
Given to a married woman by a third person in consideration of her husband's giving to him a like note, and she transfers the note with her husband's consent.... ....(Mass.) 606
Executed on Sunday but bore date the following day........(Ark.) 607
Payable on a day named "or before, if made out of the sale of J. B. Drake's horse hay-fork and hay-carrier"..................(Ill.) 608
Cancelling the signature of makers of a note dishonored and writing "paid" on the note, corrected before the note is sent back to the plaintiffs by a memorandum thereon "cancelled in error." (Eng.) 609
Made payable to the maker, no validity until endorsed by him.(Ill.) 610
Law in force when a note is made and endorsed, regulates...(Ala.) 611
Accommodation paper.......................................(N. Y.) 612
Payable upon the condition that a railroad be built to a place named on or before 20th of February, 1871.....................(Colo.) 613
When without consideration...............................(Ala.) 614
Action on, by administrator of payee, there was evidence that, on death of payee, the note, in a division of personal property made before the appointment of administrator, fell to a daughter, who by agent demanded payment of principal maker, who replied it was not convenient for him to pay, but agreed to pay "interest at eight per cent.," which rate the agent wrote on the note.(Mass.) 615
Authority of an agent or attorney to execute promissory note. (Kansas.) 616
Where a party pays a forged note through mistake, supposing the signature to be genuine.................................(Mass.) 617
Payable "on or before six months from date" was declared upon as payable six months from date...........................(Vt.) 618
Otherwise negotiable, is not rendered non-negotiable by the addition of a stipulation to pay costs of collecting including reasonable attorney's fees..(Kansas.) 619
When time of payment is not stated.....................(Oregon.) 620
Forged note paid by mistake on the part of creditor............. 621
Transferred without endorsement........................(Oregon.) 622
Agreement to deposit purchase-money notes with an attorney, and from the proceeds of such notes outstanding liens on the land should be paid......................................(Texas.) 623
Secured by deed of trust, part of which is paid and a new note given for the balance. The purchaser of the new note may enforce the deed of trust to secure the payment thereof.............(Miss.) 624
Maker promised B. if he would endorse his note he would get C. to

endorse it also, who on application refused, unless he had a note for same amount from first endorser as security, which was given him..(Vt.) 625
Bona fide holder of a note, who purchased it for value before it fell due and without notice of payments made thereon.........(Cal.) 626
Written contract between payer and payee, made at same time the note was, and in which the note is clearly referred to, must be read in connection with the note......................................(Cal.) 627
Need not prove execution of note if the maker omits to file an affidavit denying it...(Mich.) 628
The consideration of a note is open to inquiry of all interested therein...(Mich.) 629
Partnership paper given *mala fide*..............................(Mich.) 630
Contemporaneous and subsequent guarantees...............(Mich.) 631
Subsequent endorsement does not make the endorser jointly liable with his principal..(Mich.) 632
Note received after it became due.............................(Canada.) 633
Given to new firm formed after dissolution of old, in satisfaction of a guarantee to the old firm for advances made by them.(Canada.) 634
Plaintiff's evidence admissible to prove the note, though dated at Montreal, was made at Quebec.......................(Canada.) 635
Endorsement—Protest..(Ohio.) 636
When endorser has protected himself...................................... 637
When endorser has security in his own hands..............(Maine.) 638
Where endorser waives demand and protest................(Conn.) 639
When endorser was held liable................................. 640
Endorsers held responsible where demand was a day too late.(Miss.) 641
Second endorser with ample security from first endorser was held. (Miss.) 642
Want of the words " Value received "...................(Canada.) 643
Passed without endorsement...............................(Canada.) 644
Renewal note retained, but sued on old notes before second came due...(Canada.) 645
" Paid Dec. 15th, 1872, $500 on acct. of this note to revive the same." (Md.) 646
Signed by married woman without authority of her husband. (Canada.) 647
Signed with an x in presence of a witness...............(Canada.) 648
Endorsed before maturity by a party who has since become bankrupt..(Canada.) 649
Signed by a married woman authorized by her husband, but not shown that she is separate in property, etc. ....(La.) 650
Joint note by two parties, one paid half the amount, and was released by the payee...(Penn.) 651
For patent right...(Ohio.) 652
Maker of, after judgment rendered against endorser, not a competent witness..(Del.) 653
Bank being the holder of a promissory note protested for non-payment, has not the right to credit it with deposits...........(Del.) 654
Agreement by the bank to credit on the note such fees as the debtor might earn from the bank as its notary public...........(Eng.) 655
To release the surety, time must be given, and for a consideration. (Eng.) 656
" My note becoming due the 10th inst., good for ten days after date." The note to which reference was made became due on the 11th, there was no other note.....................(Canada.) 657
Memorandum made by a party on a note in his possession....(Ky.) 658
Payable at and discounted by an incorporated bank, stand as foreign bills ....(Ky.) 659

Alterations, erasures or mutilations on a note ....(Ky.) 660
Minor's note..(Canada) 661
Taking a note for an antecedent debt, imposes upon the creditor an
    obligation to wait for his pay............................(Me.) 662
Promising to pay A. or his order on account of B., payment must
    be made to A. not to B................................(Canada.) 663
Where room is left by the maker on the note for making additions
    without defacing..(Ky.) 664
R. held the note of the firm of T. G. & Co. After it was given
    some of the members retired from the firm, leaving assets suffi-
    cient to pay all debts and binding the remaining firm to pay them.
                                          (Ohio.) 665
Signed by procuration................................(Canada.) 666
Executed by the maker's mark, if endorsed..............(Canada.) 667
Transfer of after maturity..............................(Canada.) 668
Accommodation endorsers who are protected by a mortgage.(R. I.) 669
Not paid or protested at maturity, but some time afterwards en-
    dorsed and paid out by the holder....................(Canada.) 670
Given by insolvent debtor a few days before the insolvency to secure
    parties who were creditors on accommodation paper...(Canada.) 671
Obtained by surprise and false representation............(Canada.) 672
Where maker absconds before due.....................(Canada.) 673
Given by an insolvent to one of his creditors in settlement of a claim
    of the creditor against another party for whom the insolvent was
    security. The creditor refusing to sign composition deed of in-
    solvent unless such a settlement was made...........(Canada.) 674
Pleaded want of notice of protest, but produced no affidavit in sup-
    port of such plea....................................(Canada.) 675
Payable in this country must be made in money current in this
    country...(Canada.) 676
Holder being requested by a surety to proceed against the principal
    maker..(Colo.) 677
Stamp of a bank on a note............................(Canada.) 678
Holder and owner of a note may cancel any of the endorsers.
                                          (Canada.) 678½
Given by an insolvent to a creditor for the balance of his claim in
    consideration of his having signed a deed of composition.(Canada.) 679
Action to recover the amount of an "I. O. U."............(Eng.) 680
Part payments by indorsers.............................(Canada.) 681
As follows: "12 mos. from the 26th June, 1873, I (defendant) will
    pay J. C. (plaintiff) $90 for D. P., or otherwise settle the sum of
    $90 for him, on a note, that he says he gave J. C. for $100.(N. B.) 682
A promise in writing to pay on a day certain £250 to A. B. or order,
    with an engagement to pay in cash or in goods, if the holder
    should choose to demand the latter....................(Canada.) 683
A promise to pay a note to the holder which is not endorsed and
    which fact the drawer was aware of..................(Canada.) 684
Writing merely certifying that a person is indebted to another in a
    certain sum of money................................(Canada.) 685
Issued under fraud....................................(Canada.) 686
Suit before due because of the maker's insolvency and going away.
                                          (Canada.) 687
Executed in 1863 for the balance of a note executed in 1853...(N. C.) 688
Payable on demand sued thirteen years after its date.....(Canada.) 689
Issued by the secretary-treasurer of a municipality.......(Canada.) 690
When plaintiff need not allege in a suit to recover endorsement sub-
    sequent to the defendant.................................(R. I.) 691
Action on note made in the United States, and payable there, defend-
    ant after action brought, tendered the amount in Canadian cur-

rency equal at the current rates of exchange to the amount of
American currency....................................(Canada.) 692
No set form of words is requisite to constitute a promissory note.
  (Canada.) 693
Illegal consideration..(R. I.) 695
Suit brought against maker of note in name of party who received
  payment therefore from one of the endorsers............(R. I.) 696
An obligation before a notary to pay a certain sum of money.
  (Canada.) 694
An action in name of the bank which had previously received pay
  for the note from one of the endorsers in whose behalf suit was
  brought..(R. I.) 697
Signed by G., payable to order of W., who endorsed it, and before
  issue F. endorsed it. At request of W. and G. changed his signa-
  ture to "G., agent"..(R. I.) 698
Due presentment of a note, when denied, is sufficiently shown by
  evidence that the note was in the bank where it was payable.(Ky.) 699
Property in—Right to sue..............................(Canada.) 700
Date of issue..(Canada.) 701
When payable...(Eng.) 702
Given in discharge of antecedent debt......................(R. I.) 703
Given on a precedent debt.................................(R. I.) 704
In the possession of a regular purchaser before maturity has valid
  title, though the vendor was not the owner................(La.) 705
Maker and endorser are liable for the whole debt............(La.) 706
Pledge or sale of, before maturity, carries with it all the liens by
  which it is secured.......................................(La.) 707
In an action at law on a, facts which constitute mere matter of de-
  fence, and are available as such........................(Ohio.) 708
Burden of proof in a suit by the assignee against the assignor..(Ill.) 709
When purchased by defendant for the plaintiff's intestate with
  money furnished by the latter..........................(Iowa.) 710
When held as collateral security..........................(Iowa.) 711
Issued as partial payment for work yet to be done..........(Me.) 712
Action on an unendorsed note.............................(Ind.) 713
Payable to her order, and assigned by a woman by delivery, and
  who afterwards marries the maker.......................(Me.) 714
Evidence to impeach a....................................(Me.) 715
And mortgage given by married woman with consent of husband.
  (Ind.) 716
Holder of a solidary note..................................(La.) 717
Of a married woman which was taken for value before maturity.(La.) 718
Time in which to present for payment....................(Pick.) 719
Renewal by an administrator of a matured note executed by his de-
  cedent..(Ind.) 720
Accepted bill on a firm, the protest must state who compose the
  firm, etc..(N. Y.) 721
Protest, when may be served by mail. What is good protest by
  mail..(N. Y.) 722
Where indorser lives in a different place from that in which demand
  is to be made..(N. Y.) 723
Where note held in New York was payable in Kurtztown, Pa., and
  the holder placed it with a New York city bank for collection,
  which sent it off, and it passed through several other banks before
  presentation..(N. Y.) 724
Action by an assignee on a note...........................(Ind.) 725
Defendant pleaded a general denial, there having been no notice of
  protest...(Canada.) 726
Endorsed note discounted by a bank for the drawer, at maturity, he

took it up by a similar note on which last the indorsement was
    forged...(Penn.)   727
Secured by a mortgage, which latter is transfered without the notes.
                                                            (Mich.) 728
Given for stock in a manufacturing company, the note to be paid
    upon agreed conditions...............................(Penn.)   729
Protest irregular..(Ca.)   730
Garnishee order, note not yet due.........................(Irish.)   731
Payable "Twelve months after date (or before, if made out of the
    sale of a machine), I promise to pay to J. F. H. or bearer, &c."
                                                            (Penn.) 732
Sale, delivery and endorsement thereon is a warranty of the genuine-
    ness of it...(Vt.)   733
Oral evidence with regard to agreement when endorsement was made.
                                                            (Mass.) 577
Endorser, who, before the St. of 1874, c. 404, wrote his name upon
    the back of a negotiable note........................(Mass.)   578
Where note is paid with currency to an agent, which currency the
    principal refused to accept, when a new note was made and deliv-
    ered...(Va.)   582
Endorser's liability released for want of proper notice......(Va.)   584
Given by an assignee of a bankrupt towards payment of moneys re-
    ceived and misused by him............................(Mass.)   588
Person who receives two notes upon an agreement to release a de-
    mand upon their payment at maturity..................(Mass.)   590
Note payable to the order of A., is given by him to the maker with-
    out endorsing his name on it.........................(Mass.)   591
Joint note signed by one as principal, and another as surety, and
    payable to the order of a bank, with which certain bonds are
    given as collateral..................................(Mass.)   592
Land that has been mortgaged to secure a note which was sold
    under a power contained in the mortgage bringing less than the
    amount of the note...................................(Mass.)   593
A waiver of demand and notice upon a note before or after the ma-
    turity...(Mass.)   596
Delay in enforcing the note against the maker.............(Mass.)   597
Memorandum of "F. & L. bonds as collateral" on a joint and sev-
    eral note, signed by one as principal and another as security.
                                                            (Mass.) 598
Note payable to A. or order (secured by mortgage), who borrowed
    money of B., and indorsed the note to B.'s order. Afterwards A.
    paid B., who wrote his name on back of the note under the name
    of A., and delivered it to A., and also executed an assignment of
    the mortgage and note to A., after which A. sold for a valuable
    consideration both to a savings bank which sued B......(Mass.)   576
Delivery of note to one of the partners, and its cancellation by him,
    though unpaid..   588
A borrowed money of B. giving him therefor his note and a mort-
    gage on real estate. Afterwards A. paid the note to B. before its
    maturity, when B. assigned the mortgage to A., and put his name
    on the note. A. sold them to a savings bank, which sued B.(Mass.) 578

Protest—Of note endorsed by husband for his wife. He being uni-
    versal legatee.......................................(Canada.) 734
Omission to state in a notarial protest that it was made in the fore-
    noon...(Canada.) 735
Non-exhibition of the note to the maker when protesting.(Canada.)   736
Described as E. B. P. instead of Joseph B. P. in protest and declar-
    ation..(Canada.) 737
Waver of notice...(Canada.) 738

Dated at Montreal and payable at a bank in Albany, New York, a notice of protest mailed at Albany addressed to an endorser at Montreal according to the laws of the State of New York.(Canada.) 739
Draft is not an obligation within the meaning of the proviso of the act of 16th of April, 1850..............................(Penn.) 740
Addressed to a female endorser........................(Canada.) 743
Must be evidence of diligence of protest................(Canada.) 744
Notice of, may be given by a holder and in his own language provided the paper has been legally dishonored............(Mich.) 745
Must prove a legal notice of protest....................(Kansas.) 746
Where holder and party to whom notice is to be given....(Kansas.) 747
Holder may give notice to all prior parties or only his immediate predecessor...(Kansas.) 748
Banker or agent to whom paper has been sent for the purpose of obtaining acceptance or payment, is to be considered as though he were the real holder..............................(Kansas.) 749
Where note provides that the indorsers "waive presentment for payment, protest, and notice of protest and non-payment".(Ind.) 750
When protest is waived, need not aver such notice...........(Ill.) 751
Due notice of, sent to the address of the defendant where he formerly long resided, but at, and for several years preceding the maturity of this note, he lived elsewhere. There were three post-offices at his former residence, to one of which notice was sent of the dishonor of a note maturing earlier than this one, at same bank, which was responded to by him....................(Me.) 752
Waiver of, by accommodation indorser, who wrote the cashier of the bank where the note was payable on the day it fell due, the bank being just then ignorant of its existence.............(Vt.) 753
Endorser resided in A., but before the note came due he went beyond the Confederate lines. When note was protested notice was served at endorser's residence, but he had no agent there. (Va.) 741
Where a note is purchased at a much less value than the amount of the note at a public sale..................................(Va.) 742

Purchaser—At public judicial sale........................(Mich.) 754
Of land, with notice of outstanding equities.................(Ill.) 755
Creditor who makes advances under the security of a deed of trust, in good faith, and without notice of a vendor's equitable lien for purchase money..(Ark.) 756
Option of..(R. I.) 757
To become a *bona fide*.....................................(Minn.) 758
Insolvency of..(Eng.) 759
Creditor taking a chose in action as collateral for a pre-existing debt. (Penn.) 760
Deed made to defendant under a verbal agreement that he and wife would execute and deliver a mortgage to the vendor, to do which the wife afterwards refused..............................(N. C.) 761

Quantum Meruit—Although an action cannot be maintained upon a verbal contract not to be performed within one year....(Ohio.) 762

Receipt—For a lost note...................................(Iowa.) 763
May be explained or contradicted by parol evidence......(W. Va.) 764
Of bank check as payment of antecedent debt................(Ga.) 765

Receiver—Right to bid in property..........................(Ill.) 766
When creditor's bill charges that the debtor has choses in action, &c. in his possession..(Ill.) 767
Of a bank, under Gen. Stat. (R. I. cap. 140), may bring suit in his own name..(R. I.) 768

Redemption of Real Estate—sold under foreclosure, may be redeemed from the purchaser by the judgment creditor..............(Ind.) 769
Replevin—No previous demand upon a *bona fide* purchaser of a chattel from one who had no authority to sell it is necessary.(Maine.) 770
Sheriff cannot sell goods covered by a writ of replevin previously served upon himself..(Mich.) 771
Goods commissioned to M. by D. for sale. D. pledged them for a loan of money to another, who knew they belonged to M. Held, M. could recover by replevin without tendering repayment of loan...(Penn.) 772
Where property bond was given and the lender retained the goods. (Penn.) 773
There is no set-off in replevin.... ....(Penn.) 774
Where party declines to accept payment except in a way he is not entitled..(Penn.) 775
Representations—Damages not recoverable for loss of speculative profits..(Mich.) 776
Recission—of contract can only be by the acts or assent of all the parties..(N. H.) 777
Stock sold with agreement to take it back.................(Penn.) 778
Damages for refusal by vendee to accept goods sold him....(Penn.) 779
Retrospective operations of Statute of Limitations—Act 145 of 1871 amended the Statute of Limitations so as to run against Canadian as well as domestic creditors.. ....(Mich.) 780
Revivor of Debt—When a note and mortgage are once barred, a subsequent revivor of the note by a part payment, promise, or acknowledgment of the payer... ....(Kansas.) 781
Sales—What is considered a dealer........................(Mich.) 782
Of goods—Contract—Fraud—False Pretences—Pawning of Property...(Eng.)782½
Under the guise of a renting of personal property............(Ky.) 783
Parties considering sale complete as to price and delivery.....(Ga.) 784
Consent to a sale may be inferred........................(U. S) 785
Induced by fraudulent means..............................(N. J.) 786
Personal property. Purchase of one in possession..........(Miss.) 787
Sale—After which replevin is applied to as a relief from consequences of a breach of the agreement..............................(Mass.) 786½
Of goods in the hands of a bailee is good against an execution creditor...(Penn.) 787½
Sale to a party who has agreed to buy in for another.. ....(Penn.) 788
Of goods not accompanied by immediate delivery...........(Colo.) 789
By debtor to his creditor who credits the latter on his account and instantly resells the goods to the debtor....................(La.) 790
Implied warranty..(Vt.) 791
Of personal property by a debtor there must be a real, permanent delivery and change of possession........................(Ill.) 792
Conditional sale and delivery wherein the property is not to vest until the purchase money is paid..........................(Neb.) 793
Warranty—Implied acceptance.............................(Vt.) 794
Satisfaction—Payment of part of a debt without release under seal, although received in full satisfaction....................(Penn.) 795
Savings Bank—Loss of deposit book......................(Mass.) 796
Securities—Stolen, may be followed and reclaimed..........(Penn.) 797
Confession of judgment by principal. Its effect upon the security. (La.) 798
When release of collateral security does not discharge a surety on the note..(Minn.) 7½?

Set-Off—H. being indebted to W. on a note under seal bought a note issued by W., which he desired to set-off ....(Del.) 800
When set-off can be made................................(Mass.) 801
Debts are not mutual, when one is by defendant as principal and surety, to the plaintiff as trustee for a minor...............(Ga.) 802
Assignee of a mortgage, unless the mortgagor has estopped himself, holds it subject to all the equities to which it was liable in the hands of the assignor....................................(Penn.) 803
Subsequent assignee may avail himself of "no defence" given to the first..(Penn.) 804
B. borrowed money of an agent of a trust company, giving stocks, &c., as collateral. The agent borrowed of A. and afterwards took an assignment of B.'s note and collaterals...............(Penn.) 805
Whenever a demand is for damages which the law is capable of measuring accurately by a pecuniary standard................(Ala.) 806
The right of set-off in an action is governed by the law of the place where the action is brought............................(Ohio.) 807
A set-off may be pleaded in an action brought by a receiver of an insolvent national bank................................(Ohio.) 808
When a bank can retain the deposits in set-off against the notes held by it..(R. I.) 809
Legacy presently payable, cannot be set-off in equity against a debt of the legatee to the estate, not yet due..................(Del.) 810
In a suit against a party and his sureties....................(Ill.) 811
Demand against one person cannot be set-off against him and his nominal partner...(Miss.) 812
When a surviving partner purchases from the administrator of his deceased partner, the interest of the latter in the firm property, while he has a claim due him from the said deceased partner.(Ind.) 813

Shareholders—Wherein a shareholder who has become such in a company incorporated by letters patent, issued under 27 & 28 Vict. ch. 23, by the purchase of partly paid-up shares of stock is not responsible for debts of the company.............(Canada.) 814

Signature—Genuineness of, ceases to be presumed the moment the defendant denies it in his plea supported by affidavit...(Canada.) 815
Proof of...(Canada.) 816
On check forged by a clerk whom the principal has trusted to report the condition of his bank-book as being correct, and has otherwise shown great confidence in him, and thus created confidence in said clerk in the minds of the officers of the bank.(N. Y.) 817
How proven.......................................(Ohio.) 818
Comparative evidence offered as a standard by the presentation of a receipt..(Ohio.) 819
Action against endorsers who deny their signatures......(Canada.) 820
Verification of....................................(Canada.) 821

Stated Account—Burden of proof on the party impugning the accuracy thereof..(R. I.) 822
What constitutes is a matter of evidence....................(R. I.) 823
Balance shown in an account and claimed in a suit as such.(Texas.) 824

Statute of Limitations—A promise by A., that "he would see his brother and would pay the debt"........................(N. C.) 825
Residence and not citizenship is contemplated in the Statute of Limitations upon the time of bringing actions...............(Iowa.) 826
Part payment of the consideration of a parol promise not to be performed within the year...................................(Ohio.) 827
Are in force when the remedy is sought, and not that existing when contract was made...(Me.) 828
Runs against an infant having only a color of title...........(Vt.) 829

Can apply to future transactions only, unless expressly given effect..(Mich.) 830
Credit upon an account after cause of action on the same is barred, not always considered as part payment..................(Ohio.) 830½
Began to run during the life of the devisor................(Ark.) 831
Payment of interest on a note barred. Effect on surety....(Mass.) 832
Payment upon a bond by the administrator of one of the joint makers within the statutory period......................(Mo.) 833
When the, begin to run on an administrator's bond........(Mich.) 834
When plaintiff shows that defendant was a non-resident, the latter must show he had owned attachable property within the state.(Vt.) 835
Commence running from time of a loan payable on demand, and no note or other obligation is given........................(Cal.) 836
When a payment by one of several makers of a joint and several note will take it out of...................................(Vt.) 837
Payment made by the treasurer of a partnership from partnership funds, and by him indorsed on the firm note...............(Vt.) 838
Partial payment of a debt raises only a *prima facie* presumption.(Ind.) 839
Are pleaded a reply that such money is a part of a mutual running account...(Ind.) 840
As to married women.....................................(Ill.) 841
Payment of interest year by year by the principal..........(Md.) 842
Acknowledgment of a debt made, not to the creditor, but to a stranger...(Kansas.) 843
Act of Limitations to suits on bonds does not change the presumption held heretofore, that after a lapse of twenty years, a bond has been paid...(W. Va.) 844
A promise by a member of a late firm, made after dissolution and before a suit is barred by the statute of limitations to pay firm debt..(Florida.) 845
Defendant must insist on statute as a bar in his answer.....(Ohio.) 846
Debt was due Oct. 6th, 1862, suit was brought Oct. 6th, 1868.(Penn.) 847
Receipt for $900, borrowed to be returned "when called for". (Texas.) 848
Construction of act of 1868, ch. 357.......................(Md.) 849
Defendant's letter said: "in regard to settlement that he was ready any day after that week, and willing to leave it out to be settled" (Vt.) 850

Stock—As between a corporation and corporator...........(Penn.) 851
Was pledged as collateral for a note, and pledgee took a mortgage as further security......................................(Penn.) 852
A. agreed, for a valuable consideration, to purchase from or sell to B., at the option of the latter, a certain number of shares, within a limited time at a specified price......................(N. Y.) 853
Agreement to carry stock on margin, right to sell when margin not kept good...(N. Y.) 854

Stockholder—If any one stockholder is required to pay debt due by the corporation, he is entitled to contribution from all the others, unless he has not paid up his subscription................(Md.) 855
Presumed to be owner of stock if his name appears on the books. (U. S.) 856
Party who made a contract with an organization which had attempted to irregularly create itself into a corporation.....(U. S.) 857
Subscriber to railway shares who fails to pay his subscription must pay interest...(N. Y.) 858
Restraint from transferring stock by articles of association...(Del.) 859
Liability of, for corporation debts........................(Mich.) 860

Subrogation—How and to what extent......................... 862

Allowed principal and surety............................(N. Y.) 861
When a surety pays the debt............................(Ark.) 863
Sunday—Contracts made on that day, but bearing the date of another.
(Iowa.) 864
When made for a charitable purpose....................(Ark.) 865
Promissory note dated on Sunday............................ 866
Action on assumpsit to recover money paid on Sunday contract.
(Mc.) 867
Sureties and Surety—Not creditors of the principal, until they pay
the debt for which they are bound......................(Del.) 868
Contribution from estate of co-surety...................(Ark.) 869
On a joint and several bond, given by them with A. and B. as principals...(Mass.) 870
To entitle a surety to an assignment and execution against his co-sureties..(Md.) 871
When all the stockholders of a corporation give their joint and
several note..(N. Y.) 872
Where one person becomes surety for the payment of money by
another, who is himself a surety for a third person........(S. C.) 875
Where a party refuses to sign as surety unless another person will
first sign, the latter's signature is forged by the maker of the note.
(Ill.) 876
Verbal notice by a surety on a note to the holder thereof, to proceed
at once to collect the note of the principal...............(Ind.) 877
Extension of time of payment upon consideration that maker will
annually pay interest on the note........................(Ind.) 878
Surety cannot be held under a judgment void as to his principal.(La.) 879
Mortgage given to secure payment of notes; their time of payment
was extended..(Penn.) 880
Holding several securities by way of indemnity............(U. S.) 881
Married woman as surety for her husband.................(Mich.) 882
Part payment of a debt already due......................(Ohio.) 883
Surety who takes of the debtor a mortgage for his indemnity as such
surety...(Ohio.) 884
A *bona fide* purchaser of a debtor's land from a frudulent vendee,
without notice of fraud................................(Ohio.) 885
Undertaking by an infant as surety for the stay of execution.(Ohio.) 886
Or indorser of a bankrupt is released from liability by the bankrupt's payment of the debt to the creditor, who accepts payment
in fraud of bankruptcy..................................(Ky.) 887
Security taken by one of several co-sureties..............(N. Y.) 888
Where one of two co-sureties pays the debt of their principal.
(N. Y.) 889
Where surety does not assent to an alteration of the terms of his undertaking...(Ky.) 890
After judgment surety continues for most, if not for all purposes.
(Ky.) 891
A surety against whom judgment has been rendered, may off-set.
(Texas.) 892
Cannot benefit by an exception personal to the principal......(La.) 893
Neglect of a privileged creditor to sue......................(La.) 894
In an action on a bond against a surety, judgment having been obtained against principal, he is a competent witness.......(Penn.) 895
Signing on faith of that of co-surety, whose signature proves to be
forged...(Mo.) 896
Judgment rendered against one of the makers of a note.....(Ohio.) 897
Agreement between payee and principal of a note for extension of
time for a fixed period in consideration of same rate of interest as
named in the note....................................(Ohio.) 898

Release of by failure to present debt against estate of deceased principal..(Ill.) 899
One of several apparently joint makers appears, and upon default of his co-defendants, and without any notice to them other than the original summons alleges, and obtains judgment against them, that they are principals and he a surety only........(Ind.) 900
Surety paying a judgment against his principal and himself...(Va.) 873
Bond on which principal and surety are both bound, once paid by the surety in the lifetime of the principal, without assignment by the creditor, or agreement to assign........................(Va.) 874

Taxation—Profit upon the capital or investment of a corporation, either made or passed to the stockholders without declaration of a dividend..(Penn.) 901
Solvent debts, promissory notes and mortgages.............(Cal.) 902

Tax-exemptions—The return of the city tax assessor, setting forth the amount of the taxable capital of a banking corporation, will be held as true...(La.) 903
Capital invested in United States bonds....................(U. S.) 904
Deposits of United States currency........................(U. S.) 905
United States currency and national bank notes are part of assets. (U. S.) 906

Tax Sale—Made on a day other than that provided by law....(Miss.) 907
Deed describing the land conveyed as "200 acres in sec. 2, T. 12, range 1 east"...(Miss.) 908

Taxing Stock of Corporation—When its capital is represented by shares of stock which are not the property of the corporation. (Cal.) 909

Tax-Titles—Purchaser of, holds *prima facie* after the delay for redeeming has expired.....................................(La.) 910
Deed of a State tax collector is not conclusive of the legality of the title...(La.) 911
Power to sell land for non-payment of taxes is a naked power.(N. H.) 912

Tender—Of payment to one of several creditors and a demand from him of an assignment of the security......... ....(Del.) 913
Where a debt is unliquidated the acceptance by the creditor of money tendered by the debtor as "in full of all account"...(Vt.) 914
Demand for stock purchased and is ready to pay the price..(N. Y.) 915
Endorser of a note, on a tender of payment may insist on its delivery to him..(N. Y.) 916
There must be a production and manual offer of the money.(N. Y.) 917
By the president of a bank, in money belonging to the bank, to his private creditor..(N. Y.) 918
Offer in writing, effect of, when not accepted............(Oregon.) 919
Of advances and charges on goods to a warehouseman......(Colo.) 920
Does not extinguish the right of action but only precludes a claim for interest...(N. Y.) 921
Of interest—How and to whom made......................(N. Y.) 922

Trade Mark—The right to label goods with maker's own name, or that of his mill..(R. I.) 923, 924
Goods stamped with a particular mark or brand..........(U. C.) 925

Transitu—Stoppage of goods in............................(Mass.) 926

Trustee—Promise to allow personal debt as credit..............(Ga.) 927
Father made a deposit in his own name as trustee for his daughter, and died shortly after.....................................(R. I.) 928
No presumption of a resulting trust arises from a wife's possession of premises conveyed by her husband....................(N. J.) 929

Person acquiring legal title with notice of equitable interest in some other person...(N. J.)	930
An habitual drunkard conveys lands without consideration..(N. J.)	931
Trust Fund—That has been perverted......................(U. C.)	932
Trust Assignment—Mutual rights of beneficiaries............(Tenn.)	933
Trust ex Maleficio—Agreement to purchase at sheriff's sale for another having an interest in the land to be sold.........(Penn.)	934
Trust and Trustee—Deposits in bank by B., in trust for R., the deposit book being given to R.............................(R. I.)	935
Usages of Trade—Party conversant with the rules and usages of the Chicago Board of Trade, employs a commission merchant to buy grain for future delivery..................................(Ill.)	936
Usury—Note and mortgage executed to secure a loan of gold at a higher rate of premium than the market value of gold....(Iowa.)	937
Surety cannot avail himself of usury paid by his principal.....(Vt.)	938
Code does not deprive a party of existing remedies for relief against payment of illegal interest.........................(Md.)	939
Bill filed to restrain the execution of a judgment of fraud....(Md.)	940
Allegation in answer that the complainant, as executor, received a certain amount usuriously..................................(N. J.)	941
Must describe the usurious contract with precision..........(N. J.)	943
Suit by a national bank upon a bill of exchange. Defence, usury. (U. S.)	942
When the complainant voluntarily confesses the taking of usury. (N. J.)	944
Consideration of contract to forbear........................(Miss.)	945
In usurious contract it is immaterial in an inquiry as to the validity of the sale, the distribution of the proceeds is only affected.(Md.)	946
Plea of usury by indorser of notes in an action of recovery from him...(N. Y.)	947
Factor and broker..(Tenn.)	648
Money lent for a year at 8 per cent. on a note stated to be at 6 per cent. Surety's rights...(Penn.)	949
Usurious contract, whether expressed or implied, at the time of or subsequent to the entering into the agreement...............(Ill.)	950
Overdrawing the account at bank, and at the end of each sixty days the bank compounds the interest..........................(Ill.)	951
Bank-book settlements cannot be re-opened on charge of usury.(Ill.)	952
In suit on a note defendant averred that the loan for which the note was given had been carried by her father for two years previous at ten per cent. interest................................(Penn.)	953
Four notes payable in one year, with interest at ten per cent., secured by mortgage. After maturity plaintiff endorsed thereon: "For value received I promise to pay twelve per cent. from maturity until paid, Nov. 29, 1871".........................(Neb.)	954
Unless there is a law which limits the rate of interest to be charged. (Ark.)	955
Weight of evidence in favor of usury......................(N. J.)	956
Liquidated damages...(Ill.)	957
Purchaser of notes and mortgage brings suit against the purchaser of the equity of redemption, who sets up usury............(Vt.)	958
Party loans money, and at same time sells lots to the borrower at a fictitious value...(Ill.)	959
No one but the person paying usury........................(Vt.)	960
Purchaser of mortgaged property..........................(Ga.)	961
Recoupment...(Ind.)	962
Recoupment—Repeal of statute.............................(Ind.)	963

Taint of usury cannot be eradicated..........................(Penn.) 964
Usurious brokage taken by third person.....................(N. J.) 965
Where usurious interest is reserved or charged on a note or bill discounted by a national bank.................................(Ohio.) 966
What renders a transaction usurious........................(N. Y.) 967
Taking more than legal interest by mistake.................(N. Y.) 968
When principal and interest are both put at hazard.........(N. Y.) 969
Contract depending on contingencies........................(N. Y.) 970
Where one man advances money to buy lands for the benefit of himself and others...(N. Y.) 971
Loan of money upon condition that the borrower would sell to the lender, real estate of a speculative character.............(N. Y.) 972
No usury on a loan of chattels unless intended as an indirect loan of money...(N. Y.) 973
Loan, secured by pledge of stock agreeing to let lender have benefit of their rise...(N. Y.) 974
Fiction of a resale to cover usury..........................(N. Y.) 975
Agreement to sell land for $10,000 cash, but for which a bond and mortgage for $12,000 on same is given with interest........(N. Y.) 976
Usurious loan on a contract to procure assignment of choses in action which have then no existence...........................(N. Y.) 977
Loan made by insurance company, on condition that borrower effect an insurance..(N. Y.) 978
Authorized to loan on pledge and to charge interest for a full month when for a period of over fifteen days has passed..........(N. Y.) 979
Giving a note for a larger sum than the party discounting it expected to advance..(N. Y.) 980
Reservation of interest, payable quarterly.................(N. Y.) 981
On a bill of exchange......................................(U. S.) 982
Bona fide contract for the delivery of chattels..............(N. Y.) 983
Note with interest from a day past.........................(N. Y.) 984
Taint of usury attaches to all successive obligations......(N. Y.) 985
Discounting a note on the theory that 360 days is a year...(N. Y.) 986
Loaning money by check payable in current funds............(N. Y.) 987
Taking security bearing interest, and giving check for the amount, payable in six months without interest.....................(N. Y.) 988
There must be a loan, a taking of more than lawful interest, and a corrupt agreement..(N. Y.) 989
Agreement to pay more than legal interest, made at the time of the loan...(N. Y.) 990
Agreement by borrower to receive uncurrent notes at a higher rate than their market value....................................(N. Y.) 991
Accommodation paper..(N. Y.) 992
Accommodation note negotiated upon a usurious consideration. (N. Y.) 993
Where party gives his bond for the par value of stock which is depreciated in the market...................................(N. Y.) 994
Loan of notes at their nominal value, which are actually worth less than that amount..(N. Y.) 995
Credit given on a payment in advance for a larger amount than actual payment...(N. Y.) 996
Taking a note, interest on which is computed to day of sale, and giving therefor another note payable at a future day, with interest without rebate......................................(N. Y.) 997
Two persons exchange notes, for the purpose of raising money, and one procures the other's note to be discounted at a premium exceeding lawful interest...................................(N. Y.) 998
An exchange of notes, for the purpose of enabling one of the parties to sell the other's note at a usurious rate of discount..(N. Y.) 999

An accommodation note sold at a usurious rate of discount.(N. Y.) 1000
Fact that the maker of an accommodation note takes security for
 his indemnity..(N. Y.) 1001
Exchange of notes with a commission of two and a half per cent.
 (N. Y.) 1002
In an action defendant answers that such note is the last of a series
 of usurious renewals of a usurious note..................(Ind.) 1003
When usury was set up the agreement having been made in another
 State, it appearing that a premium had been taken for the loan.
 (N. J.) 1004
Vendor—Guaranty of title.......................................(La.) 1005
Lien on real estate for purchase money....................(Iowa.) 1006
When legal title is retained until the notes of purchaser are paid.
 (Miss.) 1007
Note for the purchase of land payable in Mississippi certificates of
 indebtedness...(Miss.) 1008
Person who having discovered a flaw in land purchases the title for
 speculation..(N. J.) 1009
Of land, who had taken a note therefor reserving title and endorsing
 sells it..(Ohio.) 1010
Delivery of the deed...(Mich.) 1011
Giving a receipt or taking a note, with security, from the purchaser,
 or taking a note of a third party, where the title remains in the
 vendor...(W. Va.) 1012
An acceptance of an order for goods by the vendor without further
 notice to the vendee......................................(N. C.) 1013
Warehouse Receipt—A receipt for goods not in the warehouse at
 the time of the execution thereof.........................(Ky.) 1014
Party may sell his property in store in the absence of a warehouse
 receipt..(Ky.) 1015
Third party must present receipt and written consent of the holder
 to get property..(Ky.) 1016
Warranty—Contract in writing, reciting that it was A.'s "own prop-
 erty, and free from all encumbrances and all of the crop".(Mass.) 1017
Breach of warranty set up as a defence without returning the goods.
 (Mich.) 1018
Implied that it is a valid and subsisting security for the amount
 expended..(N. Y.) 1019
Under contract received of L. $700 in part payment of 500 barrels
 of strained rosin, to be delivered, &c.," after which L. examined
 and selected the number he purchased...................(N. C.) 1020
Courts interpret written instruments......................(Penn.) 1021
Agreement not in writing for the sale of personal property at a price
 not less than fifty dollars...............................(Oregon.) 1023

www.ingramcontent.com/pod-product-compliance
Lightning Source LLC
Chambersburg PA
CBHW032118230426
43672CB00009B/1778